MYSTERIOUS ISLANDS

FORGOTTEN TALES OF THE GREAT LAKES

Editor: Deborah Wise Harris
Cover Painting by: James Flaherty
Typesetting and design: Russell Floren, Lynx Images Inc.
1st Edition, August 1999

Printed and bound in Canada by Transcontinental Printing Inc., Métrolitho division

Canadian Cataloguing in Publication Data

Gutsche, Andrea, 1964-
    Mysterious Islands: Forgotten Tales of the Great Lakes

Includes bibliographical references and index.

ISBN 1-894073-11-8   Book
ISBN 1-894073-10-X   Video
ISBN 1-894073-12-6   Book/Video Package

I. Islands - Great lakes - History. 2. Great Lakes Region - History. I Bisaillon, Cindy, 1948-   . III. Title.

F551.G87 1999   977'.0094'2   C99-931533-1

MYSTERIOUS ISLANDS

FORGOTTEN TALES OF THE GREAT LAKES

WRITTEN BY
ANDREA GUTSCHE
CINDY BISAILLON

PROJECT PRODUCERS
RUSSELL FLOREN
BARBARA CHISHOLM

LYNX
IMAGES

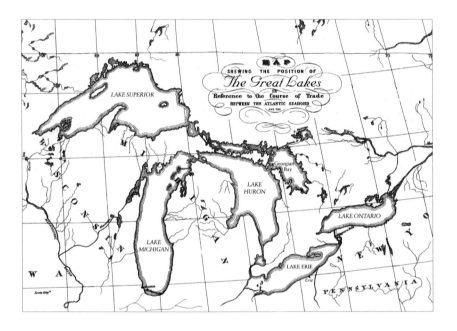

TABLE OF CONTENTS

Manoeuvring surfboats through treacherous seas earned life savers the nickname, "storm warriors."

To those who lived it...

John Hillis
Pat Johnston
Merritt Strum
&
Dave Thomas

INTRODUCTION

As the water flows, it is over one thousand miles from the Apostle Islands at the west end of Lake Superior to the Thousand Islands at the confluence of eastern Lake Ontario and the St. Lawrence River, the outlet to the Atlantic Ocean. Thousands of islands dot the five Great Lakes, ranging from rocky shoals to Manitoulin, the largest freshwater island in the world. Some islands are close and accessible pleasure grounds, open to the public. Others are remote and rarely ever visited. In native cosmology, some islands took on spiritual or mystical qualities. One island floated mysteriously, while another was lined with golden sands. Even today, their separation from the mainland makes islands feel worlds away. And this is part of their allure.

Surprisingly, these places that now feel lost to the mainstream world were, in earlier years, on the front lines. For at least two hundred years from the early 1600s to the early 1800s, the importance of the Great Lakes made them a stage for violent conflict. Native nations vied for territory, as did the British and French. Then there was the American Revolution, the War of 1812, and the Upper Canada Rebellion of 1837. With the frontier between British Canada and the U.S. running through the Lakes, the islands were strategic bastions (however humble), the sites of battles, and sometimes of refuge. Now with the longest undefended border in the world running through the Lakes, the swirling waters have left behind these former outposts of empire.

For centuries, goods were transported through the Great Lakes, the water highway to the interior. Islands were more accessible than many points inland, and as their resources began to be exploited, there was work for the willing. Picking up steam in the nineteenth century, thousands of immigrants made their start in the New World on islands in the Great Lakes. They came to mine, quarry, timber, farm and fish. When these resources were depleted, many of these people moved on, and the quarries, mines and fields were gradually reclaimed by the encroaching forest. Some of these immigrants set down deep roots, and generations of descendants still call these islands home.

As railways and roads opened up the interior of the continent in the latter years of the nineteenth century, many settlers and workers drifted away from their water-bound worlds. But the islands were soon to reinvent themselves—as summer getaways. Around the 1880s, there emerged the romantic notion of escaping the urban pressures to relax in nature's beauty. What better place to provide such simplicity and isolation than an island? For the extravagantly wealthy, this meant building a castle rivalling those on the Rhine. Most built modest cottages and cabins, or "summered" at one of the many opulent hotels and resorts that drew hordes of pleasure seekers every season.

Isolation made islands the setting for some of the most amazing, bizarre, and heroic events in Great Lakes history. Some islands are imprinted with the strong characters who made empires of those islands—whether commercial, religious, or simply a place of their own. Some saw the islands as havens from religious persecution. For the more reclusive, they were simply a refuge from the stress and disappointments of mainstream life.

Formed from tremendous forces—volcanoes, a tropical sea, even a meteor strike—many Great Lakes islands are tough remnants of geological time. They have resisted millions of years of erosion. Survivors of the Ice Ages and their meltwaters, they have been pounded by thousands of years of wind and waves. The results of eons of crafting are islands marked by a remarkably diverse beauty. Recent centuries have laced their history with the passions and tragedies of human endeavour. Though many stories in this collection have faded from memory, the islands' shores are yet marked by the passage of these fascinating times.

Skipping stones at Kelleys Island, Lake Erie

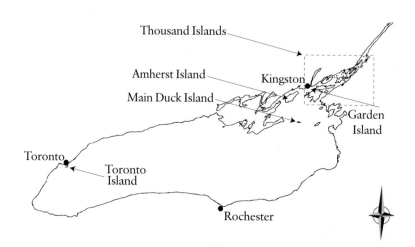

Thousand Islands

Amherst Island
Main Duck Island

Kingston

Garden
Island

Toronto

Toronto
Island

Rochester

LAKE ONTARIO

LAKE ONTARIO ISLANDS

Lake Ontario is the smallest of the Great Lakes, and arguably the gentlest. Most of its islands are nestled close to the mainland. Some, like Amherst Island, have pastoral settings and were homesteaded by 19th-century European settlers. Wolfe Island, off Kingston, and Toronto Island are a short ferry ride from mainland communities, and generations of city people have spent leisure-filled summer days on their cool and breezy shores.

Water from the Great Lakes system flows through Lake Ontario last before reaching its outlet, the mighty St. Lawrence River to the Atlantic.

Escaping the city doldrums: at the turn of the century thousands flocked to the islands for boating, swimming and other recreation.

At this confluence of lake and river, the international border runs through the maze of islands known as the Thousand Islands. Over the years these islands have served strategic and commercial interests—both legal and not. The area was fortified, saw skirmishes during the various British and American wars, and was even the haunt of Pirate Bill Johnston. Later in the nineteenth century, a timber rafting and shipbuilding operation, one of Canada's biggest enterprises, was based on tiny Garden Island. During American Prohibition (1920-33), rumrunners prowled the region using the islands, some only metres from the international border, as transit points for sending Canada's finest to the thirsty population to the south. Yet what endures about the Thousand Islands is their beauty. The tumble of islands has long been a summer paradise, dotted with cottages ranging from the modest to the majestic.

Despite their close relationship with the mainland, islanders on Lake Ontario have always retained their differences: a lifestyle less hectic; traditions better kept. Perhaps it is this close juxtaposition with the mainland that makes Lake Ontario's islands most interesting and their differences that much more charming and noticeable.

TORONTO ISLAND

The Island that Wasn't

Toronto Island began as a peninsula tipped by a series of fingerlike sandbars and marshes, created by eroded sediment from the bluffs further east. In the early 1600s, explorers, missionaries and fur traders were acquainted

In 1793, John Graves Simcoe arrived to build a fort on the mainland, and a military outpost on the peninsula that later became Toronto Island. Note Gibraltar Point lighthouse at right.

Toronto Island began as a series of fingerlike sandbars, marshes and ponds at the end of a long peninsula. Inset) John Graves Simcoe and wife Elizabeth

with the fine bay on the Lake Ontario, protected by the large sweeping sand bar. Rather than paddling around the peninsula, voyageurs often portaged across it. By the early 1700s, the area was home to the Mississauga nation. A French fur trading post on the mainland here became so profitable that the British built their own post on the southeast end of Lake Ontario at Oswego. There was a French presence here until France formally lost the Great Lakes to the British with the Treaty of Paris in 1763.

In 1793, Colonel John Graves Simcoe arrived with his wife Elizabeth, two children, their domestic help and his Regiment, the Queen's Rangers. Simcoe had chosen York (now Toronto) as the site of Fort York, a British fort. Simcoe placed a military outpost and several cannons at the end of the peninsula. Elizabeth Simcoe nicknamed the location Gibraltar Point*.

In unfavourable winds, the peninsula impeded sailboats and ships from entering and leaving the bay. Smaller boats were sometimes dragged across the point. By the early 1800s, the population of the town of York had reached 700, and a lighthouse was needed to aid the increasing water traffic. Completed in 1809, Gibraltar Point lighthouse was the second light tower to be built on the Great Lakes. (*In Simcoe's time, Gibraltar Point was closer to the location of the garrison on the peninsula, but now the location of the lighthouse is known as Gibraltar Point.)

TORONTO ISLAND

Murder at Gibraltar Point Lighthouse

Lightkeeper James Durnam had been working on his garden most of the summer afternoon, around 1833. He stuck the spade into the earth and tossed the soil onto the growing pile. Then he hit a stone. Trying to dislodge it, Durnam inhaled sharply. It was a human skull. He dusted the dirt away, exposing a wide grimace and a shattered forehead. Durnam saw horror locked in the peat-filled sockets of the eyes. He was sure he had found the skull of J.P. Rademuller, Gibraltar Point's first lightkeeper, missing since 1815.

On a cold, moonless night in January 1815, J.P. Rademuller vanished from his post without a trace. The case was short on clues, but not on speculation. Fond of good ale, Rademuller had brought his brewing skills from Germany. He tended his brewing operation as carefully as he trimmed the lamp wick on the tower light. He was friendly and generous, happy to share his beer with friends and passing strangers. British soldiers from the outpost on the point dropped by routinely.

On a winter night in 1815, so the tale is told, three soldiers hammered on the keeper's door, drunkenly demanding beer. Rademuller gently tried to send them away, which only made them more belligerent. The keeper held his ground, suggesting the soldiers sleep there for the night. Incited all the more, one man threw a piece of firewood at Rademuller's head while the

Excessive drinking was such a problem at Fort York (on the mainland) that on pay day the night guard stayed late to ensure all the soldiers returned to the Fort.

Built in 1809, Gibraltar Point lighthouse is the oldest remaining lighthouse on the Great Lakes.

others started beating him. The lightkeeper lay crumpled on the floor. As the theory goes, the soldiers then dragged his limp body up the spiral steps to the top of the tower, and threw him off.

The mystery of Rademuller's disappearance was never solved. When keeper James Durnam found the human bones seventeen years later, no one doubted the remains were Rademuller's. Durnam had his own reason for certainty. It was the strange echo he had heard in the tower, like heels being dragged up the steps. The sound became familiar to generations of keepers at Gibraltar.

An eerie stillness fills the clearing where the lighthouse stands. The low-arched wooden door, with its heavy iron hinges, looks like the secret entrance to a castle. Built near the western end of Toronto Island in 1809, Gibraltar Point lighthouse is the oldest standing lighthouse on the Great Lakes. Discontinued in 1959, it now stands amid the trees, mostly forgotten.

Lightkeeper James Durnam (right) being interviewed by reporter about the discovery of Rademuller's remains.

TORONTO ISLAND

The Storm That Made an Island

For years, only a handful of people lived on the long, curved sandbar facing Toronto Harbour: the lightkeeper, a few soldiers and fishermen, and sometimes natives, passing through. The peninsula was a quiet spot, and residents of York visited from time to time for picnics, hunting and horse racing. Around 1835, the newly incorporated City of Toronto's population had reached 9,000. Some citizens started a lobby to cut a canal through the peninsula in order to improve shipping access to the harbour. The debate continued until the winter of 1858. That year, several hotels were operating on the peninsula, including the Quinn family establishment.

Mrs. Quinn walked over to the window, wringing her hands. The waves had picked up, and were slamming up against the cedar-post breakwater. They had postponed the celebration for the men who had renovated the hotel and Mr. Quinn had returned the workmen to the mainland. Jenny was with him on the lake.

Seven-year-old Jenny Quinn was close by her father's side when the men had climbed into Quinn's boat. Jenny had hoped they would have time to see a few shops in Toronto but the weather was turning and her father insisted they return home right away. Back on the lake, it was only minutes before a hurricane was unleashed from the northeast.

Her baby boy in her arms, Mrs. Quinn moved back from the window, and began to pace the lobby. The breakwater had been swallowed up by the surge of foam, and the waves were clawing deep into the shoreline. The walls shook with the first wave that hit. Terrified, Mrs. Quinn backed toward the centre of the room, clutching her son to her chest and shouting for her daughter, Elizabeth. Another massive thump sent a chunk of plaster toppling from the ceiling. Suddenly the entire wall bent with the wrenching

Privat's hotel as it appeared before the Quinn's purchased it in 1853. In a sense, it was Toronto Island's first amusement park, including a bowling alley and merry-go-round.

sounds of snapping beams and boards.

As they tried to land, John Quinn and his daughter Jenny saw the nightmare unfold. The shoreline had vanished. The hotel was engulfed in water. Smashed by massive waves, the hotel's walls collapsed. The roaring wind and sea swallowed up John Quinn's screams. He pulled the boat into the hotel. Dishes and a dustpan swirled

Soon after John and Jenny Quinn departed from Queen's Wharf (pictured above) the hurricane struck threatening the rest of the Quinn family stranded at the hotel.

around him in the waves. John struggled through the water towards his wife who was afloat upon a piece of wood, the children gripping tightly to her. John hauled the three into the boat and retreated inland to the family's emergency shelter. Soon afterwards, one enormous wave took out the rest of the hotel, allowing the giant surge of water to rush across the peninsula. After hours of clawing, the storm had carved a five-foot channel. And so on April 13, 1858, the peninsula became Toronto Island. A month later, the gap was wide and deep enough for two schooners to sail through.

THE TORONTO ISLAND ARCHIPELAGO

WARD'S ISLAND

In the 1830s, fishermen started to build crude log houses on the peninsula (later the island), setting up wooden reels for drying fishing nets. Of

the men who harvested the local waters, it was one in particular, William Ward, who began making a place

In the early 1860s, fishermen operated from the island. This is what the Toronto waterfront looked like the year Ward's five sisters drowned.

When William Ward and Bob Berry reached the Schooner Jane Ann Marsh, they had to chop ice from the crew members who had frozen on the rigging.

for himself in the annals of Toronto Island history.

Young William Ward was an island child, born with water in the veins. His father had a fisherman's respect for the lake. He had warned young William to stay put this blustery day. But William was impetuous and petulant. The lad herded his five younger sisters into the family sailboat and off they went to enjoy the wind. It was not long before the weather turned foul. The vessel capsized, tossing the Ward children into the water. The girls quickly swam to their elder brother, grabbing on to him as swells pushed them under. William righted the sailboat and pulled himself aboard. He yanked three of his sisters from the lake but it was too late—they had drowned. Then the boat flipped again and he watched helpless as the waters swept away the bodies of all five of his sisters.

In one version of the story, after losing her daughters, Mrs. Ward took to wandering the shore. Mr. Ward moved his fishing operation inland, to a location known as Ward's Pond. (The island has been significantly altered since that time. Now Ward's Pond is essentially the water that divides Centre and Olympic Islands.)

Sally Gibson's *More Than an Island* follows the incredible life of William Ward. The loss of his sisters haunted the young man. Ward made it his mission to rescue people off Toronto Island. The first of many rescues happened on December 7, 1868 when he was twenty years old.

Peering through the grey blanket of falling snow, the fishermen could just make out the rocking masts of a wreck. William Ward and Robert Berry struck out to meet the sailors, floundering on the stormy lake. But the storm proved too much. Their boat flipped, striking Berry so sharply that his head split open. Three times the boat capsized, and hand over hand, fishermen dragged the rescuers back to shore. Ward and Berry finally made it to the ship, freeing the crew of the ice that had encased them. One of the sailors fell into the lake, but he floated, ice-encrusted, and was rescued. It took seven hours to save everyone.

In the following year, Ward's urge to rescue reached almost mad proportions. He joined a volunteer lifesaving crew headed by Thomas Tinning. The morning of November 14, 1875, the rescue team saved the crew of the *Olive Branch*, thanks largely to Ward who swam through 14-foot waves to deliver a lifeline to the schooner. A second ship foundered the same afternoon. Tinning declared the seas too dangerous after the lifesaving crew failed to reach the vessel. But Ward was determined to save the crew. He punched Tinning, starting a rumble on the beach. William Ward later tried to reach the ship alone but he was unsuccessful. The crew of the *Fearless* had to stand all night waist deep in freezing water, waiting out the storm.

By 1880 Ward was captain of the lifesaving crew. He was also a fisherman, island constable, and he ran a modest two-storey hotel. That year, the Royal Canadian Yacht Club moved onto the island, and a public park was established. But it was the 1882 opening of Wiman Baths, public swimming baths on the Eastern Point, that most ignited public interest in the island. People came in droves, and William built a new elegant three-storey hotel to accommodate them. This area was later named Ward's Island for lifesaver and hotelier William Ward.

By the 1890s, the population of Ward's Island was only 100, mainly patrons of Ward's Hotel and some tenters. More and more, the island became a popular retreat for Toronto's less affluent. They slept in Victorian-era tents with wooden floors and root cellars. People cooked on

Ward capitalized on the island's popularity as a vacation destination. He built a modest 2-storey frame hotel in 1876. This second and grander Ward's Hotel followed in 1882-3 complete with sixty-foot-long verandahs allowing curious guests to observe bathers at the nearby Wiman Baths.

open fires, built windmills to pump water, and dug wells. The tent city brought with it issues of sanitation and overcrowding.

In 1920, wooden verandahs were all the rage on Ward's Island, and no tent was without one. Against regulations, Islanders began to construct wooden walls—inside their tents! The first cottage appeared in 1929, built with a special permit for a man's disabled son. In 1931, residents were

The tent city on Ward's was a summer vacation spot for Toronto residents. While Ward's Island regulations allowed "tents only," some people built wooden verandahs and walls to increase comfort.

The tents were fairly simple affairs

finally permitted to build small cabins, no larger than 840 square feet. Friction developed between the would-be cottagers, and those wanting to preserve the unique tent city. The *Ward Island Weekly* implored, "No matter what we live in, let us hope the old camping spirit remains around here."

By 1937, only 32 tents remained, and 130 tiny cottages lined the boardwalks. Through changing politics and politicians, Ward's Islanders struggled to maintain their historical community. In 1956, Metropolitan Toronto acquired the island, and began to bulldoze and burn buildings as the leases expired. The land was to become Metro's first major park. Those remaining Islanders intend to continue in the tradition that began more than a hundred years ago.

William Ward lived to see the island named after him change radically.

CENTRE ISLAND

Along the Boardwalk

To escape the heat on a Toronto summer's day, families can take a ten-minute ferry ride to Centre Island where they can picnic, enjoy amusement rides, and walk, bike or inline skate along the boardwalk.

From the 1880s until the 1950s, the boardwalk was lined with grand, Victorian summer homes. Trimmed in lacy gingerbread, they had spacious, wooden verandahs. White columns were entwined with ivy. Elegant ladies in white cotton dresses strolled along the boardwalk, parasols in hand. To own such a cottage was the height of civilized living. At the end of a demanding day, it was a short ferry ride from the mainland to the

Visitors flocked to Toronto Island.

Toronto, 1912. The industrial city's smoke-filled streets drove many residents to seek out cleaner environs of the island.

shade of a lake-cooled garden. Summer residents included Dr. W.T. Atkins, president of the Toronto School of Medicine, politician Michael J. Woods, and George Gooderham of Gooderham and Worts Distillery. By 1900, 3,000 summer residents lived on Centre Island.

Of course, not everyone could afford this summer bliss. Over the decades, thousands of visitors enjoyed the boardwalk breezes, staying for the day or overnight at the hotels. In the post-war boom of the 1950s, the Toronto City Council ordered the grand houses removed, and transformed the Island into parkland. The ghostly tangle of overgrown lilac, forsythia and lily of the valley, and the pathways that lead nowhere are some of the only reminders.

One of the waterfront features of Toronto Island, Hanlan's Hotel burned in 1909.

*Previous page top right & right)
Many beautiful Victorian summer homes were bulldozed to
make Centre Island a public
park.*

*Gorman's famous diving horses
were a favourite attraction at
Hanlan's Point Amusement Park
on Centre Island.*

MAIN DUCK

The Fishing Sloop and the Thrashing Machine

1868. The wind rippled across the field of golden oats and barley on
Main Duck Island. Sanford Davis pondered his crop with mixed feelings.
It was a fine harvest. A good thousand bushels. But Davis did not look forward to thrashing all that grain by hand. Even with help from Howard,
from up the Bay of Quinte, and Henry Selleck, from over at Point Traverse.

It wasn't easy to farm this tiny island at the eastern end of Lake Ontario.
Everything had to come by water. Once Captain John Walters had agreed
to bring two bulls on his old fishing boat, the *Gentle Jane*. He tied them
securely head to tail, fore and aft. Lucky thing they were as gentle as *Jane*.
Davis then convinced the captain to bring over a good-sized flock of sheep,
a few sheep at a time. How many were there now? Four hundred?

The *Gentle Jane* was gone now, and she could not have held the thrashing machine he wanted anyhow. He had seen the machine of his dreams for
rent the week before. It was an "open cellar" horsepower thrashing
machine for rent and couldn't shake it from his mind. Maybe the brothers

from Port Ontario, N.Y. could bring it in their fishing sloop?

Sanford Davis sent Howard and Henry to find the brothers, and bring back that thrasher come hell or high water. The four men found the thrasher but soon realized that, even dismantled, it would not fit down the boat's single hatchway. The only answer was to put it on deck amidships, and secure it to the bulwarks. They had to raise the boom to make it fit. Meanwhile the skies had clouded over, so they waited for a day or two, to be sure of better weather.

Isolation made island farming a challenge.

On the last day of August they sailed off with their cargo. They had only twenty miles to go, but with such an awkward, heavy load, the open lake stretched out before them. Henry was worried. A man of 37, he was thinking of his new bride. Muffled by the creak of rigging and the surge of spray, he murmured a quiet prayer. The exposed Duck Islands were notorious for their shoals and shipwrecks.

Everything was going well. Then, a few miles off Main Duck, the sky turned an ominous slate grey. The wind blew hard, pushing the sloop wildly onward. Then, as the island came in sight, a squall hit them full force, capsizing the boat. The thrashing machine sank like a stone. Without a lifeboat, the four men clung desperately to a hatch cover and an oar.

Meanwhile, Sanford Davis had been waiting for weeks for his thrasher to arrive. He was generally a patient man. But as the days wore on, his composure was giving way. After all, he had a farm to run and crops to harvest. He finally sent one of his boys to Point Traverse. The boy learned that the sloop had sunk, and that the Port Ontario brothers had turned up dead. But there was no news about Henry and Howard. Later, a newspaper report said Howard's body had washed up in the Bay of Quinte, as if he had been heading home. The body of Henry Selleck had floated almost to the doorstep where his bride had been waiting in distress.

Sanford Davis and his wife

MAIN DUCK LIGHTHOUSE

A Sailor's Intuition

Main Duck Island, a curve of wooded land, lies 19 miles (30 kms) off the northeastern shore of Lake Ontario. With its spine against the northern winds, it cradles two protected bays that serve as ideal shelter in a summer storm. But late in the fall, raging gales whip up the water, and scant shelter can be found. Since 1914, the 74-foot (22-m) Main Duck light tower has stood guard over the stormy November seas.

During a violent blast on November 17, 1920, lightkeeper Bougard woke in the small hours of the morning to thumping sounds and faint cries at his door. Captain Harry Randall and his crew of five were collapsed at his doorstep, panting with exhaustion, and freezing in drenched clothes. Their eyes were hollow. Bougard hurried them inside.

Harry Randall was captain of the *John Randall*, his family's little steamer. A sturdy vessel only 116 feet (35m) long, she shipped small cargoes across the eastern tip of Lake Ontario. Her crew of five worked hard for their money, from early spring until the winter freeze. On this very journey, the *John Randall* had set out from Oswego, New York, laden with coal. The lake had been still, and the skies uncertain. But as the *John Randall* steamed into the night on the 12-hour route to Belleville, a sudden storm hurled itself onto the lake. As the little vessel swallowed massive waves, the crew struggled to pump it out. Before long, the water ripped the lifeboats from the deck, and the crew's strength was fast depleting. The ship was sinking.

In an effort to reach shelter, Captain Harry pointed the steamer towards the Main Duck lighthouse. Within a mile of the island, the crew made a

Main Duck light station. The lightkeeper recalled Captain Randall's cryptic words when the following year Randall, his crew, his wife and two children were lost at sea.

panicked leap into the icy water. Somehow, each one found the strength to make it to the shore, and to drag their numb limbs through the bush to the lighthouse on the island's northern tip. All six men were safe. With no way to send word to the mainland, their anguished families lived for eight days fearing the men were dead. The little steamer was pulverized on the rocks of the "protective" southern bays of Main Duck Island.

In the comfort of the lightkeeper's home, the Captain's spirit seemed heavy as he gripped a warm mug of coffee. Losing a ship was not just a financial blow. In some ways, it was like the death of a friend. That evening the captain confessed to lightkeeper Bougard that for weeks he had felt a sense of impending doom. A part of him was relieved when the ship had foundered, and no one had been killed.

Captain Randall replaced the vessel. The next year—to the very day—the lake swallowed up the new boat. Randall, his crew, his wife and two children were lost.

AMHERST ISLAND

An Irish Tale

In the mid 19th century, hundreds of thousands of Irish emigrated to North America in search of new beginnings.

Fighting off sickness and fatigue, Alexander Caughey climbed to the windswept upper decks of the ship and peered out over the bow. Only the featureless grey waters of the Atlantic lay before him. Alexander and his three children had been at sea nearly four weeks. Fresh food and water were running low; the lower decks of the rickety old ship were infested with vermin and lice and the floors were covered with human waste. Typhus had begun to spread among the passengers, and for the first time, Alexander doubted their decision to abandon Ireland for the New World. Straining his eyes for the first sight of land, Alexander tried to imagine the life that awaited him, but the last five years of pain kept intruding in his thoughts.

At the Liverpool docks signs for Quebec enticed Irish emigrants to come to Canada.

When the first potato crop failed in 1845, Alexander was not worried. He lived in Ballymullen in the north of Ireland, a region that had survived food shortages before. Here loyal Scots (transplanted after Oliver Cromwell's invasions of the 17th century) had built a relatively prosperous community, with strong fishing, shipbuilding and linen industries. The Caugheys were lucky. Further south, Irish peasants were dying by the thousands.

But two years later crops were still failing and things in Ballymullen had grown worse. Food was scarce and the sickness had arrived. Cholera attacks its victims slowly, beginning as a fever and becoming an excruciating intestinal infection. In town, entire households lay empty, their inhabitants ravaged by the disease. In 1848, Alexander's wife Mary died during childbirth. It was one of the worst winters of the Great Irish Famine. The following spring, crops failed for the fifth year in a row, swelling the ranks of the poor, the destitute and the starving. There were whispers of violent revolution. Irish society stood on the brink of collapse.

Fearing the worst, Alexander and his family packed up and made their way to Liverpool, the dirty, crime-ridden port of choice for thousands of Irish seeking passage to the New World. Swindlers tried to sell the Caugheys bogus tickets to New York and Boston for the outrageous sum of 4 to 5 pounds each. Alexander bought cheaper tickets subsidized by the British government—destination: Canada. Some time later, the Caugheys reached their final destination: Amherst Island, a narrow, ten-mile strip of land southeast of Kingston on Lake Ontario. It was a huge relief to arrive in the summer. The island's rich farmland, grassy meadows and plush forests were the ideal setting to begin again.

By 1850, Amherst Island was already home to an established, tight-knit Irish community, mostly from the Caugheys' region of northern Ireland, the Ards Peninsula. The first Irish families had arrived by 1827, becoming successful farmers, labourers, sailors and fishermen. The Irish joined a flourishing settlement of United Empire Loyalists, who had been living comfortably on large estates along the north shore since the 1790s. Life on Amherst Island was civilized and peaceful. By 1850, the island had its own local market, churches and small businesses. Land, food and employment were abundant. The tensions of the Old World—religious, political and social—were not nearly as profound. Newcomers like the Caugheys were welcomed warmly. They were often given credit and contacts so they could purchase their own land.

The Caughey children—daughter Mary and sons David and Robert—made friends quickly, as they fished, hunted and explored the windswept harbours of the southern shore. Cold winter nights were spent around the fire with family and friends listening to Amherst Island legends. The two boys were particularly curious about the Mississauga and Iroquois hunters and traders who used its sheltered harbours to fish and to protect themselves from enemies. A favourite story was that of Catherine Maria Bowes, who was a major landowner of Amherst. A notorious gambler, Bowes once staked the entire island on a single hand of high-stakes poker—and lost.

There were also the harrowing tales from the Rebellion of 1837. In June of 1838, a group of armed rebels led by Pirate Bill Johnston raided the north shore of Amherst Island as part of William Lyon Mackenzie's ill-fated revolution. Houses were plundered, several women threatened and at least two men were wounded. But the Islanders got their revenge five months later when the local militia took part in the decisive Battle of the Windmill at Prescott near Kingston, and helped turn the tide against the rebels. The story became a source of pride for Islanders—a symbol of their loyalty to King and Country.

Despite fondness for their new home in the Canadas, most immigrants maintained a strong emotional connection to their Irish homeland. Many families, including the Caugheys, had left loved ones behind, agonizing over the separation. In her book, *A New Lease on Life*, Catherine Anne Wilson recounts the story of the McGrattons. In 1848, without telling his wife, David McGratton sailed his small fishing boat for Ireland. The couple had moved to Amherst Island years earlier, but had been forced to leave their youngest daughter behind with her grandmother. David planned to surprise his grief-stricken wife by retrieving their daughter and re-uniting the family in Canada. Only a few miles off the coast of Ireland, a violent storm capsized David's boat and he drowned while trying to swim ashore.

Caughey homestead, Amherst Island

Meanwhile, Jane McGratton kept a candle burning every night for a full year in hopes of her husband's safe return. When Jane eventually learned of her husband's demise, she arranged for her daughter to come to Canada. For the grandmother in Ireland, the departure of yet another relative was too much to bear. Legend has it that the elderly woman died soon after.

Amherst Island had its high life. Major Radcliff, the island's rent collector, had a two-storey home and estate complete with servants' quarters, piano, billiard table, yacht and horses. It was often the site of high society soirees attended by Old World officers and aristocrats visiting from Kingston. After one such party in 1849, an editorial appeared in the *British Whig*, "society in this flourishing island is placed on a most delightful basis, far different from what is generally found in other parts of Canada. Several old country families of good birth and high respectability have settled... and maintain all the amenities and courtesies of well bred European life."

Like many Great Lakes islands, Amherst's population declined over the years. Between 1851 and 1901, the number of residents peaked at 1,287, and then fell to 544. In the same period, the population of Canada had more than doubled. Industrialization, railway construction and international trade transformed the shores of Lake Ontario. Towns like Hamilton, Toronto and Kingston became burgeoning cities plagued with congestion, pollution and social chaos. Amherst Island remained quiet and insular. Its small communities retained their traditional cultural identity and customs. Visiting in the early 1900s, a doctor was amazed to find Irish home remedies still in use by some of the locals. For example, a trip to the healing waters of the island's spring wells was recommended for most general afflictions, while sucking on a rag soaked with whiskey or tossing an infant's clothes into the fire were cures for convulsions.

Today, for many, Amherst Island is a small, peaceful island where tourists and cottagers gather to escape the city heat. However, for the Caugheys and hundreds of other Irish and Loyalist immigrants, Amherst Island symbolized a new beginning and an opportunity to live a prosperous and peaceful life.

WOLFE ISLAND

Baseball and Wolfe Island:
A Perfect Match

With a man on first and second and one out in the eleventh, the number six hitter, Billy Little, stepped up to the plate. The stocky first baseman had struck out his last time at bat, but now with the game on the line in extra innings he had a chance to be the hero. The Wolfe Islanders had already defeated Tamworth, Yarker and Picton in this year's (1924) Ontario Baseball Association (O.B.A) playdowns, but no one had expected them to do so well against Kingston. With the score tied 8-8, Little watched the first two offerings from Kingston's pitcher, Bennett, go by for strikes. The infielders were playing straight away, the outfielders shallow, hoping to throw out the lead runner at the plate. Little tightened his grip around the bat. Bennett entered his windup... The pitch...

...Whack! Little felt the ball give effortlessly under his bat and take flight towards the outfield. The players on the Wolfe Island bench leapt to their feet as the crowd began to roar. The first runner scored, giving Wolfe Island the lead. The second baserunner rounded third and headed for home. The Kingston fielder picked up the ball and fired to second. In a cloud of dust, Little slid safely into second, with the game-winning, two-run double.

Thanks to Billy Little's late-inning heroics, the Wolfe Island baseball team advanced to the next round of the O.B.A. playdowns in 1924. However, before their next game, the team was discovered playing Sunday baseball in Clayton, New York. At that time, the O.B.A. forbade games on the Sabbath, and so the Wolfe Islanders were disqualified and banned from competition.

Baseball has a rich history on the islands of the Great Lakes. In 1914, a 19-year-old pitcher George Herman Ruth (you know him as "the Babe") hit his first professional home run at Hanlan's Point stadium on Toronto Island. The ball sailed over the right field fence and—legend has it—straight into Lake Ontario. Sixty years earlier, in the 1860s, Confederate Civil War prisoners learned the game while interned on Johnston's Island on Lake Erie. After the war, they returned home and were among the first to introduce baseball in the American south.

The people of Wolfe Island, Ontario were also early converts to the game. The island's population never climbed higher than its 1861 peak of 3,600, shrinking to half that number ten years later. But by 1909, the small community supported no fewer than six baseball teams: the Head, Village (Marysville), Foot, Ridge, Buxton Bay, and Boxton Harbour.

Why was baseball so popular among these peaceful, island farmers? The large, wide-open spaces might have inspired their interest. The largest of the Thousand Islands, Wolfe Island is over 54 square miles, most of it farmland that was cleared by Scots and United Empire Loyalists at the beginning of the 19th century. Maybe it was the island's proximity to baseball-crazed towns in upstate New York. As early as 1802, a ferry operated between the island and the U.S. mainland, and by the end of the century, American tourists frequented Wolfe's two hottest vacation spots, Hitchcock House (which is still standing) and the Wolfe Island Hotel (now The General Wolfe). The island's baseball mania may have been sparked by the Wolfe Islanders' famous victory at the Cape Vincent, New York Fair of 1885. That year, a group of ballplayers from the island went undefeated in three straight games to capture the championship.

Apart from great baseball, Wolfe Island at the turn of the century had the advantages of a quiet life. But this came with a price. Getting on and off the island could be a challenge, especially in winter. When the cold weather arrived and ice formed on the St. Lawrence, ferry service to Kingston and the Cape Vincent was suspended until the spring thaw. For months, an ice bridge—not always stable—was the only link to the mainland. Islanders used sleighs, skis and iceboats. They drove their horses, and later cars and trucks, across the frozen bridge. One employee from the Island quarry twice fell through the ice in the late 1800s and survived by pulling himself out with a long pole. That man was Alexander Mackenzie, the second Prime Minister of Canada.

The Wolfe Islanders won the intercounty league championship three times in the 1920s. Pictured here are the 1921 champs.

Boxscore from the 1924 game between Wolfe Island and Kingston.

Even in summer, islanders' lives were shaped by limitations on transportation, which sometimes even played havoc with the baseball season. In 1905, a contest was halted after only six innings when the visiting team from Kingston hastily left the field to catch the last ferry home. A week later on the mainland, a team from Wolfe Island faced the same dilemma, and ran for the ferry docks in the eighth, with a 14-13 lead. Yet despite the occasional "ferry-out," baseball flourished on the island. Every spring, young boys dusted off their old baseball gloves, stored in the barn all winter. They dreamed of becoming the next Lou Gehrig or Babe Ruth. Their fathers told stories about Tris Speaker, Three Finger Brown, and the 1885 champion Wolfe Islanders. In the 1920s, the islanders won the Intercounty League championship three

Hitchcock House has welcomed Island tourists for well over a century.

years out of five. Year after year, baseball was a constant on Wolfe Island.

The early history of Wolfe Island is also peaceful. Archeological discoveries suggest that the first inhabitants arrived about 2000 years ago and called the island Ganounkouesnot (roughly translated as "long island standing up"). In the centuries that followed, successive waves of aboriginal peoples passed through, including the Owasco, the Iroquois and the Mississauga. The island offered excellent hunting, a temperate climate, and good fishing. The first Europeans did not arrive until the 17th century when King Louis the XIV of France granted Fort Frontenac (at present day Kingston) to LaSalle, along with a seigneury that included Wolfe Island. LaSalle then promptly conveyed the island to James Cauchois, whose descendants owned the land through the next century when it was often known as Hog Island, in honour of its most numerous inhabitants.

In the 17th century LaSalle was granted a seigneury that included Wolfe Island.

In 1792 Lord Simcoe renamed the island after British General James Wolfe, the victor of the Battle on the Plains of Abraham. And despite its new military name and strategic location at the mouth of the St. Lawrence, Wolfe Island managed to escape conflict. The War of 1812 passed without incident. A detachment of soldiers was stationed on the island during the Rebellion of 1837, but the action was limited to catching the odd deserter. In the late 1850s, in hopes of establishing a profitable new rail link to the United States, Kingston businessmen built a canal through the centre of the island, hoping to create a bustling new trade route. But modern commerce passed Wolfe Island by. Tranquility prevailed. The canal officially closed in 1932 and today is a popular fishing spot.

A ferry has connected Kingston to the island since the early 1800s. Visitors have enjoyed the island's fishing, hiking and open spaces for nearly 200 years.

GARDEN ISLAND

The Island Enterprise of D.D. Calvin

At its height in the 1880s, D.D.Calvin's timber and shipbuilding business on Garden Island was one of the largest firms in Canada. Calvin owned the sixty-five acre Garden Island and had established a self-sufficient community, geared entirely to his company's success. An American most of his life, Calvin traveled in lofty circles of Canadian society, counting Sir John A. Macdonald, the first Prime Minister of Canada, among his close friends.

Dileno Dexter Calvin had established a modest timber operation in upper New York State in the 1820s, rafting timber down the St. Lawrence River to Quebec City. His business acumen led him to search out a new location at the head of the St. Lawrence River, the gateway of the Great Lakes navigation system. In 1836 he found the ideal site at the eastern end of Lake Ontario. The sheltered bay on the southeast side of Garden Island was excellent for unloading timber from other Great Lakes ports. The bay was big enough to hold large timber shipments, and to allow the great logs to be built into rafts to take down river to Quebec.

At first, Calvin rented the southeastern part of the island. By 1844, he he had moved there to provide his constant supervision. His second wife and six children from his first marriage moved with him. The island was beautiful, and the growing business was evolving its own community.

Top) D.D. Calvin: an astute businessman and progressive thinker. Bottom) Timber rafting down the St. Lawrence River was the core of Calvin's business.

As business changed from timber rafting to shipbuilding in the 1870s, the village continued to grow with the addition of a large sail loft, a boiler shop and a marine railway.

By the 1860s there were six more Calvin children, and a community of 750 people. The village was alive with the sounds and smells of industry. The docks clanked with the noise of anchors and chains. The machine shops roared and

Calvin's ships delivered square timber from around the Lakes to Garden Island to be lashed into rafts.

whined and hammered. The smells of fresh hot bread wafted from the bakery. The smoke from extra timber smoldered in the school's wood stove. The town had a general store, a butcher, customs officer, and a post office. Garden Island even had company-issued money, printed from engraved plates. The islanders had one of the finest Mechanics' Institutes in Canada, with a library of 1,600 volumes. There was a Masonic

Calvin's business brought together an eclectic mix of workers including French Canadians, Scots, Irish, Americans and Natives.

lodge, an Orange lodge, and a Temperance Society. There was no alcohol. And surprisingly, there was no church. While Calvin was a devout Presbyterian, he was also a progressive thinker. The company town brought together French Canadians, Scots, Irish, Americans,

The Calvin family home

and native people. Calvin saw no point in a church that would accommodate one faith at the risk of antagonizing others.

Calvin's business boomed. He oversaw a fleet of vessels bringing oak and pine squared-off logs from as far away as Michigan and Minnesota. His impressive operation assembled rafts from a series of "cribs," floating frames sixty by forty-two feet, made without bolts or nails. Four or five cribs were fastened together to make a "dram" 250 to 300 feet long. Then the huge timbers or "sticks" were strapped onto the frames with "withes," saplings made flexible by being twisted or crushed. Initially softening the withes was tedious work, as tens of thousands were needed in the course of a season. In 1854, the company invented a horse-powered withe-making machine that replaced the work of twelve men. By 1880, a steam-powered machine did the job even better.

By the 1860s teams rafted thousands of squared pine and oak timbers every year making Calvin's business one of the largest in Canada.

Teams of expert rafters, mostly French Canadian and native, took the rafts down river towards Quebec. The men built cooking and sleeping sheds on the main raft or "home dram," and stocked up on supplies. The trip by oar, sail and current lasted several weeks. Later, steam-powered vessels towed the rafts, considerably shortening the trip.

Members of the Calvin family and their guests would often go along for the adventure. One of Calvin's grandchildren, Marion Calvin Boyd, recalled her experience,

> It had a charm all its own, to sit on the shady side of a cabin and watch the shore sliding calmly by. Motion, until the rapids were reached, was almost imperceptible... It was an excellent way to see the beauties of the Thousand Islands, as one had plenty of time to admire.

The pace picked up considerably once they hit rapids,

> The raftsmen kneel down for a brief prayer before entering the rapids. A thrilling moment was when we were in the grip of Lachine [Rapids]. We would be perched on the roof of our little cabin so as to keep dry... We felt great admiration for the foreman's skill and nerve... the slide was over all too quickly.

Sometimes a dram would burst apart in the swirling rapids, and the crew would have the tricky task of collecting and reassembling the logs that had broken loose.

The profits kept the company afloat until the 1870s when a depression dropped timber prices through the floor. Rather than laying off his employees, Calvin embarked on a shipbuilding enterprise. The islanders built one ship a year, launching each one as a major event. School closed for the occasion. By this time, the town boasted a large sail loft, a boiler shop, a pattern storage loft, a marine railway, and more solidarity than ever. The first—and largest—ship

The raft was the workers' home day and night for weeks as they travelled down the St. Lawrence River.

Along the St. Lawrence rafts had to flow over five sets of rapids.

was a sea-going vessel, appropriately called *Garden Island*. Launched on May 8, 1877, it was used to transport the company's timber to England. In later years it carried coal, wheat, sand for glassmaking,

Skilled at running rapids, raftsmen still prayed before embarking on tough runs.

sugar, and rice as far away as Cuba, Colombo and Rangoon.

Calvin ran the company with generosity and kind-heartedness. That is, until his sailors signed up with the Great Lakes Seamen's Union and launched a wage dispute. Eighty-year-old Calvin did not care for this threat

New sailors from Glasgow, Scotland were shocked to learn they were strike breakers.

Tugs, steamers, sidewheelers and barges were built and launched at Garden Island. The largest of Calvin's fleet was an ocean-going vessel, the Garden Island.

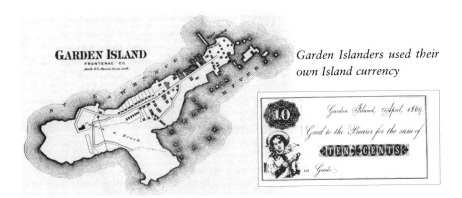

Garden Islanders used their own Island currency

to his authority. He fired his unionized sailors and hired new men from Glasgow, Scotland. When the new men also joined the union, Calvin got rid of all the sailors, and converted his schooners into barges. He towed them on Lake Ontario with a new steam barge, the *D.D.Calvin*. Calvin died at the age of 86 in 1884.

Calvin converted many of his ships to tow barges.

With one of his sons at the helm, the company carried on successfully until the outbreak of World War One, when timber-rafting ceased on the St. Lawrence. The Calvin family still owns Garden Island. The homes are rented out as summer cottages and many of the buildings are still intact. In the bay, the ribs of the sunken *D.D. Calvin* thrust out of the water, a reminder of the once enormous enterprise. (Garden Island is private property.) The Marine Museum of the Great Lakes at Kingston has a display about Garden Island's history, (613) 542-2261.

Garden Island, 1999. Many of Garden Island's ships have been scuttled around the island.

THE THOUSAND ISLANDS

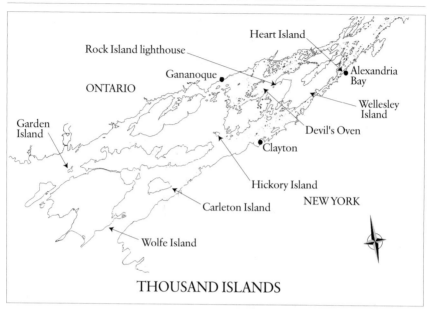

THOUSAND ISLANDS

In the Thousand Islands

CARLETON ISLAND

Fort Haldimand

August 8, 1778. British Lieutenant William Twiss called out to his oarsmen to row harder. The British boat pushed through the dark water of the St. Lawrence toward the limestone cliffs of Carleton Island. It had been two years since the war had broken out against the rebel army of the Thirteen Colonies. Twiss had been commanded to find a site to build a fort and navy base along the frontier with Lower Canada. Carleton Island was ideal. A month later, carpenters, blacksmiths and several detachments of soldiers had swung into action on the two-acre island, building a fort, complete with parapets and protective trench, high upon the cliffs.

Ruins of Fort Haldimand

In the summer of 1779, the American army marched northward, leaving fields and orchards burning in its wake. The British at Carleton Island, preparing to confront the rebels, recognized the importance of allying with the local native groups. Soon Mohawk war parties—led by British officers—were launching successful raids to the south.

For the next two years, ruthless skirmishes followed, often led by the British-educated Mohawk chief Thayendangea, also known as Joseph Brant. Clad in feather headdress, red sash, and loose European cotton shirt, Brant made the fort his base and refuge. However, the most sought after British ally was Molly Brant, Joseph's sister. A skilled interpreter and shrewd negotiator, Molly smoothed over relations between the British and the natives. According to the British, her influence was "far superior to that of all their chiefs

The Fort's barracks and magazine

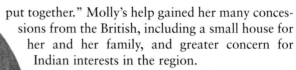

put together." Molly's help gained her many concessions from the British, including a small house for her and her family, and greater concern for Indian interests in the region.

Native attacks from the north were not the only difficulties that the Americans endured. There were internal conflicts as well. A considerable number of settlers in the Thirteen Colonies did not side with the rebels. A steady stream of these Loyalists fled their homesteads and travelled north, seeking refuge in British North America (now Canada). Many found a temporary haven at Fort Haldimand on Carleton Island.

Joseph Brant

April 1783 brought the Treaty of Paris, ensuring American independence which had been declared seven years earlier in 1776. An international boundary was decreed between British North America and the new United States, running midway through the Great Lakes and along the middle of the St. Lawrence. Britain lost Carleton Island—and their fort. But it was more than a decade before the Carleton garrison gave up the fort, leaving it partly dismantled, and transferring to Kingston.

When the War of 1812 broke out, the island garrison consisted of one sergeant, two women, and three invalids. Their capture by a boatload of Yankee farmers ended the British presence on Carleton. Soon the island became a peaceful domain for settlers and smugglers, the fort's crumbling stone chimneys its only remains.

HICKORY ISLAND

The Woman Who Saved Upper Canada From America

New York State, 1838. The men stamped the snow from their feet as they entered from the cold February air. Through the smoky haze of the tavern, they could see shadowy figures at every table and crammed against the walls, listening intently to the speech. Here in this tavern, William Lyon Mackenzie, the Canadian rebel and fugitive on an anti-British crusade, was mainly preaching to the converted. These Americans already hated all things British, and the more Mackenzie exposed British injustice, the more they grew convinced of their duty to liberate their neighbours to the north. More and more men enlisted in the secret Patriot Army and joined the Hunter's Lodge meetings to overthrow the British.

Elizabeth Barnett in later years.

Mackenzie was more than just a travelling inspirational speaker in the Upper Canada Rebellion of 1837-38. He spearheaded a major offensive against the city of Kingston, strategically located at the outlet of Lake Ontario. He had enlisted the help of American General Van Rensselaer, and an already famous rebel nicknamed "Pirate Bill" Johnston. Johnston had become the Admiral of the "Patriot Navy," which consisted of skiffs rowed by a dozen men and some boats with cannons perched at their prows. Under Mackenzie's direction, the rebels would capture the fort at Kingston, gain control of the munitions and use the strategic post as the hub from which to overthrow the government.

Pirate Bill's "Patriot Navy" consisted of some boats with cannons perched at their prows.

In mid-February 1838, hundreds of men left Clayton, New York on foot and horseback and streamed across the snow-covered ice of the St. Lawrence River to Hickory Island. They were armed with rifles, ammunition, and a few cannon that they had "liberated" from various military holdings. It was from this island that they would attack the Canadian town of Gananoque

Rebels mustering. The army was comprised of men who wanted to liberate Canada from Britian's Imperial yoke.

and then "on to Kingston" (their attack slogan). According to the plan, sympathizers at Kingston's Fort Henry would open the doors when the forces arrived.

The rebels chose Hickory Island because it was only five miles from Gananoque, and most importantly, it was located just inside the Canadian border. The U.S. Congress had distanced itself from the rebels' cause by voting for neutrality. Not wishing to contravene American law, the rebels launched their offensive from within Canada. Besides, Hickory had plenty of fields for the anticipated 2,000 rebel troops to camp out on. They set up tents around the Livingston family's farmhouse. The rebels huddled by fires, liberally dispensing whiskey that further fueled the Patriots' resolve.

Elizabeth Barnett paced up and down her family's guest room in Lafargeville, N.Y. Her bags sat packed by the front door as she waited for her horse and cutter. Her family had tried to convince her to stay and see a local doctor. But Elizabeth insisted on returning home to Gananoque, keeping the details of her "illness" vague.

Soon Elizabeth was bundled up and clutching the reigns as she charged the ten miles across the St. Lawrence River back to her home. American born, Elizabeth had joined her brother in Canada. After one year in Gananoque, Elizabeth had become a schoolteacher, passionately loyal to her new home. While visiting her family back in the U.S., she had overheard rebel plans to attack Kingston and her hometown from Hickory Island.

Once back in Gananoque, Elizabeth's news of the rebellion spread like wildfire. Within hours, sleighs loaded with women and children exited the town. Meanwhile, the militia built a timber wall from which to fire on the unsuspecting rebels. Scouts confirmed Elizabeth's story—hundreds of armed men had gathered. In Gananoque, guns were cleaned and readied and every able-bodied man squeezed into the blockhouse to plan the town's defence. The Kingston militia was notified, and on its way to Gananoque. They were ready—all they needed now was a spy to keep them up to speed on rebel movements.

A patrol struck out over the ice at 5 a.m. At Mudlanta Island, a resident revealed he had spied the Patriot Army skulking off, bit by bit, back home to the U.S. The two Canadians hurried on to Hickory Island. There they found Mrs. Livingston alone in her farmhouse, with the surrounding snow trampled for as far as they could see. The rebels were gone.

For the rebels, things just kept getting worse. First, only a small fraction of the 2,000 men who had pledged to fight actually showed up. The weather was bitterly cold, and the men ill equipped. Then, the news shot through the camp that the enemy had learned of their surprise attack. Now the rebels found themselves about to face six companies of the Leeds Militia, the Brockville Rifle Company, the Frontenac Cavalry, and a contingent of Mohawks. Fearing slaughter, the men slipped, one by one, into the night. By morning, Admiral Bill Johnston and General Van Rensselaer had scarcely any soldiers left to charge on Kingston. The action was aborted. As for Mackenzie, he had pulled out long before, said to have lost confidence in the General and his love of drink.

Upon Barnett's return the town of Gananoque sprang into action. Women and children fled by sleigh, and men readied weapons and planned their defence against the impending rebel attack.

Having saved the town, Elizabeth Barnett met Warren Fairman of the Leeds Militia during defense preparations. They were married within the month. The historical significance of Elizabeth's act cannot be underestimated. If rebel forces had taken Kingston, it would have been an inspirational victory for Americans who were sitting on the fence about the Patriot cause. As it happened, the failure of the Hickory attack so diffused rebel resolve on Lake Ontario that it never recovered. But Pirate Bill was not finished yet. He had his swan song with the burning of the steamship *Sir Robert Peel* the following spring (see below). (For more about the Rebellion of 1837-8 see Pelee Island, Lake Erie p.83.)

WELLESLEY ISLAND, DEVILS OVEN

Pirate Bill Johnston

Johnston's posting at Rock Island

It was a strange fate for a pirate, ending up as lighthouse keeper at Rock Island. Truly, it was amazing he had not been jailed for life or hanged for his deeds. But here, in the serene days of his life, he could almost see the spot where he'd committed his most notorious act, if he gazed across the waters toward Wellesley Island.

Bill Johnston had been a pirate and smuggler long before he had declared himself Commander in Chief of the Patriots' Naval Forces in 1838. Born to a poor Quebec family in 1782, from his youth, Bill was preoccupied with money. He built a small ship and took up freighting. He learned his way through all the nooks and crannies of the Thousand Islands, a skill that would later assist him as a smuggler.

In 1811 he sold his vessel and opened a store in Kingston. Johnston sold contraband—rum, ground ginger, peppermint cordial, Scotch, snuff and cigars by the hundreds—acquired from his old smuggling associates south of the border. When the War of 1812 broke out, Johnston's fraternizing with the enemy displeased British authorities. He was arrested and his land, house and store were confiscated. Sentenced to confinement in the Kingston gaol, the wily Johnston took to a small canoe, crossed the treacherous Lake

Pirate Bill Johnston was both feared and admired, depending on whose side one was on.

Ontario, and escaped to the United States. Johnston swore revenge on the British—a pledge that would fuel him the remainder of his days.

Johnston took up spying for the Americans, intercepting military dispatches en route along the river between Kingston and Gananoque, seizing boats, stripping passengers for their money, and generally wreaking his own personal havoc under wartime cover. After the war, Pirate Bill spent three decades in and out of either jail or hiding. His feisty daughter Kate—a sharp shooter known as the Queen of the Thousand Islands—helped Bill out of tight corners.

In 1837, another cross-border conflict also marked the peak of Bill's pirating career. In Toronto, William Lyon Mackenzie was inciting rebellion against British rule in Canada. When his skirmish failed, he fled to Buffalo, gathering American sympathizers and founded his own government on Navy Island, upriver from Niagara Falls. A Patriot vessel called the *Caroline*, attempting to bring supplies to the island, was captured by Loyalist Canadians, set fire and cut adrift to hurtle over the Falls.

News of the *Caroline's* fate inflamed Bill Johnston's anger and his inspiration. In late May of 1838, Pirate Bill proclaimed himself Commander-in-Chief of the Patriot Navy—which did not yet exist. Bill and two dozen supporters devised a scheme to capture a British steamship, the first vessel in the naval fleet. They set their sights on the *Sir Robert Peel*. Owned by a group of businessmen from Brockville, it ferried passengers through the Thousand Islands, and was the best boat in its class on the lake.

Rain battered the Commander and his men the night of May 29, as they crouched in wait for the *Robert Peel* near the Wellesley Island dock. The men's faces sported Mohawk war paint. Commander Bill relished the disguise, remembering the

Bill Johnston wanted to revenge the burning of the Patriot's ship Caroline *by Loyalists.*

Pirate Bill found his revenge May 29th, 1812 when his navy captured and burned the Robert Peel *near Wellesley Island.*

terror the Indians had unleashed in the War of 1812. He hoped the rain wouldn't wash the paint away too soon.

The chug and churn of a steam engine came toward them in the gloom. The *Robert Peel* loomed out of the dark and glided in to dock. A crewman stepped ashore to moor her and was swarmed by a band of natives, their bayonets and rifles threatening. "Remember the *Caroline*!" was their curious war cry. The painted marauders forced the crew into submission and went to rouse the sleeping passengers. Bewildered men and women were pushed from their berths and forced off the ship. Passengers and crew were put ashore, shivering in the driving rain.

Neither Bill nor any of his "Navy" men knew how to get the vessel going. The more they tried and failed, the more the Commander's frustration grew. Then the sight of the flaming *Caroline* flashed in Bill's memory. He ordered his men to strip the ship of its valuables and set it on fire. Soon the *Robert Peel* was a hot orange blaze reflecting in the still, black water. The burning vessel began to drift downstream, coming to rest against a rock where it burned down to the water.

To Pirate Bill, this revenge was gentler than the high drama of the *Caroline's* plunge over Niagara. But he had netted a decent haul from the well-heeled passengers, a rumoured $175,000. Lord Durham, Governor General of Upper Canada, offered a $1,000 reward for Johnston's capture. Commander Bill issued a manifesto in local papers, proclaiming his goal to liberate Canada from Britain. The U.S. government distanced itself from Johnston by offering a $500 reward for his capture and $250 for each of his followers. Within three days, nine of Bill's men had been picked up and jailed. A team of British and Americans wove through the myriad channels of the islands, hunting for Bill and the rest of his followers. Johnston eluded them for months. He purportedly hid out in a cave on a tiny island called Devil's Oven. His daughter Kate brought him food and the latest news on his would-be captors.

The search party eventually caught up with him. Johnston was arrested in November, tried, and sentenced to a year in jail. Kate asked permission to spend the time with him. After six months, the two escaped, emerging later with a long petition asking for his pardon. The pardon was eventually granted by U.S. President Franklin Pierce in recognition of Johnston's service in the War of 1812.

Pirate Bill's career finally took a peaceful turn as William Johnston, lighthouse keeper of Rock Island where he resided until February 17, 1870, at the age of 88. Alexandria Bay residents honour Bill Johnston in the annual Pirates' weekend festivities.

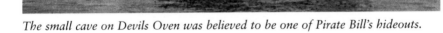

The small cave on Devils Oven was believed to be one of Pirate Bill's hideouts.

HEART ISLAND

Castle of the Heart

Pushing gently through the sparkling water at the eastern end of Lake Ontario, the tour boat wends its way past island after island, some with modest cottages, and others with grand Victorian summer homes. Suddenly a castle appears, straight out of a storybook, six storeys and two dozen spires piercing the sky. Gracing the centre of Heart Island—a heart-shaped island—is Boldt Castle. A millionaire's folly. Inspired by love.

Born in 1851 in Prussia, as a child George Charles Boldt loved the castles on the banks of the Rhine. He emigrated to the U.S. at age thirteen and worked in a hotel kitchen in New York City. Slowly he saved enough to buy a chicken farm in Texas but a flood swept it away. He went back to New York and gradually worked his way up in the restaurant business, landing a job as steward of the exclusive Clover Club in Philadelphia. From their first meeting, the owner's daughter, Louise, took his breath away. They were married two years later. Soon they had a son and a daughter.

Boldt prospered in Louise's loving company. The members of the Clover Club were impressed with him, impressed enough to help him start his own

George Boldt, the wealthy manager of the Waldorf Astoria Hotel in New York City, built Boldt Castle as a gift to his wife.

hotel. One night, a gentleman arrived wanting a room. Although the hotel was fully booked, Boldt, the gracious host, gave up his own quarters. That man was Waldorf Astor and when the Waldorf Astoria opened in New York, Astor asked Boldt to be his manager. Within a decade, Boldt was director for several trust companies, president of an import firm, trustee of Cornell University, and the most successful hotel magnate of his day.

In 1895, he and Louise visited the Thousand Islands, the newest playground for the nouveaux riches. They fell in love with an island owned by Congressman E.K. Hart and began to build Boldt's dream estate. First he renovated Hart's mansion, then built a boathouse large enough to accommodate three yachts and ten guests. Next came the powerhouse. It had a clock tower with chimes like London's Westminster. Then he built the Alster Tower (also known as the playhouse) that housed a theatre, dance hall, billiard room and bowling alley. A stone archway, styled like the Arc de Triomphe in Paris, led to a network of gardens, promenades, pavilions and lagoons.

Boldt delighted in the fairytale grandeur of the island, and in the joy it gave Louise. In 1903, he was seized by his greatest inspiration yet. He would remove the original mansion, dwarfed as it was by the other fine buildings, and replace it with the most extravagant gift a man could give his wife: an authentic castle like those along the Rhine.

Barges brought tons of granite upriver from Boldt's own quarry on Oak Island. Loads of oak arrived for floors, wainscotting, and the grand spiral staircase. From Europe came pink marble, crystal chandeliers, tapestries, and mosaics. Three hundred workers—

The lavish interior of Boldt Castle

Romantic drawing of Boldt Castle

architects, engineers, carpenters, masons, artists—worked to make Boldt's fantasy come true.

As the castle took shape, its creator became fixated on hearts. Boldt demanded that the island's contours—already somewhat shaped like a heart—be smoothed out to make a perfect shape. He changed the island's name from Hart to Heart and embedded a heart-shaped rock in the sea wall. He insisted on hearts in stone, wood, wrought iron and plaster. He even designed a family crest, featuring a heart beneath a deer, or "hart" in German.

By January 1904, the ground floor was complete and Boldt had spent $2.5 million. But on January 7, the workers received a telegram from New York: "Stop the work. Mrs. Boldt is dead." Boldt died in 1916 having never returned to Heart Island.

The castle stood abandoned for decades. Birch trees pushed up through the burnt roof of the powerhouse. Floors collapsed in the playhouse. Visitors, lured by the mystery of the place, wandered through the castle's mouldering hallways and cob-webbed salons. Vandals smashed its three hundred windows. In 1977, on the verge of being condemned, the estate was deeded to the Thousand Islands Bridge Authority. Twenty years and $9.5 million later, the estate has been restored beyond Boldt's wildest dreams, down to heart-shaped garden beds filled with bleeding hearts. Every year, almost 200,000 visitors amble on the paths and sweep down the spiral staircase, their hearts full of romance.

1894 government publication listing the Thousand Islands for sale

THE THOUSAND ISLANDS

A Bootlegger's Paradise

United States Border Patrol agent Archie Denner had heard about a bootlegging operation run from a tiny Canadian island, just a few metres from American waters. The Canadian who ran the operation was one of dozens of new smugglers in the region, looking to profit from prohibition.

Cutting the engine, agent Archie Denner quietly advanced his boat through the narrow channel, drifting silently into a cove. Jagged rocks lurked just below the surface and overhanging branches scraped the boat, but Archie knew these waters well. His father was a ship's captain and the Denner family owned nearly a hundred islands on the river. As children, Archie and his brother Henry chased each other in small boats, hiding in secluded coves and harbours, exploring hidden caves and beaches. Now, instead of chasing each other for fun, the Denner boys chased rumrunners for a living. An ideal childhood playground, the very same features made it a smuggler's paradise.

Ahead through the darkness, he saw a faint light flickering from a cottage. He could see a slim man smoking a cigarette and moving cases in and out of the cabin. Denner's voice drifted across to the man on shore, "A case of yer best whiskey." Minutes later, a shadow rowed out of the darkness with the expensive merchandise. Denner kept his pistol ready. Some of the big-time bootleggers were armed, and when smuggling deals had gone sour,

Border agents on the Great Lakes were up against a multi-million dollar smuggling industry.

people had gone missing, and bodies had washed up on shore. Border agents had been shot at before.

Denner could make out the sharp features of the bootlegger's face. The man was crouched down in his boat, peering at Denner. Something was wrong. The bootlegger reached into his boat. Denner leapt into the rowboat, and sent the stunned man flying. He was caught red-handed, literally. Dazed and sprawled out over a case of whiskey, the bootlegger clutched a broken bottle of fine scotch in his hand, its reddish-brown liquid trickling down his arm...

For centuries, the Great Lakes region has been a centre of international trade, not all of it legal. In January 1920, the U.S. Congress passed the Volstead Act prohibiting the purchase, sale, manufacture or transport of liquor and beer over 0.5% alcohol content. A flood of illegal booze began to flow in from the Canadian border. Until Prohibition was repealed thirteen years later, the Thousand Islands were a major battleground for the U.S. government's war on smuggled alcohol. Bootleggers ferried their beer and liquor from places near Kingston and Belleville to American destinations at Sackets Harbour and Oswego. Smugglers used islands such as Main Duck, Wolfe and Simcoe for storage and for shelter from bad weather and border patrols. To the east, where the river narrowed and the islands dominated, they ran booze south through the maze of islands to the U.S. shore. Only a handful of border agents were on duty, up against a multi-million dollar industry.

Prohibition era cartoon

Most of the action happened during night patrol. Invisible in the dark, smugglers' small boats could hide almost anywhere. They were mainly youth or small-timers sneaking across the border with a few cases. But sometimes the agents would come across longer craft carrying more than 1,000 cases of beer or whiskey. With powerful motors and machine guns mounted on their boats, most bootleggers got away. When chased, they used decoy boats, opened fire, or tried to draw their pursuers onto the rocks. Many border patrol agents preferred to wait for the smugglers to reach shore before giving chase, thus avoiding life-threatening encounters on the water.

The ones who didn't escape often found ways to conceal their merchandise: in secret boat compartments; in haystacks; stuffed into large fish. Large shipments were dumped overboard packed in salt-filled sacks that sunk to the bottom. A few days later the salt would dissolve and the bootlegger—released from jail due to lack of evidence—could return to pick up his contraband, now floating on the surface. But not all of the liquor was recovered. Cases of fine old Canadian whiskey are rumoured to lie at the bottom of the St. Lawrence River.

(*This story is partially based on information from Shawn Thompson's* River's Edge: Reprobates, Rum-runners and Other Folk of the Thousand Islands.)

Sunset cruise in the Thousand Islands

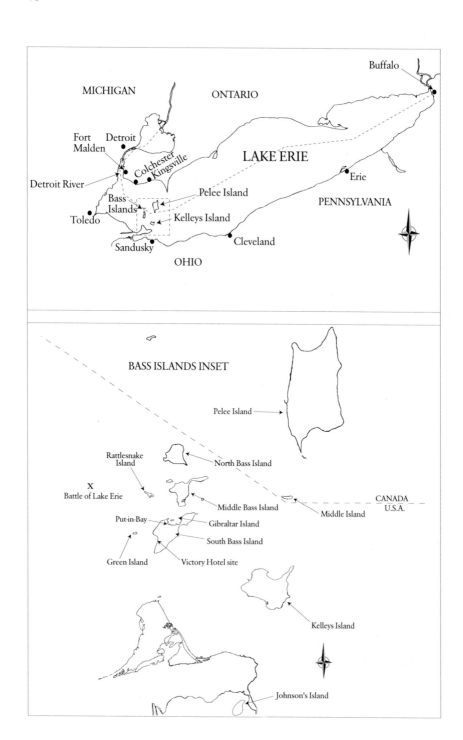

LAKE ERIE ISLANDS

Born of a Tropical Sea

The islands of Lake Erie were born of a tropical sea. Three hundred and fifty million years ago, the area from Ohio to Ontario was positioned near the equator, and warm waters blanketed the region. The shells of early aquatic life sank to the lake bottom creating a thick mud floor. When the sea eventually evaporated, this muck turned into limestone. Fossils from the ancient tropical sea can be viewed at Kelleys Island.

Volcanic action pushed up the limestone in the locations of the future Erie Islands. During the Ice Ages, debris carried by the glaciers carved the limestone. As the final glacier retreated about 10,000 years ago, it flooded a vast region with its meltwater. The lake settled to its current level, exposing Erie's archipelago, a series of islands at the western end of the lake, the largest being Pelee, Kelleys and South Bass. The islands are low, flat and marshy, clustered together in what is the shallowest water in the Great Lakes.

In the 19th century, the Lake Erie islands took on a strategic and political importance. They were on the front lines of both the War of 1812 and the Upper Canada Rebellion of 1837. Battles fought on or near their shores helped to draw the border that today divides Canada and the United States. Confederate officers were imprisoned here during the Civil War.

Drawn by the temperate climate, European and United Empire Loyalist settlers cleared the land and planted vineyards. In the later 19th and 20th centuries, most of these soft and tranquil islands became magnets for summer holiday makers. Large hotels and resorts, cottages and clubs appeared on the shores of South Bass and Gibraltar Islands. Private boats and island steamers cruised the waters, bringing sightseers and tourists, birdwatchers and fishermen. Serene and accessible, many of the islands are inhabited and are linked to the mainland by regular ferries and by generations of fond summer memories.

SOUTH BASS ISLAND

The Visitors Paradise

Around the turn of the century, tourists flocked to South Bass Island, made famous by the 1813 Battle of Lake Erie. Crowds poured in by steamer, drawn by the island's celebrated restaurants, dancing, swimming, fishing, caves and extensive vineyards. Guests of the palatial Victory Hotel rode a trolley car for free, while others paid a fare of 75 cents (72 cents more than a regular city fare).

Today, tourists still cram into the town of Put-in-Bay, soaking up Lake Erie's restorative effects, and taking in the fishing, swimming, cycling and golf. Many century buildings—housing restaurants, bars and shops—have been beautifully preserved. Sights include the world's longest restaurant bar, Perry's Cave, Crystal Cave, Heineman winery (the only South Bass commercial winery still in operation). The island has three historical museums: Perry's Victory and International Peace Memorial about the Battle of Erie, (419) 285-2184; the Lake Erie Islands Historical Society Museum offering a rich look at the history of South Bass, (419) 285-2804; and Stonehenge wine-making museum in a nineteenth-century stone house, (419) 285-2585. For ferry information call Island Transportation Inc., (419) 285-4855. For camping on South Bass, contact South Bass Island State Park (419) 285-2112 or (419) 797-4530.

Tourists flocked to the Columbia Restaurant in the Round House, built 1873

By 1878, there were 71 grape growers producing wine on South Bass.

Advertisers hailed islands where "the song of the Mosquito is never heard and there is an entire absence of dew," and travellers by the thousands came by steamer.

SOUTH BASS

"We have met the enemy and they are ours"
The Battle of Lake Erie

The defeat of Canada would be "a mere matter of marching" Republican congressmen had assured President James Madison in the spring of 1812. After all, British forces in the colony numbered only a few thousand, and most of them were stationed in far away Quebec. Besides, most of the settlers in Upper Canada were of American stock. Surely they would not fight their own kin. But the Canadas would not fall so easily. After a year of humiliating defeats at Detroit, Queenston, and Mackinac Island, American troops were stalemated along a one-thousand-mile front from Lake Champlain to the Upper Mississippi in the summer of 1813.

The war was generally little understood, on both sides of the border. Most Canadians were more concerned with their crops and trading with the United States than responding to British calls for duty to King and Country. For the most part, their American neighbours agreed, especially in the northeast where opposition to the war was so strong that some states refused to contribute troops or money to "Mr. Madison's War." But the fight continued. It was a matter of "national honour," insisted the war-hawks in Washington and London. America could no longer tolerate the harassment of its ships on the high seas by the British fleet. Britain, engaged in a desperate war with the French, could not permit America's continued trade with Napoleonic France. The matter would be settled on the battle-fields and lakes of North America, in the War of 1812.

At only 28 and with limited naval action, Oliver Hazard Perry was called to lead a battle on Lake Erie in the War of 1812. The pressure and the stakes were high. Whoever controlled the Great Lakes, basically controlled the war—the Lakes were the supply route and the communication line. In the fall of 1813, the British held Lake Erie. A victory could reclaim American control, making way for Northwest expansion.

When Perry arrived at the military base at Erie, Pennsylvania, he found it was a base in name only—it was actually a construction site. Neglected and defenseless, it had a single gun and no completed ships. At the other end of the lake, at the established Fort Malden, the British were well armed. Yet for both sides, the first stage of preparation became a ship-building contest.

In this frontier region, it was a challenge to recruit seamen and to rally

R)American Oliver Hazard Perry began his naval career at 13 but did not see action until he was called to lead the Battle of Lake Erie. He was 28 years old.

L)In the Battle of Lake Erie, Britain's Robert Heriott Barclay was 26 years old and had been at sea since the age of twelve. Experienced in naval battle, he had lost an arm in 1807 in an expedition off France.

supplies, carpenters and blacksmiths. Iron was in such short supply that treenails had to be used. To make matters more difficult, the lumber was green, cut from massive trees from nearby forests. "Plain work is all that's required," master shipwright, Noah Brown told his workers, "[The ships] will only be wanted for one battle." By mid-July, the Americans had eleven vessels to the British effort of only six. However, Perry had other factors to consider.

The British had more guns which could fire a greater range. If Perry were to succeed, he would have to use his cannon—which were shorter in range but greater in firepower—tactically. A closely fought battle with the wind in his favour was imperative. Furthermore, Perry was short of crew, and was concerned because his men had been struck with "lake fever" or dysentery. The British commander, Captain Robert Heriott Barclay was, like his youthful adversary, only 26 years old. But unlike Perry, Barclay was a seasoned seaman who had lost an arm earlier in the Napoleonic Wars. Yet Barclay too was desperately short of experienced seamen.

At their new base at Put-in-Bay, on South Bass Island, the Americans awaited British provocation. It finally came. At dawn on September 10, a

Perry raised this flag to rally the seamen. He borrowed his battle slogan from the dying words of his friend, Captain Lawrence, killed June 1, 1813.

lookout spied the British on the lake 10 to 12 miles northwest of Put-in-Bay. By six a.m. the Americans were underway to meet them.

It was a perfect late summer day and the sun sparkled silver on the blue water. Fifteen vessels converged gracefully, their white sails luffing in the gentle breeze. To the distant eye, they could have been toy sailboats on a pond.

Within three to four miles of the enemy, Perry rallied the seamen. He raised a handmade ship's flag. "My brave lads," he began. "This flag is inscribed with the words, 'Don't give up the ship.' Shall I hoist it?" "Aye, aye, sir!" the crew sang out in chorus. Their three cheers echoed across the water.

At a quarter to noon, and a mile apart, a bugle sounded on the British ship *Detroit*. Shouts rose, and the first British cannonball hurtled toward—but missed—the American *Lawrence*. Then the carnage began. The *Lawrence*'s surgeon, Usher Parsons, was a witness. "Little could be heard but... the crash of balls dashing through our timbers, and the shrieks of the wounded." Blood spilled over the decks. The dead and the suffering were everywhere.

Perry remained surprisingly unfazed by the destruction. He had been standing with an officer who, in the next moment, was struck in the thigh by a cannonball, shattering him horribly. Perry coolly ordered him to be taken below. "His countenance was as calm and placid as if on ordinary duty," recalled Dr. Parsons.

For the next two hours, the American flagship remained Commander Barclay's principal target. The wind was not in his favour, so Barclay tried to get enough shots in from a distance before Perry was able to pull into close range. Perry did not intend to surrender. Pushing the *Lawrence* through the barrage of cannonballs, Perry got within 300 yards of the *Detroit* and opened rapid fire with all his starboard guns. Three other American vessels moved up to take on the smaller ships. The *Niagara* hung behind.

When Perry's flagship Lawrence *lay destroyed, Perry made the unusual move of switching to the* Niagara.

Bombarded for two hours, the American *Lawrence* was doomed, its sails in tatters. Perry abandoned her and ordered the first cutter. "If victory is to be gained, I'll gain it," declared the captain, as the crew rowed with all their might toward the *Niagara*, their ship that had hung back. The British commander spotted Perry, standing in the *Lawrence's* cutter, and read his plan. Perry had already severely damaged the *Detroit*. Barclay did

Nine American vessels battled six British vessels. While the Americans had a larger fleet, the British had more guns.

not relish the thought of another onslaught from a fresh ship; he ordered every gun to fire at the cutter.

As legend has it, Perry continued his proud stand in the boat, as cannonballs fell all around. He reached the *Niagara*, took command, and sped toward the enemy. Barclay himself had his one good arm shattered in the barrage and was taken below deck. Meanwhile, to use their remaining guns to best advantage, one of Barclay's junior officers ordered the *Detroit* to come about. The British *Queen Charlotte*, not responding effectively to this move, ran her bowsprit into the rigging of her sister ship, *Detroit*. With the British ships entangled, the *Niagara* slipped between them, and gave the British everything it had, blasting the ships from both sides. In 15 minutes, a white flag was flying on the deck of the *Queen Charlotte*, and before long, the *Detroit* had also raised her flag of truce. By three in the afternoon the battle was over.

Commodore Perry sent General Harrison a dispatch that would go down in history: "We have met the enemy and they are ours. Two ships, two brigs, one schooner and one sloop... O.H. Perry"

After the war, Perry had a short and checkered military career, and he died of yellow fever in Trinidad at the age of 34. The Battle of Lake Erie left British Captain Robert Heriott Barclay further physically impaired, both arms now rendered useless. Spectators at his court-marshal—a standard procedure when British vessels were lost at war—wept at his appearance.

While Perry's victory did not win the war, it did win back control of Lake Erie, and it helped secure Ohio for the U.S. The battle also won Oliver Hazard Perry a hero's place in history: it was the first time an entire British fleet was conquered.

SOUTH BASS

Perry's Victory and International Peace Memorial

The monumental stone column is visible for miles. It is Perry's Victory and International Peace Memorial, the third tallest national monument in the United States. An awesome 80,000 cubic feet of pink granite, it is crowned with an eleven-ton bronze urn, and towers at a height of 352 feet.

The memorial was constructed from 1912 to 1915 to commemorate the American victory in the Battle of Lake Erie (September 10, 1813). It is as massive and permanent a monument as the battle was short-lived.

An on-site museum depicts the Battle of Lake Erie. Visitors take an elevator to an observation platform 317 feet (95m) above the lake, offering a spectacular view. For information on the Perry's Victory and International

The burial procession for six British and American officers following the Battle of Lake Erie. On the American flagship, Lawrence, *83 of the 103 on board were killed or wounded.*

Left) Man standing beneath the massive 11-ton bronze urn crowning the Perry Monument
Below) Postcard of Perry's Victory and International Peace Memorial

Six officers (three British and three American) were buried in a common grave in Put-in-Bay. A willow shoot left on the grave sprouted into "Perry's Willow," a popular, tourist site around the turn of the century. It was rumoured that when the tree fell over in 1900, it was cut up and sold as souvenirs.

In September, 1913, the six officers were exhumed in Put-in-Bay, placed in a single casket, and moved to their new resting place in a crypt beneath the floor of the monument.

Peace Monument, call: (419) 285-2184; or contact: www.nps.gov/pevi

For the British point of view of the battle, visit Fort Malden in Amherstburg, Ontario near the mouth of the Detroit River, where Barclay and his fleet were stationed before the battle. Displays include artifacts from the Royal Navy stationed at Amherstberg and information relating to the Battle of Lake Erie: (519) 736-5416. Web site: www.ont_fort-malden@pch.gc.ca

Monument under construction showing the crane. The tower was faced in granite and then concrete was poured.

SOUTH BASS ISLAND

Enchanted Caves

Of the twenty caves discovered on South Bass Island, all but one was formed by rainwater seeping into the rock which gradually dissolved pockets of gypsum, leaving dome-shaped cavities. Crystal Cave is one of a kind on South Bass. Samples of Crystal Cave celestite—a white mineral containing strontium—are on display at the Smithsonian Institute in Washington D.C. After the cave had formed, water mineralized with

Crystal Cave was discovered in 1880 during the digging of a well. They broke into the opening full of crystals at a depth of about thirty feet. In 1898, Gustav Heineman opened the cave to the public.

L) Perry's Cave guide, John Gangwish, claimed he had received hundreds of letters from people whose wishes had come true after visiting the "wishing well," the pool of water in Perry's Cave. R) John Gangwish, loved to thrill guests by planting props, such as old boots, that he claimed had belonged to sailors from the War of 1812.

Daussa's Cave, opened in 1899, was sold in 1913 and renamed Mammoth Cave. Gustav Heineman managed the cave along with his own Crystal Cave and winery. He closed Mammoth in 1953, after showing stockholders that large rocks had fallen.

Captain John Brown Jr. came to South Bass for solitude in 1862. (This was about three years after his father, John Brown the abolitionist, was hanged for treason after he tried to take over the federal arsenal at Harper's Ferry.) Brown, a surveyor on the island, was fascinated by the caves and served as the unofficial tour guide for visitors and scientists.

celestite, creating gem-like formations that lent the cave its nickname, the "fairy grotto."

From the Victorian era onward, it was all the rage to visit the caves at Put-in-Bay, and the marketing began. Daussa's Cave had women attendants to assist unescorted women and children. Stronita Cave boasted, "Don't miss this wonderful cave. Six lawyers from different states are fighting for it." Paradise Cave lit its interior with coloured lights. Crystal Cave was advertised as a "casket of jewels." Today only Perry's and Crystal Caves are still open for public viewing. Perry's Cave: (419) 285-2405; and Heineman Winery and Crystal Cave: (419) 285-2811.

SOUTH BASS

Fall From Glory: Hotel Victory

So grand was the Hotel Victory that steamer captains reportedly could see its glow from 30 miles away. Also known as "Tillotson's Palace" after the hotel's first owner John Tillotson, it was indeed a palace, with a 600-foot verandah, ballroom, three dining rooms and more than 800 guest rooms. The exquisite Belgian rug in the lobby was so large that a wall had to be removed just to install it. A 23-piece orchestra entertained at fancy dinners. Equipped with all the latest modern amenities, rooms had private bathrooms, light fixtures, and electric call buttons to ring the bellhop. Electric trolley cars could hold 150 people, and transported guests to the hotel and around the island. But astoundingly, not long after opening in 1892, the Victory was already bankrupt, sitting empty, and nicknamed "Tillotson's Nightmare."

When the trolley service ended after the Hotel Victory was destroyed by fire in 1919, Heineman purchased twenty Yellow Ribbon Taxis to transport visitors to Perry's, Mammoth and Crystal Caves.

The Hotel Victory was advertised as the world's largest resort hotel, and as the "Florida Hotel of the North."

Owner Tillotson had trouble bankrolling the lavish venture. Soon his extravagance and slippery financing caught up with him. Construction had just begun when most investors pulled out, leaving Tillotson with only $1,000 in cash. Nearly complete, the hotel had accrued a huge debt, and a long line of angry, unpaid creditors. In August 1893 the Victory went bankrupt. The hotel remained empty until April 1896, when it was sold off—for a fraction of its value—to the architects who built it. They dumped the struggling enterprise only five years later. Hardware merchants, the Ryan brothers, picked up the white elephant in 1899 and

The Victory's grand dining room

brought aboard a manager who turned it all around. Thomas McCreary had a feel for the times. He was gregarious and friendly, considered the "perfect host." He set exactly the right tone: replacing Black waiters with waitresses in the dining room; encouraging men and women to swim together, considered risqué in those days. McCreary kept the hotel humming with guests drawn in by his marketing brochures. Filled with an arsenal of clichés, they

offered something for everyone: "the Mecca of the Tourist; the Historic; the Garden Spot of the Great Lakes; Nature's Beauty Spot; the Children's Paradise; the Boon of the Invalid; a First-class place for first-class people...."

When McCreary died in 1908, the hotel lost its direction once again, closing due to lack of business. Several would-be hoteliers tried their hand at the Victory but were unsuccessful. Then, on an August evening in 1919, with only thirty guests inside, a fire started in the wiring. The burning Victory was a bright and dazzling sight, beheld even in Detroit. But the Victory in ashes signified the end of grandeur on South Bass Island.

The August 1919 hotel fire was visible in Detroit. By morning the Victory was reduced to rubble.

GIBRALTAR ISLAND

The Man Who Financed the Civil War

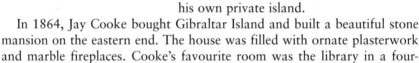

Jay Cooke was not born into wealth. He began his career modestly, a bank teller in Philadelphia. He rose quickly through the ranks, until one day, with enough capital and clout behind him, he started his own bank. He eventually became one of the country's richest men, the man—it is said—who financed the Civil War.

At the time of the Civil War, Jay Cooke's innovative idea of selling war bonds saved the American government from financial ruin. It was going to be a costly war to fight. If bonds were priced within their reach, ordinary citizens could support the Union cause. Soon every northern newspaper advertised the bonds, and the money flowed—through thousands of Cooke's agents. Now Cooke was rich. And a rich man needs a place to spend his summers: his own private island.

Jay Cooke

In 1864, Jay Cooke bought Gibraltar Island and built a beautiful stone mansion on the eastern end. The house was filled with ornate plasterwork and marble fireplaces. Cooke's favourite room was the library in a four-story, seven-sided tower.

Cooke was known to be generous—distributing oysters, candies, and boxes of pictures and books to Put-in-Bay residents. As a devout Christian, he frowned on the drinking and revelry that tourism brought to Put-in-Bay. Cooke built a Protestant Church and hosted an annual picnic for local residents, presenting each child with a new Bible. When General William Tecumseh Sherman arrived unannounced once on the Sabbath, Cooke hid inside the mansion, and had his housekeeper turn away the famous guest.

Then, in 1873, Jay Cooke lost his fortune overnight. In order to build the Northern Pacific Railway, the financier had

Jay Cooke's monument to the Battle of Lake Erie.

Gibraltar Island was the summer home of Jay Cooke, "the man who financed the Civil War."

borrowed heavily against his own bank and had been selling shares in Europe. The timing could not have been worse. As the Franco-Prussian War began, all loans were called in. Jay Cooke's property was sold to pay off debts, except for "Cooke's Castle" on Gibraltar, which could find no buyer.

Jay Cooke had left many small investors teetering on the edge of ruin. But while panic raged in the money markets, Cooke remained steadfast and cool. Speculators offered ten cents on the dollar, but Cooke advised investors not to sell their shares. Those who trusted Jay Cooke saw their accounts restored, not a single dollar short. Cooke managed to regain his fortune and pay off his debts.

On a fine summer day in 1879, Jay Cooke returned to his refuge on Lake Erie. The flag blowing in the light breeze, the former staff was assembled on the dock, the castle cleaned. The Cooke family owned the mansion until the mid-1920s when it was sold to Julian Stone, a Columbus industrialist. Stone donated the "castle" to Ohio State University for the study of flora and fauna. Permission must be obtained from Ohio State University to visit the site.

Cooke hosted an annual picnic for residents of Put-in-Bay

ERIE ISLANDS

Truth and Lore

In the War of 1812, Commodore Perry anchored his fleet in the harbour at South Bass Island, awaiting the inevitable British attack. This historic event left the Erie Islands rife with folklore.

Workers raising Perry's Niagara for restoration in 1913. The ship is now in Erie, PA, and in 1994 had its third rebuilding. (The ship was restored in 1913, 1936, and 1994.

People used to boat over to Misery Bay in Erie, PA to view the remains of the Niagara, the flagship of Perry's famous fleet. The U.S. Navy scuttled the ship in 1818 after the Rush-Bagot Agreement called for the disarmament of the Great Lakes.

Ballast Island was named for the limestone cut for ballast in Perry's ships.

GREEN ISLAND LIGHTHOUSE

Frozen Fire

It was New Year's Eve, 1863. As he swirled his girlfriend around the dance floor, Pit Drake was feeling slightly apprehensive. It was warm outside, startlingly so, with the temperature in the mid-60s, and a light rain falling. Pit was the son of the lighthouse keeper on Green Island in Lake Erie. He had come two miles across the water to a dance at Put-in-Bay, leaving his family on the tiny island.

Soon the air was suddenly very cold. A wind from the northeast had reached gale proportions. The dance hall trembled with icy gusts and snow rushed at the windows, and the revelers left the dance floor to huddle around the wood stove. In a few hours, the mercury had plunged to 25°F below zero. As the clock neared midnight, the full moon seemed to rise over the water. It was not long before they realized in horror that it was actually the lighthouse on Green Island. On fire.

Colonel Drake was a rugged man who had weathered many harsh winters as keeper of the Green Island light. This New Year's Eve, he lacked his former vigour. Sitting down to a special dinner, he reflected on his family—his elder daughter and her husband, Gregorier, a likeable fellow whose strength he admired; his grandson; and Drake's charming, younger daughter, Sarah. She

The keeper and family escaped and kept warm in the stable when the Green Island lighthouse burned during an 1863 New Year's storm

was wearing a short-sleeved cotton dress on this balmy evening. He smiled at her as they began their meal. His only regret was his son Pit's empty chair.

Near the end of dinner, a chilly wind had risen, sending Sarah to fetch her shawl. There came a peculiar sound from upstairs in the light tower. It was the family cat clattering on the wooden floor, and howling wildly. Sarah padded up the stairs to find the cat. She opened the door where the cat was trapped, suddenly overwhelmed by billows of smoke. The cat streaked through her legs as Sarah rushed downstairs.

The smell of smoke flung the family into action. Gregorier propped a ladder against the tower while others carted buckets of water, and hurled

The second Green Island light, built as replacement after the fire.

them through the window. The wind blew harder, fanning the flames. With mounting dismay, the colonel feared their efforts might be hopeless. The whole tower was alight with the growing blaze. In a frenzied burst of energy, Gregorier rushed in to save whatever was at hand. The big, old government clock was striking midnight as he hauled it down into the snow, now whirling around the house.

Midnight struck Pit Drake like a sword. He could do little more than watch the blaze. In his short sleeves, Pit burst out the door, rushing toward the lake. His friends seized him just as he was climbing into his dingy, determined to row the treacherous, two miles back to the lighthouse.

Their possessions seemed absurdly out of context in the swirling snow. Rocking gently on her slippered feet, Sarah was in shock. Drake knew their only chance was to send Gregorier to fetch some mattresses. He would have to climb the burning stairs. Flames danced at Gregorier's face and hands as he plunged through suffocating smoke into a bedroom, seizing two thin mattresses, and hurling them through the window before jumping out himself.

The lake had become a seething mass of ice and angry surf. Spray exploded forty feet into the air, hissing into steam as it met the flames. Cascades beyond the fire's reach froze into strange shapes, made grotesque by the crimson glow.

Drake dragged the mattresses to the stable. He instructed his family to lie down tight together on one mattress and he put the other one on top of them. Realizing that Sarah was ailing badly, Drake put Sarah's feet into a large iron pot he salvaged from the fire. He collected hot bricks and placed them in a circle around the bed. Darkness and frigid cold descended. An entire night of this and they might all succumb.

By dawn the storm had abated. At Put-in-Bay, Pit Drake stood by the dock, surveying the surface of the lake. The calming water was freezing quickly in the harsh air. But was it thick enough to hold several rescuers? Pit summoned his friends to gather wooden planks. He stepped gingerly onto the first plank, crouched and moved his way along it. A friend passed him a second board and he proceeded along the ice as it groaned and cracked beneath his weight. Encouraged by Pit's progress, a few of his friends began their own slow paths across the ice.

At last they reached Green Island and the smouldering black ruin of the lighthouse, its ghostly ice formations hanging in the air. Pit scanned the scene for signs of life, finding nothing but embers and tumbled, blackened stone. He rushed into the stable. Seeing the mattress, he flung it back. A groan came from one of the prone figures. They were alive. Only Gregorier, with his burned hands and face, and Sarah—her arms frozen stiff—showed serious signs of their ordeal.

A second lighthouse was built as a replacement, but only its ruins remain. The light on Green Island now beams from an automatic beacon atop a metal skeleton tower.

RATTLESNAKE ISLAND

Sea Serpents

As early as 1721, Rattlesnake Island's reputation was already known to early missionaries and priests travelling Lake Erie. Father Charlevoix noted that *Isles aux Serpents* were so plagued by snakes that "the air is infected with them." Seventy years later, things had not improved much. The Vicomte de Chateaubriand noted in his *Travels in America* in 1792,

> Lake Erie is famous for its serpents. In the western part of the lake, [the] Viper Islands... are covered with serpents entwined in one another. When the reptiles happen to move in the sunshine... you can distinguish nothing but sparkling eyes, tongues with a triple dart, throats of fire...

Rattlesnake Island and the surrounding tiny islands known as "the Rattles" were not the only ones abundant with reptiles. In 1793, a group of explorers went ashore on Middle Bass and found it seething with rattlesnakes. A greater horror still was the appearance of a monstrous snake

Henry Rowe Schoolcraft, Indian agent and native historian, made this sketch from a rock painting of various Ojibwe images of Mishepeshu. The underwater manitou was depicted both as a horned lynx and a horned sea serpent. It is interesting to note that, in 1920, two settlers from Sugar Island on the St. Marys River spotted a fifteen-foot serpent with "two nubs" on its head.

over sixteen feet long—that chased them for a hundred yards. Perhaps it was the same creature reported by the schooner *Madelaine* the previous year,

> Captain Woods saw the waters of the lake lashed into foam about a half a mile ahead. Drawing near, to the surprise of all aboard, a huge sea serpent was seen wrestling about in the waters, as if fighting with an unseen foe... about 50 feet in length and not less than four feet in circumference... Its head projected from the water about four feet. He says it was a terrible looking object. It had viciously sparkling eyes... fins were plainly seen... the body was dark brown....

Similar sightings were reported as recently as 1947 when more than a dozen people on the steamer *City of Detroit III* claimed they observed a 60-foot sea serpent in Georgian Bay. Convincing sightings throughout the lakes have made the existence of the creature more credible. However, a hoax was exposed in the 1930s when wired sections of a 30-foot wooden serpent were found on a Michigan beach.

Central to Ojibwe mythology is the god of the waters, Mishepeshu. Capable of whipping up waves and whitewater, Mishepeshu was known to capsize canoes and drown humans. To this day, some Ojibwe elders will not speak Mishepeshu's name in summer for fear of invoking its wrath. They reserve stories about Mishepeshu for winter when the serpent is trapped beneath the ice.

As for the verifiable reptile population on the Erie Islands, most of the snakes were eaten by domestic hogs that were imported by settlers in the early 1800s.

MIDDLE BASS

Lonz Winery

Andrew Wehrle's residence. Golden Eagle Winery was once the largest wine producer in the country. Middle Bass Island was used as a key location for freeing slaves through the Underground Railroad.

The sprawling stone Lonz Winery on Middle Bass Island is visible from the town of Put-in-Bay. Development of a wine industry began here in the mid-1850s, when immigrants bought land and planted grapes. One such man was Andrew Wehrle who foresaw a good future in the wine business. Around 1863, he cut a 14-foot deep cellar out of the limestone, and built a grand house for his vineyard. Within a decade, his Golden Eagle Winery had become the largest wine producer in the United States. Over the years, the operation passed through the hands of several owners before the main building burned down in 1923. Two companies merged to create the Lonz Winery. George F. Lonz constructed the current building over the original Wehrle vaults. In the summer months, the winery is open to visitors and wine tasters. Lonz Winery: (419) 285-5411. Ferries arrive from South Bass Island and the mainland.

The Lonz Winery was built after the Golden Eagle Winery burned in the 1920s.

NORTH BASS ISLAND

In the mid-1800s, two French-Canadian brothers, Simon and Peter Fox, cleared 500 acres of land on North Bass Island for livestock and a winery. In 1863, they joined a Detroit financier in purchasing the steamer *Philo Parsons*, for plying the route between Sandusky and Detroit. (The *Parsons* gained notoriety when it was used in a conspiracy to rescue prisoners of war incarcerated at Lake Erie's Johnson's Island-see page 96) With two more steamers, they were able to compete with the steamship business of Ira and Datus Kelley from Kelleys Island. Today, the Fox brothers' 1860s home is still standing, and is maintained by the present owner. The island is owned privately.

Simon and Peter Fox's farm, c.1870s

KELLEYS ISLAND

Wine and Lime

The island that Datus and Irad Kelley purchased in 1833 had its problems. The island's tiny community was being terrorized by Benjamin Napier, War of 1812 veteran, and his gang, in an attempt to seize control of the island. It took several years before the Sheriff's Deputy forcibly removed the thugs, and thereby resolved the problem.

Three industries flourished all at once on Kelleys: vineyards; limestone quarries; and the cutting of red cedar to feed the steamship furnaces. The Kelley Island Lime and Transport Company bought out several quarries in the late 1890s, taking possession of nearly all the island's quality stone. Unfortunately, in the drive to cut blocks and crush stone for the company's lime production, one of the world's natural wonders was destroyed. Millions of years of glaciers have left in their crushing wake, the largest glacial grooving in the world on

Datus Kelley

Only 396 ft. (119m) of the world's longest glacial grooving have survived the quarry industry. The remaining grooves are now protected by Kelleys Island State Park.

Kelleys Island. Some grooves are 2,000 feet long and 17 feet deep. Quarry operations destroyed all but 396 feet of the grooves, which are now protected by the Kelleys Island State Park.

The largest of the American islands on Lake Erie, Kelleys has a charming town in South Bay with many Victorian homes. To view the glacial grooves and for camping and hiking trail information, contact Kelleys Island State Park (419) 746-2546. The island also has museums and gift shops, golf cart and bike rentals. Neuman Cruise and Ferry Line: (800) 876-1907; Kelleys Island Ferry Boat Lines (419) 798-9763.

Covered in over 100 aboriginal pictographs, Inscription Rock on Kelleys' shore is considered one of the finest pictograph sites on the Great Lakes. Most of the drawings have worn away with the passage of time and the impact of careless visitors so the interpretive panel is helpful.

KELLEYS ISLAND

Quarry Life

Kelley Island Lime and Transport Company had what the region wanted-limestone. Limestone for the canal at Sault Ste.Marie, for the streets of Detroit, the Cleveland breakwater, and to produce fertilizer for crops in the Midwest. In its day, KL&T Co. was one of the largest limestone quarry companies in the United States.

At its height in the early 1900s, the quarry employed a thousand workers. Broken stone was loaded onto freight cars that were pulled by narrow gauge steam engines on a network of moveable railway tracks. There was a stone crusher four stories high, a long row of lime kilns sixty-five feet tall, and a loading bay with a 600-foot steel trestle. In 1912 alone, the quarry loaded over half a million tons of stone into 459 wooden barges that were towed by steamship to almost every port on the Great Lakes.

In the early days of quarrying, limestone was blasted out with black powder and fuses. In later years, holes were drilled, driven by compressed air, and shots of dynamite were set off with electricity.

Top) Young couples without children lived in the frame, barrack-styled house, nicknamed the "incubator house." R) Quarry labourers were from so many European countries that signs were posted in seven languages.

The quarries, in conjunction with shipping companies, sent agents to southern and eastern Europe looking for workers. Young, able-bodied, married men came from Hungary, Russia, Greece and Italy. At one point signs had to be posted in seven different languages. The newcomers came alone, saving their money to send for their wives. All of the reunited couples moved together into a bunker-like building nicknamed the "Incubator House." They were only eligible for private—although crude—accommodation once their first child was expected. Essentially the workers lived by the good grace of the company, and pretty much under its thumb: their lodgings were near the quarries, and they spent their pay cheques in the company-owned store.

In 1912 alone, over half a million tons of limestone were loaded into 459 wooden barges and towed by steam freighters to almost every port on the Great Lakes.

Sixty-foot-high limestone burners on Kelleys Island

Kelleys' original inhabitants were predominately British and German. They did not—as one current resident recalled from his German father— mix much with the "foreigners." When the quarries closed in the 1940s, these immigrants provided mason work expertise in Lake Erie cities such a Cleveland and Marblehead, and many became very successful.

Today red cedar trees slowly renew the island. The abandoned quarry sites have become a source of Christmas trees for residents. When visiting the glacial grooves at Kelleys Island State Park, visitors can look down through the fence onto the island's quarries, operated between 1830 and 1940, now overgrown with cedar. Limestone is still quarried on the island.

Satellite image of the many scars the giant quarries have left on Kelleys

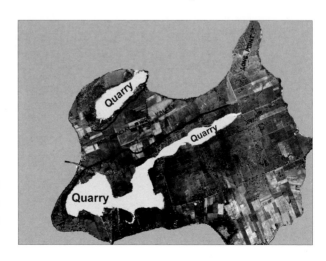

KELLEYS ISLAND

The Rescue

"I'll never forget the day of that storm, even if I live to be a hundred," Hazel Hamilton wrote. She touched the heavy gold pendant hanging from a scarlet ribbon. It had been her father's. On it was inscribed, "For heroic daring in saving life, June 29, 1902."

James Hamilton was mayor of the village on Kelleys Island when an awful gale hit in June of 1902. Many islanders stood near the shore, watching mesmerized as the huge waves came crashing in. Mayor Hamilton, standing with his daughter Hazel, agreed with fisherman Fred Dishinger that these waves were the largest they had ever seen. Early that morning, the steamer *George Dunbar* had foundered just a few miles east. The first lifeboat quickly capsized, plunging its five passengers into the lake. The remaining five aboard the *Dunbar*—including the Captain Little, his wife and daughter—were lowered into the lake aboard the second lifeboat. But it was unequal to the seas and, in only moments, it had flipped. Dumped into the raging waters, the Littles clung fiercely to the *Dunbar* as the wind and current swept them toward Kelleys Island. For a moment Captain Little glimpsed over the great, green walls of water and caught sight of Kelleys Island on the dim horizon. He noticed a cluster of small shapes—people—on the distant shore. Each time the waves thrust them high upon a crest, the Littles waved frantically to the people on the shore.

Meanwhile on Kelleys, a fisherman thought he spotted something strange, but decided it was just flotsam from the storm. Young Hazel Hamilton focused on the floating objects. She was positive that she saw somebody waving. Alarm mounted through the crowd. Then James Hamilton seized Fred Dishinger by the coat sleeve.

The two men and the fisherman's grown son rushed off to find a boat. They found an old flat-bottomed skiff, not ideal for such a sea. "They carried and dragged the skiff a considerable distance to the bank. They were pretty well used up before even launching the craft," remembered Hazel.

The men had barely climbed into the vessel when it was already swamped. The younger Dishinger bailed furiously, while his father and Mayor Hamilton rowed with fierce concentration. On the shore frightened whispers rumbled through the crowd as the rescuers disappeared between waves. Many feared the mission doomed. Hazel stared into the waves, afraid to blink and forever lose sight of her father. "I'll never forget the awfulness of seeing that little boat tossed about in that heavy sea."

As the rescue skiff and the lifeboat returned to view, hopeful cries shot up from the shore. But frightened and exhausted, Captain Little was not convinced the approaching boat was real. He held desperately to his wife and daughter. His daughter had lost consciousness, only her life preserver kept her afloat. His wife's eyes seemed miles away.

The shouts were close now. Captain Little grabbed the end of a rope that was thrown to him, and with frozen fingers, he tied it to their life preservers. Soon, he felt the blessed rush of being pulled through the water. He closed his eyes. When the pulling stopped, arms seized him. White water surged and pounded all around.

The rescuers barely noticed their boat splintering into the rocks. Stumbling and floundering in the heavy surf, against the undertow, they hauled the Little family to shore. The onlookers rushed forward as the three men tottered with exhaustion. Captain Little, his wife and daughter lay lifeless, blue with cold, but safe. They would all survive. And James Hamilton, Fred Dishinger and his son were each awarded a national gold medal for the heroic rescue.

MIDDLE ISLAND

The Southernmost Point in Canada

You won't find Middle Island on most maps of the Great Lakes. Perhaps the mapmakers consider it too small and insignificant. You can't blame them really. At only 20 hectares, it barely qualifies as an island. It is more like a rock. Its shorelines are rather ordinary; its vegetation and mineral deposits are no different than the surrounding islands. In fact, no one has lived there since the late 1940s. But just ask some of the residents living on nearby islands about Middle's history, its reputation. You will soon learn that in the 1920s and 30s this modest looking rock was once one of the most lively islands on the lake.

Location is Middle Island's greatest asset. It is the southernmost point in Canada, at the same line of latitude as northern California. When borders were drawn on Lake Erie following the War of 1812 and the Treaty of Ghent (1814), Middle Island wound up just half a mile north of the U.S.-Canadian boundary. It lies just four miles south of Canada's Pelee Island and the same distance northeast of America's South Bass Island. For the bootleggers and smugglers of the Prohibition era, it was the perfect drop point—quiet, uninhabited and just out of the reach of American Revenue agents.

During Prohibition, liquor seizures were common along the Windsor-Detroit "funnel", but smugglers around isolated Middle Island were rarely caught.

In January 1920, the United States Congress passed the Volstead Act forbidding the purchase, sale, transport and manufacture of alcohol for public consumption. Reformers across the country rejoiced. At last, a sober America would be free of the social evils associated with drink. Workers would be more productive, men more responsible to their families, crime and corruption a thing of the past. But just 13 years later, Prohibition—America's "Great Experiment" as an alcohol free society—was over. Foiled by the smugglers.

The residents of Put-in-Bay, Ohio, on South Bass Island were among the many Americans who opposed, or were indifferent to Prohibition. They considered it an unjust law, one that robbed the working class of a most basic pleasure—the right to enjoy a drink or two after a hard day's work. Before the 1920s, saloons and bars were more than simple watering holes. They were community meeting places where people came for the camaraderie, food, music and dancing. They were social institutions where one could find employment information, newspapers, and occasionally even postal service. They hosted weddings, meetings and celebrations. A decade before Prohibition there was one saloon for every 300 Americans. They were more common than churches, schools or parks. They were a fixture on the American social landscape.

In 1920, Put-in-Bay supported anywhere from 15 to 25 saloons and bars, mainly in hotels. Drink was popular, especially with local fishermen and summer tourists. When Prohibition was proclaimed and traditional liquor supplies dried up, the locals had to turn elsewhere. That's where Middle Island came in.

"People from Put-in-Bay always seemed to know when the next shipment was coming in," recalls local resident Joe Parker,

> They used to take their boats over there to Middle Island to pick up the beer, wine and brandy. It was mostly small timers that I remember—three or four cases at a time. They would bring it back to South Bass and bury it at various places on the island—in the vineyards and the cisterns. Some of it was trucked over to the mainland and then on to Detroit. A lot of that stuff was marked grape juice (to fool the authorities) but it wasn't grape juice, it was wine! Of course everyone knew that.

In later years, the abandoned Middle Island Clubhouse was remembered as a hotspot for booze and gambling in the 1920s and 1930s.

Joe recalls one instance in 1926-27 when the police came searching for illegal booze at the house of a local man on South Bass. "I used to play with his daughter, and when the revenuers came by one day, he had us sit on a carpet over the opening that ran under the porch where the booze was hidden. They never found the stuff; the old house is still there."

It is estimated that between 15 and 20 bootleggers operated during Prohibition between Put-in-Bay and Middle Island. Most were ordinary folk—fishermen, merchants or the unemployed—who never considered their activity dishonest or criminal. After the Depression hit in 1929, bootlegging was just another way to make a living. You could get as much as $5.00 a bottle, a full day's wages in the 1920s.

The liquor on Middle Island came mainly from suppliers on Pelee Island and other towns in southwestern Ontario. It was easy to find liquor for smuggling here. According to Prohibition historian Larry Engelmann, as much as 25% of the Canadian population in the Windsor-Detroit "funnel", may have been connected to the illegal liquor trade in the early 1920s. Hundreds of thousands of cases—destined for the U.S.—were shipped there every year from distilleries in Ontario and Quebec. In 1928, the liquor

Members of the Detroit-based Purple Gang. Operators on Middle Island were rumoured to have had links to organized crime.

industry in Canada accounted for more than one-fifth of the country's tax revenues. A single fair-sized boat could transport thousands of cases of liquor and earn its owner in excess of $10,000—in one month. The lure of such profits inevitably attracted criminal elements. Most restricted their operations to the Detroit area, but rumour has it that a few operated gambling joints and "blind pigs" (underground drinking establishments) further south, including at Middle Island.

With the right connections, a man could arrange to visit the Middle Island Clubhouse, a rather modest-looking, wooden structure. Gambling, prostitution and fine Canadian Whiskey—all were rumoured readily available at this exclusive establishment. Some whispered that the ownership was linked to the infamous Purple Gang from Detroit, a group associated with Al Capone and connected to the notorious St. Valentine's Day Massacre of 1929. The club was shut down in the early 1930s.

Little physical evidence remains of Middle Island's days as a hotbed of the illegal liquor trade. There are no aging storage houses or loading docks. No buried treasure has ever been found. Only the stone walls of the clubhouse, and the crumbling foundation of the old lighthouse offer any evidence of past human habitation on this small island. Still, Middle Island remains Canada's most southern piece of land, regardless of what the maps say. The ferry doesn't stop there, but you can visit Middle Island by private boat. Don't be surprised if some of the locals eye you suspiciously and inquire about your business. After all, Middle Island has a reputation.

PELEE ISLAND

The Vineyard Paradise

Pelee Island's climate, flora and fauna are more typical of the southern United States than of Ontario. Newcomers were attracted to the island because of this, and because just after the Civil War, some on the losing side felt more comfortable remaining in the "Queen's Dominion." There were the Wardroper brothers from Alabama, Thaddeus Smith and the Williams Brothers from Kentucky. There was also the matter of land prices to consider. American islands had soared from $10 to $400 an acre. Pelee Island prices had not exceeded $100 an acre. Even at these bargain prices, the island's owner was making a good profit. In 1823 he had paid in total $300 for the 10,000-acre Pelee.

By 1890, 23 of the 41 wineries in Canada were operating between Pelee Island and nearby Windsor. According to Ron Tiessen's book, *The*

Vin Villa as it appeared in the 1800s

Vinedressers, the vineyards on Pelee were Canada's first commercial wine enterprise, bottling thousands of gallons of wine and producing grapes for the fresh fruit market. Thaddeus Smith's Vin Villa proved innovative in both its production and marketing. With machinery imported from France in 1894, Vin Villa produced Canada's first champagne and a popular Communion wine, which it shipped throughout Canada, to the eastern U.S., the West Indies and Europe.

Owner of the Vin Villa winery, Thaddeus Smith (above), was attacked by lake pirates in 1877.

Vin Villa produced Canada's first commercial champagne

An example of a of wine press used at Vin Villa

   Pelee Island had its problems. One was solved quite early: mosquitoes "of the largest breed and most bloodthirsty nature," (*Amherstburg Echo*, 1887) did not survive the draining of the 4,000-acre marsh. But with no outside communication or transportation, isolation made the islanders vulnerable. In 1877, masked lake pirates raided the sleeping Smith household, beating Thaddeaus and demanding silverware, brandy, canned fruit, and money. Their boat was traced back to Wyandotte, Michigan, where the pirates had offered brandy to the Deputy Sheriff and empty canning jars to his mother.

Built in 1833, Pelee Island's light-house is the oldest on Lake Erie, and one of the earliest lighthouses on the Great Lakes.

Meanwhile, the grapes proved unpredictable. And with fluctuating markets, transportation, disease, weather, competition from cheap imports, tariffs, and even a grasshopper plague (the beach was once a foot thick in grasshoppers), interest in viniculture waned. Farmers diversified their crops, adding corn, marsh potatoes, peaches, pears, plums, peanuts, walnuts, chestnuts, hickory, and tobacco.

Today many Pelee residents have small vineyards. The only commercial vineyard is the Pelee Island Winery. Its production facility is on the mainland at Kingsville, Ontario, but it has a wine pavilion for island visitors. Remnants of the once-thriving wine industry are everywhere—bottles, wine presses, old vineyard buildings lying in ruin. Willow shoots that were used to tie grape cane to the trellises, now stand fully mature in the forest. Between the abandoned rows of grapevine have grown conforming rows of prickly ash, Virginia creeper and lilacs.

Communication and transportation to the island were difficult in early years. In winter, even delivering mail was a major undertaking.

Pelee Island is unique among neighbouring islands, having preserved its rural origins and its distinctive wilderness. Pelee has protected the Great Blue turtles, snapping turtles, foxes, endangered water snakes, and hundreds of diverse plant varieties from prickly pear cactus to wild hyacinth. In spring and summer, the island is popular with bird watchers who come to Lighthouse Point Provincial Nature Reserve to observe migrating orioles, cuckoos and warblers, to name a few. The limestone lighthouse, built in 1833, lies abandoned and in ruin. For information about Pelee's natural and human history, visit the Heritage Centre Museum, (519) 724-2291. Ferries arrive from Kingsville and Leamington, Ontario, and from Sandusky, Ohio. Call Pelee Island Transportation Co., (800) 661-2220 or (519) 724-2115.

PELEE ISLAND

The Invasion of 1837

In the 1830s, the spirit of democratic reform was sweeping across Jacksonian America, reform Britain, and revolutionary France. Activists for change rallied common people who were labouring under unjust monarchs and corrupt employers. Upper Canada, too, became caught up in the populist fervour with its own revolutionary leader, William Lyon Mackenzie.

In December 1837, Mackenzie and a ragtag army of 500 reformers laid siege to Toronto. They planned to wrest authority from the privileged class and return power to the people. But Mackenzie's dream of American-style revolution was quashed when 1,500 government troops descended on the rebels. Exiled to America, and with a price on his head, Mackenzie and his followers changed their strategy. For the next year, the would-be revolutionaries launched a series of raids against important towns and British interests in Upper Canada. The islands of the Great Lakes were on the front lines of the battle to keep Canada part of Britain.

On the morning of February 26, 1838, William McCormick rose anxiously before dawn. He'd slept miserably, troubled by a sense of dread. All week, dark rumours had flown from house to house through the woods of Pelee Island.

By December 1837, the economy had failed and poor crops led to food shortages. After rebel leader William Lyon Mackenzie's march down Yonge

Street failed, Mackenzie fled to the U.S. where he gathered allies for his cause. An internal Canadian revolt had spilled south, becoming a U.S. threat to Canada.

By early February 1838, the American rebels had swarmed Fighting Island, a distance from Pelee up the Detroit River, but British regulars and the Upper Canada militia from nearby Fort Malden had driven them off. More mischief was expected. Women and children were afraid to go out-

When rebel leader William Lyon Mackenzie fled Toronto for the U.S., he gathered an American rebel militia.

side. A rumour swelled that thousands of Yankee rebels were on their way down Erie's Canadian shore, killing as they went. William McCormick was a proud United Empire Loyalist. He was proud to own Pelee Island, to oversee ten farm families and provide for his own family of eleven. He had also had occasion to be proud of his uncanny sixth sense.

McCormick's sense of foreboding was consistent with the rumours that the Yankee rebels were creeping towards them on the ice. He knew it in his bones. He roused his family and had them bundle up necessities. He alerted the islanders and the militia. Before midday, most of the islanders had fled Pelee for the mainland.

All through the night, a large tri-coloured flag—emblazoned with two stars and the word *Liberty*—had been swaying in the hands of a young Irish American, as he marched across the frozen lake from Sandusky, Ohio. He was one of 500 zealous men, armed with muskets and high ideals, who called themselves the Patriot Army. The men were directed by self-appointed "officers": "Colonel" E.D. Bradley, "Major" Lester Hoadly, and "Captain" George Van Rensselaer. The invaders pulled several sleighs of ammunition across the jagged ice.

The sun was sparkling on the craggy shards of ice when the army saw their target on the horizon. They had hoped to reach the island still in darkness and surprise the Loyalists in their beds, but by the time they approached the Pelee shore, it was already afternoon. Finding the McCormicks' stone house empty, they smashed the fine china, pocketed the silver and slaughtered hogs. By the end of day, they had ransacked the community.

While the marauders did their damage, word of the uprising had reached Fort Malden. Scouts returned with reports that they had been fired on by a hostile faction. Three days later, Captain Glascow of the Royal Artillery was dispatched to inspect the ice. Perilously thin only a few weeks earlier, it had to hold an army and two, six-pounder cannons. The captain returned the next day, confident that the ice was sound.

On the eve of March 3, Fort Malden's Colonel Maitland set forth. He had 400 under his command, patched together from different regiments, volunteer militia and a small group of Indians. They followed the sleigh ruts made the day before by Captain Glascow. Like the rebels, they hoped to arrive before dawn, under cover of darkness. Unfortunately, the lake surface had refrozen in jagged fragments, making it difficult to cross without a light. They traded in their sneak attack for a well-lit passage across the lake.

By daybreak they had covered 18 miles and were within a mile of the island. Captain Browne led one unit to the south end of the island to intercept any rebels trying to escape in that direction. The Colonel took a second unit toward the rebel camp at the north end. By this point the Patriots had

Angry with the government, men armed with guns and pitchforks marched down Yonge Street in Toronto.

occupied Pelee for most of a week, and had chosen an excellent, defensive location for their camp. As the Loyalists approached in the full light of morning, they had certainly allowed the rebels ample preparation time. But strangely, although the Americans outnumbered the attackers, the rebels abandoned their position, retreating for the woods. Were they intimidated by the soldiers, all in red coats and with bayonets, some even mounted on horseback?

As Colonel Maitland later reported, his "troops swept through the forest to dislodge any lurking Patriots." Before long, the retreating rebels began to spill out of the woods onto the ice at the south end of the island, where Captain Browne's troops were lying in wait. Although there were

Pelee Island uprising. In total, 31 Loyalists were wounded and five were killed. Of the rebels, eleven were killed, 40 wounded and 20 taken prisoner.

three times as many rebels, Captain Browne's troops were determined to meet them head on. The rebels opened fire, somewhat sheltered by the craggy ice near the shore. As his soldiers began succumbing, Captain Browne realized he needed a new tactic. With a great cheer, his men charged ahead, bayonets at the ready. The rebels stood their ground, fired one volley, and then, unnerved by the lethal glint of the Loyalist weapons, scattered in all directions. As one soldier remembered it, they were "running like wild turkeys."

In total, 31 Loyalists were wounded, five were killed. Eleven rebels lay dead, 40 were wounded, and 20 taken prisoner. Some fled onto the ice, falling through and drowning in the icy water. The fallen flag of liberty lay beside one jagged hole in the ice. Colonel Maitland, emerging from the woods and seeing the rebels in retreat, picked up the flag, tucking it under his arm. It later became the focus of wild celebration. In the Colchester tavern, William McCormick raised his pint of ale and cheered the Loyalist victory. Back on Pelee Island, he still had to face the rebels' destruction. His fury would haunt his dreams for years.

Pelee was not the final insurrection. In December 1838, rebel forces attacked the city of Windsor. Canadian militiamen again suppressed the attack. Historians continue to debate the causes and the consequences of the Rebellions of 1837-38. The Rebellions resulted in the appointment of

Lord Durham. The release of his Durham Report recommended the creation of a united Upper and Lower Canada, and led to the introduction of
Responsible Government.

On Pelee Island, a plaque from the Historic Sites and Monuments
Board commemorates the battle. The McCormick house no longer stands,
but the Fox house (also from the era) does. The Fox house was one of the
few not destroyed by the rebels in 1837, prompting rumours that the family were rebel sympathizers. In Amherstburg, a monument at Christ
Church remembers those who fell in battle. A display at the town's Fort
Malden National Historic Park also commemorates the event. For information call (519) 736-5416.

KELLEYS ISLAND AND PELEE ISLAND

Jake's Escape

He balanced the bundle of clothes firmly on his head, pulling his
naked body through the black water. This is one way Jake Hay got across
the lake. But this was the first time he had done it at night, and these cir-
cumstances were the worst. He glanced back quickly to see if they were
in pursuit, risking the balance of his bundle. The shoreline had already
melted into darkness.

It had baffled Jake why the pleasant folk on Pelee had suddenly turned
hostile. The Kelleys Island resident owned eight acres on Pelee. When he
had checked on things six months ago, there had been no sign of trouble.
What Jake did not know was that February night in 1838, American
rebels—the Patriot Army—were marching toward Pelee Island, intent on
capture. Jake Hay's visit and departure had looked highly suspicious. The
next day, the rebels raided the island, doing a lot of damage before they
were routed by British troops. William McCormick's house was ransacked
and all his winter stocks were eaten. As Pelee's owner, McCormick took the
raid as a personal affront.

When Jake Hay returned to Pelee one fine August day, he landed his
boat close to McCormick's house. Jake knocked at McCormick's door.
William McCormick was known for his hospitality, so it seemed strange to
Jake that McCormick stared coldly in the doorway and refused to shake
his hand. After a few uneasy minutes, McCormick accused him of being a
raider, and told him to go elsewhere.

Jake found refuge with an old acquaintance, a man called Hustin. News
was spreading of Jake's return, and a hot determination grew to find—and

Jake Hay's Kelleys Island house is seen in this photo of Inscription Rock.

hang—the invader. That evening, Hustin went out for whiskey and got wind of the plan to lynch Jake. He rushed home to warn his guest. Jake made a beeline for his rowboat, only to find it had been stolen. He saw a lantern gleaming through the trees, and heard the growing rumble of angry voices. His heart pounding fiercely, he stripped off his clothes and bundled them. Setting them on his head, he waded into the lake.

With firm strokes, he swam toward but missed a distant shoal off Middle Island. He carried on to Middle Island, reaching it by dawn. His unusual arrival triggered mistrust in the only island residents, a man and a boy. The Canadians refused to return him to Kelleys Island. But Jake reclaimed a damaged canoe he'd abandoned on the beach the year before.

Jake pushed off, a board nailed over the hole, an old keg for a bailer, and a broken board for a paddle. Soon the sky darkened and the wind flared up, growing stronger as he paddled hard against it. He willed himself to reach Kelleys before the weather broke, but he was still a mile from the island when the skies opened in torrents. The howling wind drove his canoe down the open lake.

This store (right) was one of Pelee Island owner, William McCormick's enterprises. He lost many possessions during the rebel attack on Pelee and believed Hay was involved in rebel activities.

Using his shirt and the loose thwarts from the canoe, he rigged a sail to keep the canoe from turning broadside to the wind. He used his paddle as a rudder and, bailing incessantly, rode the wild ride through the darkness. Dawn brought more wind, more rain and surging waves. No land in sight. But as darkness fell there was a flash of hope. Land ahead. He recognized the rocky shore of Avon Point. The waves crashing up against it were enormous. If he let himself be carried by the water, he would be dashed to pieces. Jake's exhaustion was a deep well. But the rocks before him brought forth a sudden burst of strength and he managed to avoid the point. Swept across the great bay, once again he was swallowed by the stormy night. The next morning was calm. He drifted completely drained on the flat lake. His body was ripped apart, hollow with hunger and lack of sleep. Through heavy eyes he perceived the thin line of a distant shore. He no longer felt connected to the arm that held the paddle. A cluster of concerned faces—residents of Dover Bay—stood on shore as he approached. He fell into their arms and was taken to the nearby town of Rockport.

Jake Hay had been missing for so long that people on Kelleys were certain he had drowned.

Jake Hay's resilience was remarkable. Within a few days his strength returned, and he thought nothing of the long walk to Cleveland. He found a boat there but the crew was too drunk to take him the whole way to Sandusky. He carried on by foot, and in Sandusky he caught a boat across to Kelleys Island, two weeks since the day he left.

JOHNSON'S ISLAND

From Prisoner of War Camp to Amusement Park

In 1852, Leonard Johnson bought Bull Island, renamed it for himself, and founded a lime kiln and quarry. When the Civil War began, Johnson leased land to the Union government for a prisoner of war camp. Johnson reclaimed the land, and the surviving buildings, at War's end in 1864.

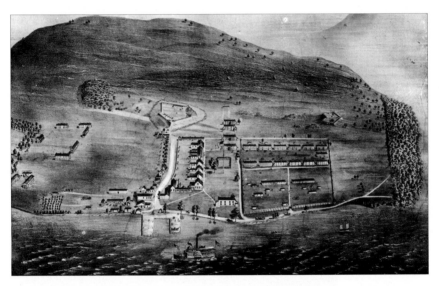

In previous wars, tradition and convenience dictated that prisoners on both sides were regularly exchanged. However, the Union's use of Johnson's Island as a prison marked a permanent change to this custom.

In 1894, nearly 90 years old, Johnson opened an amusement park and dance pavilion on the island. He charged his guests a docking fee of 5 cents, and levied a $1.00 fine to those caught disembarking elsewhere. These charges did not hamper the resort's popularity. At one point, 5,000 visitors descended on the small island in a single day, eclipsing the famous Cedar Point amusement park on Sandusky Bay.

But the high times were short lived. In 1897, a widow sued the park when her husband was shot with a security guard's revolver. The legal bills turned the park into a losing proposition, and when it was conveniently destroyed by fire, Johnson abandoned it.

By 1904, Johnson was dead and the overgrown site had been leased to a new owner. The renovated park had a vaudeville stage, a roller skating rink, a motion picture theatre, bathhouse, cottages and hotel. The owner of Cedar Point's amusement park was not amused. A ruthless businessman, George Boeckling, bought land on Johnson's Island and built an ugly fence blocking the park's finest view. But the park flourished even still. Or so the stockholders believed. In 1907, the books were probed, revealing a bankrupt operation. The resort was sold to Cedar Park's Boeckling who gleefully dismantled it.

The well-marked road off Route 163 leads right to Johnson's Island. There is a $1.00 fee to use the causeway. Civil War historians regard the island as the most significant site in Ohio. Developers are planning condominiums on the site of the abandoned quarry.

Members of the Ohio National Guard served briefly as prison guards

After the Civil War, the cemetery and its wooden crosses for the 200 interred Confederate soldiers fell into disrepair. In 1890, Sandusky citizens paid to have the graves marked with marble headstones.

JOHNSON'S ISLAND

Life in a Civil War Military Prison

One icy night in March almost a hundred years ago, a gale blew across the grassy stretch of Johnson's Island. Windswept spray froze as it fell, coating the prisoners' headstones in the Civil War cemetery. According to Nichola Rocci, a Sicilian working at the limestone quarry, it was nearly midnight when the storm peaked, and as he neared the graveyard, he beheld the strangest sight. Out of darkness came the muted call of a lone bugle. Then, moments later, silent lines of phantom soldiers emerged from the shadows. With haggard faces, tattered uniforms, and muskets on their shoulders, they advanced across the tombstones. Then, as suddenly as they had appeared, they were gone again. Within a few days, the Italian labourers of Johnson's Island fled.

Covering 40 acres, the camp held as many as 3,000 prisoners during the Civil War. Few dared escape over the 14-foot-high walls.

Today the graveyard is all that remains of the Prisoner of War camp that operated on Johnson's Island from 1861 until the Civil War ended in 1865. At one time, the Union military prison held 3,000 men, and by war's end had held a total of 12,000. The only Union prison primarily for officers, the prison had also incarcerated slaves who had refused freedom in order to stay with their masters. The prison population was made up of preachers, printers, lawyers, doctors, artisans, farmers, philosophers and poets, some of the South's most cultivated men.

One inmate, Asa Hartz, from Nashville, Tennessee, compared his prison life to the luxury he had left behind:

> *My love reposes on a rosewood frame,*
> *A bunk have I.*

A couch of feathery down fills up the same,
Mine's straw, and dry.
My love her daily dinner takes in state,
The richest viands flank her silver plate,
Course grub have I.
Pure wine she sips at ease, her thirst to slake,
I pump my drink from Erie's crystal lake.

The prison stood on forty acres with barracks for prisoners and for Union guards. It was a worthy stronghold. Its surrounding walls were made of planks 14 feet high, built on buried limestone blocks to prevent tunnelling. There was a parapet walkway from which sentinels could monitor every move. Twenty feet inside the walls was an invisible boundary called the "dead line." Crossing it meant instant death from a sentry's bullet. The few men who dared to cross the line, scale the wall and make a dash for the lake, were apprehended by the Union gunboat, the *Michigan.*

The prisoners arrived by ferry from the mainland town of Sandusky. Their money was confiscated and exchanged for notes with which they could buy food beyond their meagre rations. They could not buy better accommodations. Each of the thirteen barracks contained five rooms, three upstairs and two down, and housed 240 men. Palettes were arranged in tiers of three, with two men to a bunk.

John Bell Steele. Prisoners were society men from the South. After the Civil War, many went on to become senators, congressmen, and judges. One prisoner, Horace Lurton, studied law while incarcerated at Johnson's, and was later appointed to the United States Supreme Court.

Summer breezes blew pleasantly through the cracks in the board walls. But winter was something else completely, especially for the Southerners. On this wind-exposed island surrounded by a frozen lake, these southern men shivered in uninsulated buildings, the wind whistling through the walls. Warmth a far off dream, the men often woke up beneath a thin blanket of snow.

On fine winter days, the parade grounds of the prison were awhir with snowballs, battles fought with military tactics and Confederate yells. In

The prison included barracks, a sutler's store, hospital, the Bull Pen (an enclosed area for the prisoners to enjoy the outdoors), and kitchens with small stoves (the men did their own cooking).

summer, the same grounds became a baseball diamond. Baseball being fairly new, the Johnson's Island prisoners were the first Southerners to learn it. They learned to play it well. Those who returned home took the game with them and helped to make it a national sport.

Through cracks in the south wall, prisoners watched the passing steamers—like the *Philo Parsons* and the *Island Queen*—cruising by the shore, their passengers loudly mocking the POWs. The men devised countless ways of killing time. Some prisoners took to carving trinkets out of wood and shells that they sold or traded for books

Prison barracks were so poorly built that, in winter, the men often awoke under a dusting of snow. Newspapers provided extra cover at night.

and newspapers. One man made a fiddle, carved from driftwood with his penknife, and played it with a charm that cheered the men around him. Some prisoners mounted plays. *The Battle of Gettysburg* ran for three weeks. Formal debating groups churned with endless discussion of secession, slavery, the War's progress, and the men's longing for freedom.

The war dragged on. By the winter of 1864, the Confederate chances of victory had fallen badly. Federal forces were far better organized and had the powerful support of northern industry. The Southerners had no merchant fleet to come to their rescue. Conditions in the Johnson's Island

The Confederates were guarded by several brigades, the strangest of which was the Grey Beard Brigade, a venerable collection of fellows whose ages could be gauged by their beard lengths. Many of these men were over eighty years old.

prison declined dramatically. Food supplies dwindled to the sparsest of rations. Men grew gaunt. Lieutenant Horace Carpenter recalled getting hold of two potatoes and an onion after days of virtually nothing. Some sifted through the barrels of lake water looking for food waste that may have drifted across the bay from Sandusky. Other men were ravenous enough to eat the rats that overran the prison, and in no time, rats became as rare as steak. The cold and the lack of food took their toll. Many fell fatally ill with pneumonia and rheumatic fever.

There came a night in January so exceptionally cold that some say the coal oil froze inside the lamps, plunging the camp into darkness. The sen-

For their confiscated money, prisoners received sutler notes, good for use at the sutler store in the compound (sutlers were merchants who followed the army and sold provisions to soldiers). Virtually anything available in town could be purchased here at double the normal price.

The Johnson's Island prison

tries were taken off duty. A handful of prisoners saw their opportunity to flee. They scaled the walls and ventured onto the ice.

Broken up and frozen several times over the early winter, the lake's surface proved treacherous and slow to cross. Frozen by biting winds, two of the men sought refuge in Sandusky and were surrendered to the authorities. The other men continued westward along the shore, then struck out across the western end. Reaching Canada meant reaching freedom. For over sixty hours they trudged along without sleep or food. Close to the Canadian side, the ice began to crack. One man fell through. The others managed to haul him out. Half-dead with exhaustion and the cold, they dragged themselves the last mile to the Canadian shore, to warmth, food, and freedom.

After the Civil War, the Confederate cemetery—with its 200 wooden crosses—was neglected. The buildings were sold back to the owner of the island. A few decades later, little of the prison remained. In 1890, Sandusky citizens had the graves marked with marble headstones bearing the prisoner's name, age, regiment and company. The Follett House Museum in Sandusky displays artifacts and Johnson's Island history: (419) 627-9608. For those interested in Johnson's Island, write to Johnson's Island Preservation Society, P.O. Box 1865, Johnson's Island, OH 43440

JOHNSON'S ISLAND

Conspiracy

The Prisoners of War interred at Johnson's Island were not forgotten. Toward the end of the Civil War, they would inspire a complex conspiracy of capture, rescue and sabotage.

Prisoners were dying of hunger, cold, dysentery, and pneumonia. Word of their condition reached the ears of well-placed Confederates to the south.

Lieutenant William Murdaugh was stationed at Richmond, Virginia. He knew that a powerful Union gunboat, the *Michigan*, guarded the Johnson's Island prison and that the canals of the Great Lakes played a key role in transporting western grain to feed the Union troops. He devised a plan to capture the *Michigan*, use it to free the prisoners, and then commandeer the boat to destroy the Welland and Erie canals, sinking enemy ships and attacking Buffalo along the way.

President of the Confederacy, Jefferson Davis, approved the grand and daring scheme. It was attractive to Southerners, down on their luck by now, because it was an opportunity to undermine the Union. The element of secrecy was key. Two men were chosen to initiate the covert operation. The first man was John Yates Beall, later known as "The Pirate of Lake Erie." Raised on a large plantation in Jefferson County, Virginia, he was university-educated, handsome and loyal to the South's cause. As an officer in the Confederate Navy, he had a reputation as a fine saboteur on the northern Atlantic coast. He was also familiar with the Canadian shores of Lakes Ontario and Erie.

The second man was Captain Charles H. Cole, a con man par excellence. He claimed to be a lieutenant in the Confederate Navy, but in fact he had been a captain in the Tennessee Infantry and was discharged for chronic lying. Even still, Cole fiercely championed the Southern cause. He was assigned to research the lake defenses, become familiar with the movements and crew of the *Michigan*, and make covert contact with the Johnson's Island prisoners.

The dashing Southerner, John Yates Beall, already had a reputation as a skilled saboteur.

Posing as an oil magnate, Cole took up residence at the West House, a hotel in Sandusky, on the mainland south of Johnson's Island. His accomplice, posing as his wife, was Annie Cole, also known as Annie Davis or Emma Bison. They set about charming the Union officers aboard the *Michigan*. Parasoled and wasp-waisted, Annie delighted in sauntering by the town wharf whenever the men were due to come ashore. In their hotel quarters, the Coles loosened tongues with unlimited liquor and Cuban cigars, hoping

Union gunboat Michigan. *A Confederate scheme developed to capture the* Michigan *and use it to free the Johnson's Island prisoners. From here the ship would be used to destroy the Erie and Welland Canals, sink Union ships, and attack the city of Buffalo.*

to win the men's trust and that vital piece of information that would make their plot succeed.

Cole also befriended a few officers who guarded inmates at Johnson's Island. Meanwhile, he informed key inmates of the impending jailbreak. Inside the prison, Confederate Generals J.J. Archer and I.R. Trimble received smuggled letters with secret messages written in starch, only visible once painted with iodine. The letters triggered the formation of the Southern Cross, a select, secret society that spread throughout the prison. Tightly organized, it was prepared for the moment when, as the code put it, "the carriage would be waiting at the door."

The plan was proceeding well. The Coles had unearthed canal and shipping information, and along with Confederate sympathizers, had gone into seclusion to consolidate their plans. In the meantime, John Beall was formulating his own plan from Windsor, nearby on the Canadian shore. He and Cole had established secret communication. It was all coming together.

But Cole was so caught up in his plotting, that he failed to suspect the friendship of John W. Wilson, from New Orleans. Cole even failed to note the flaws in Wilson's Louisiana accent. John Wilson—his full name was

John Wilson Murray—was destined to be a famous detective in Canada. At the time of Cole and Beall's assignment, Murray was a gunner on the *Michigan*. Only weeks into the plot, rumours of the South's conspiracy had reached Captain Jack Carter of the *Michigan*. Carter assigned John Wilson Murray an unlimited commission to track down the conspirators.

Murray took on the task with zeal, and before long, he had infiltrated a group of Confederate sympathizers. When Murray spotted the charming Cole, he had a strong hunch this could be his man. He proceeded to track him, observed him wooing the personnel of the *Michigan*, and reported all his findings to Captain Carter. Murray agreed to stay undercover, to catch the culprits in the act.

In September 1864, several months into the plan, the two conspirators, Cole and Beall, met one last time in the West House rooms in Sandusky to finalize the details. Cole would throw a party on the evening of the raid, luring the officers from their posts in the gunboat and the prison. The whiskey would be drugged. Beall would lead the raid, first seizing the local steamer, *Philo Parsons*. After Cole signalled that his party guests were out cold, Beall would ferry *Philo Parsons* toward Johnson's Island and collide with the *Michigan*, as if by accident. They would seize her and train her big guns on the head-

quarters of the Johnson's Island prison. Finally, under a flag of truce, they would send a boat ashore demanding that the inmates be released.

On the morning of September 18, 1864, one of Beall's men, a Lieutenant Bennett Burley, visited the *Philo Parsons*

The guards were unaware of the growing plot to free the prisoners from Johnson's Island.

at her dock in Detroit. The boat did a regular run between Detroit and Sandusky. Burley asked the ship's clerk to make an extra stop at Windsor the next day to pick up friends. He explained that one of his friends was lame, and that it was easiest for him to travel by water. Next day when the steamer stopped at Windsor, four men without baggage came aboard. The one with the limp was Beall. Down river at Malden, also on the Canadian side, twenty roughly dressed men boarded with a heavy pine trunk. They looked like "skedaddlers"—draft dodgers—going for a visit to Sandusky.

The unsuspecting passengers of the Island Queen *were taken by surprise by men with hatchets and guns.*

Behind schedule, the *Parsons* arrived at Middle Bass Island. The Captain disembarked on Middle Bass where he lived, calling it a day and leaving his first mate in charge. Once the boat was underway, the "skedaddlers" threw open their pine trunk, revealing a cache of weapons. At gunpoint, Beall quietly advised the first mate to navigate to Johnson's Island.

They were in sight of their target when, for some reason, Beall had a change of heart and asked the first mate to return to Middle Bass. By the time they landed, it was dark. The *Island Queen* happened to pull in beside the *Parsons*. For Beall there was no option but to board and take her over, with her fifty local passengers, and forty soldiers heading for a posting in Toledo. Beall's men suddenly appeared, wielding hatchets and firing guns into the screaming crowd. A man from South Bass Island was seriously wounded. The ship's engineer, who couldn't hear the turmoil above the noise of the engine room, was taken by surprise and had his nose blown off. The raiders herded everyone onto the *Parsons*, and scuttled the *Island Queen*. Like a dark shadow on the water, the *Parsons* moved toward Johnson's Island, nearly invisible. It slowed and drifted on the smooth, black surface of the lake as it neared the *Michigan*. The steamer lay in wait for Cole's signal.

On the mainland, Cole's plan had not gone as expected. His party guests had not arrived and it had gotten very late. His young friend, Wilson—the undercover Murray—suggested they go down to the dock. From here, the unsuspecting Cole was conducted to Captain Carter's cabin and arrested.

The *Parsons* went on waiting for Cole's signal, a signal that would never come. Dissension and worry erupted on the ship—the armed warship *Michigan* could easily unleash its firepower. Beall argued that the element of surprise outweighed any guns of the *Michigan*. Deciding the mission was a failure, the *Parsons* steamed for the Detroit River, and dumped the kidnapped crew and passengers at Fighting Island. Arriving at their destination—a small dock at Sandwich, Ontario—the Confederates scuttled the *Parsons*.

The Philo Parsons *was used in a plot to release the Confederate prisoners on Johnson's Island.*

As for the major players, Charles H. Cole was held prisoner at Johnson's Island until the end of the war, and then moved to Fort Lafayette, New York where he was held until February 1866. Roger Long's compelling article, "Johnson's Island Prison" in *Blue and Gray Magazine* argues that Cole was actually a federal spy planted to defeat the plot from within. Why did he have such easy access to the prison? Why was he the only conspirator not to be tried for his involvement? Why didn't Johnson's Island prisoners ever see the high profile Cole after he was captured and supposedly held there?

Annie Cole was taken into custody and released for lack of evidence. John Yates Beall was captured in Niagara Falls, sentenced, and hanged at Fort Columbus, New York, on February 24, 1865. It is said that John Wilkes Booth, a friend of Beall's from university, was so enraged about President Lincoln's refusal to intervene on Beall's behalf that Booth shot him.

The graveyard is all that survives of the prison.

3

LAKE HURON ISLANDS

Lake Huron is a place of convergence. Under its waters, two geological plates meet: one of soft limestone, and the other of hard, unforgiving Precambrian Shield. The lake itself is comprised of three very distinct parts: the main lake, Georgian Bay (or "the sixth Great Lake") and the North Channel. Much of the main lake's shore is smoothly contoured and lined with sandy beaches. Except for the Fishing Islands, there are few-islands here. In stark contrast is the treacherous maze of 30,000 islands off Georgian Bay's northern and eastern shores. The impressive spine of the Bruce Peninsula separates Georgian Bay from the main lake. From the peninsula, a line of islands stretches northwestward, defining the North Channel. These are no mere rocks; the biggest, Manitoulin, is the largest freshwater island in the world.

It is also where people converged. At the geographical centre of the Great Lakes, Lake Huron has been a watery crossroads for centuries. All who were travelling east or west— natives and European explorers, missionaries and voyageurs, soldiers

Postcard of picnickers on Flowerpot Island

Nineteenth-century engraving of Arch Rock, Mackinac Island, from an 1875 guide-book to Mackinac Island.

and settlers fun-nelled through the region.

The North Channel was the corridor to Lake Superior and the west for natives and fur traders. Over the years they were fol-lowed by countless ships bearing goods and settlers. Once the railway hit the southern shores of Georgian Bay in 1850, the bulk of goods going to or coming from the west travelled up the treacherous waters of Georgian Bay. Even after lighthous-es lit the way, Georgian Bay's stormy disposition, and her maze of islands and shoals took countless ships. Around their shores, the lake bottom is lit-tered with them.

This lake at the crossroads has had immense strategic importance, and islands have been central to the lake's history. In the 1600s, the Iroquois invaded Huron and Ojibwe territories, and Christian and Frenchman Islands tell that story. In the 1700s and early 1800s, controlling the Straits of Mackinac was considered key to controlling the North American interior. Island forts—on Mackinac, St. Joseph, and Drummond Islands—changed hands several times as the French and British, then the Americans struggled for dominance of the region.

In the twentieth century, there was a new pull drawing people to the lake—leisure, travel and recreation. Old forts were converted into muse-ums; fishing cabins and trading posts were replaced by private cottages and grand hotels. The lake appeared in paintings by well-known artists; its islands acquired a reputation for beauty and sanctuary. They are places where people and history still converge.

CHANTRY ISLAND

Battle with the Seas

Looking back over his twenty-two years as lighthouse keeper on Chantry Island, Duncan McGregor Lambert could scarcely recall a moment he hadn't battled with the seas. Still, with all of the tragedies, he could not imagine another way of life.

Before lighthouses watched over the northern Great Lakes, Lambert had served as first mate aboard a steamer, the *Bruce Mines*. It was November 1854. Nearing Stokes Bay along the eastern shore of Lake Huron, the steamer hit a raging storm. She was pummeled and tossed for hours by great waves and high winds. The old wooden hull sprung a fatal leak. Lambert remembered that Captain Frazer's first order was to throw the cargo overboard. The lighter load only bought a little extra

Duncan McGregor Lambert well knew the power of Lake Huron's seas.

time. By dawn the vessel was sitting hopelessly low in the water. When the carpenter suggested they abandon ship, Captain Frazer drew his pistols, screaming that he'd shoot the first man to board a lifeboat without orders.

The ship was suddenly sucked down. Somehow in the ship's descent,

Lambert was Chantry Island lighthouse's first keeper.

the deck was torn off intact, the lifeboats and crew still on it. The men dove into the boats, Lambert, the captain of one and Frazer of the other. The carpenter fell into a panic, plunged into the foam and vanished.

Lambert started rowing. Each man took his turn at the oars, and by night they'd come 15 miles (24kms), landing on Devil's Island. They connected with the other boat by morning. Lambert recalled how fast their spirits sank when they realized they would not be found on Devil's Island. They would have to row all the way around the Bruce Peninsula to Owen Sound in order to survive. It took them four days.

The winds and cold had been severe. Lambert could still recall the ache in his arms and the hunger in his belly as they'd inched along. He also remembered they'd passed islands that were lost in the dark. It was because of disasters like the one they'd just survived that those islands would soon be lit by a grand new set of lighthouses.

Lambert took up his post at the Chantry Island light in 1858. One of his duties was tending the 540-foot (162-m) breakwater off the island's northern shoal, built at the same time as the light tower. The seas beat hard against the wall and it was a constant battle to keep up with repairs. In 1861, an entire hundred-foot section was battered away.

If the breakwater's purpose was to prevent ships from hitting shoals, then Lambert could not explain why fifteen vessels foundered there in the next decade. One foul night in November of 1864, two ships, *American Eagle* and *Lilly Dancy*, came to grief within a few hundred metres of one another. Struggling in their sailboat, Lambert, his able wife, Louisa, and their two sons, William and Ross, came to the rescue of *American Eagle*. The crew of another schooner, sheltered in the lee of the island, went to the aid of the *Dancy's* crew. After that night, Lambert asked the Department of Public Works to provide him with a proper lifeboat. Over the years, more than one drenched soul was rowed to safety in that craft.

But not all the rescues were successful. Lambert's son Ross was one who was lost to those fierce seas. Even now, Lambert's mind battled to make sense of it. When the scow, *Mary and Lucy*, struck the reef south of the island, the steamer, *Manitoba*, moored in the Chantry harbour, lowered a rescue team into those raging waters. The next thing Lambert knew, his son, Ross, had jumped in too.

Lambert knew the rescue attempt was folly. The rescue boat abandoned hope, and then tried with all its might

Duncan's son William took over as light-keeper. He is seen here holding a watch presented to him after he rescued the Nettie Woodward's *crew in 1892.*

to get back to shore. Lambert stood helpless at the dock. There was nothing he could do as the boat, caught by a massive wave, flipped upside down. Miraculously, it righted itself, and all hands were still on board. Another wave flipped it over and again the small boat righted itself. The third wave—carrying the fate of Lambert's son on its giant crest—crashed down. When the boat returned to view, Ross was gone. Scanning the water, Lambert spotted him, clinging to an oar. It was not enough to hold him up. Ross was hit by one wave after another, and soon the seas had swallowed him. Ross's death left Lambert heavy-hearted. In 1879, and at the age of 70, Lambert gave up lightkeeping. William, Lambert's other fine son, took over from his father.

THE FISHING ISLANDS ARCHIPELAGO

The Fishing Islands are a cluster of more than seventy limestone rocks and islands off the west shore of the Bruce Peninsula. These beautiful islands provided an essential fishing ground for Ojibwe and Petun. Names such as Smokehouse Island represent traditional locations (natives cured whitefish and sturgeon here).

From the late 1800s, the islands teemed with European fishermen and campers. In 1901, people started to purchase islands and build summer cottages. Irene Monkman's 1912 book, *Oliphant and its Islands*, cites a few of the characters, events and stories that gave the Fishing Islands some of their names. Here are a few:

Whitefish Island: The McAuley family of Southampton was known locally for the tragic loss of their ship *Rob Roy*, off Chief Point in 1864. Captain George McAuley's body was recovered later, having drifted to Lonely Island. A decade

FISHING ISLANDS

later, George's brothers Dan and Neil established a fishing station on Whitefish Island.

Whisky Island: Captain Alexander McGregor's workers from the fishing station on Main Station Island kept a still for making whisky on this island.

Smoke House Island: The Schell family's sawmill on the south shore ran a good business on this wooded island—until the operation burned to the ground in 1885.

Basswood Island (Deadman's Island): In the early 1900s, Allie Heuter, Chaucer Henderson, and Charlie and Edward Reckin were camping in the island's Basswood forest when they came across the grisly sight of a drowned man. The group buried him in a rock crevasse. It is not known if the body was later retrieved.

WILDMAN'S ISLAND (BOWES ISLAND)

The Life of a Hermit

It was around 1900 in the village of Southhampton. The fisherman noticed a couple glancing over warily as he unloaded a tent and supplies from his canoe. The woman came toward him, her long dress sweeping along the dock. "Excuse me," she smiled, "I know this sounds strange but a few nights ago we heard yells out on the lake and I hoped you might keep an eye out for anything unusual." The fisherman sighed as he moved a box of new cotton nets into his boat. "Where were you when you heard this?" he asked. "Camping," she replied, "on the south end of Bowes." She had scarcely uttered the words when the fisherman gave a knowing nod.

Fishermen had nicknamed the hermit "The Wildman" for his caterwauling habit. He paddled the islands in a dugout canoe, surviving on berries, trapping, and fishing from an old net. No one knew how long he had lived on Wildman's Island in his little shack of logs and driftwood. He showed no desire to make the fishermen's acquaintance; whenever they approached, he would scurry into his house or into the forest. They shared the notion that "The Wildman" had chosen a life in exile after his heart was broken by spurned love. In

Great Lakes fishermen

retrospect, the fishermen realized he was a tragic man with a tortured mind. One day, the fishermen found "the Wildman's" primitive canoe, floating empty. The hermit was never seen again, nor was his body recovered. Still the cry continued.

"The Wildman's" abandoned cabin

MAIN STATION ISLAND

Quicksilver

There were thousands and thousands of them, glistening and gleaming, swimming and darting, shining like silver. Captain Alexander McGregor stared agape into the dark water. He'd had thirty years of sights and adventures on schooners between Georgian Bay and Detroit. But in all that time, he had never seen water so teeming with fish. It was like quicksilver. He was already counting his fortune.

It was around 1831 when Captain McGregor sailed among what would later be called the Fishing Islands, west of the Bruce Peninsula, silvery swells of fish following in his wake. He searched the area for the ideal fishing station, and called it Main Station Island. It was not long before the whitefish and the herring overwhelmed McGregor, and he needed to hire French and Indian fishermen to help him. Soon he was speaking French and Ojibwe, along with his English and Gaelic.

Main Station's headquarters were both factory and home. McGregor erected a sixty-foot-long stone building. On the west side were McGregor's rooms, with a huge fireplace and mantle that displayed the black prow of a wrecked ship. Barrels were stored on the east side of the building. An early fishing method involved careful dragging of nets into the shore. One of the men would stand amid the fish with a net, and toss them on land. Others gutted the fish and packed them in brine. It might take several days to empty the net after a single haul. As the summer progressed, McGregor had thousands of barrels to sell. A Detroit buyer was happy to take three thousand barrels off his hands at a dollar per. Even after his men were paid, McGregor had never earned so much money.

*Ruins of Captain
Alexander
McGregor's Main
Station headquarters*

For all his good fortune, the Captain's reign on Main Station Island last-ed only a decade. His success sparked envy in Goderich, McGregor's hometown. The powerful Dr. William Dunlop concealed his personal jeal-ousy by wrapping himself in the flag, advocating Canadian-only enter-prise. Along with a group of envious cronies, he publicly scorned McGregor's Detroit business connection. Dunlop then used his political clout to secure fishing rights to the waters around the Fishing Islands. Under the auspices of his newly-founded Niagara Fishing Company, he and his friends gained exclusive access to the bounty of the islands. Having lost the right to fish off Main Station Island, the Captain laid off his crew, abandoning the premises he had built. The quarters were so extensive and unusual that half a century later the limestone ruins inspired tales that it had been a French fort in the 1700s.

The Niagara Fishing Co. operated until 1848 when it was sold out to Captains John Spence and William Kennedy, two early settlers of Southhampton. Captain Spence and his sons continued fishing for decades. As for Captain McGregor, he set his sails for new waters, too proud to be set back by Dunlop's trickery. For the next two decades, McGregor con-tinued fishing around Tobermory, Cape Croker, Manitoulin Island and the North Channel. But he never again found a fishing ground like the quicksilver around Main Station Island. He aban-doned his first wife, marrying a native woman. His family name lives on at Whitefish River First Nations on the North Shore near Killarney where many Ojibwe McGregors have served as chiefs.

Reels for drying nets

MACKINAC ISLAND

The Crossroads

The Ojibwe of the Great Lakes region revered Mackinac Island as the place where human life began. After the Great Flood, Michibou, the Hare, picked a grain of sand from the lakebed, and blew it dry until it grew into an island. It was here on this island that the first humans were placed, and it is their descendants who populated the earth.

The island is located in the Straits of Mackinac, at the crossroads between Lakes Huron, Michigan and Superior. This position made it significant throughout every era of Great Lakes history. Natives, missionaries, fur traders, and the military all used the strategic straits and the large island.

The military occupation so prominent in Mackinac's history began as early as the 1680s, when a French fort was established to protect fur trade interests. In 1715, the French established an outpost known as Fort Michilimackinac on the south side of the Straits. It grew to include a healthy civilian population, and became the principal summer depot for the Upper Great Lakes fur trade. Then, after the Seven Years' War (1756-63), New France and all of its forts were won by Britain.

It was a turbulent time for the Indian nations of the Upper Great Lakes. Many had fought valiantly alongside their French allies. The natives distrusted and despised the British troops and fur traders who began arriving on the Upper Great Lakes. Tensions erupted in 1763. Ojibwe and Sac warriors attacked the British at Fort Michilimackinac as part of a broader Indian anti-British offensive known as Pontiac's Rebellion.

The Rebellion awoke the British to the necessity of allying with the Indians. In the decades that followed, connections grew and the fort flourished. The civilian village enlarged to more than one hundred houses. But, amid the tensions that preceded the Revolutionary War, British authorities worried that the Fort was too vulnerable. For more security, they rebuilt on Mackinac Island, completing the new fort in 1781, at the tail end of the war.

The new location proved to be an unforeseen problem for the British. The post-war treaty awarded Mackinac Island to the newly formed United States. Britain held fast to their fort but, with Jay's Treaty in 1796, finally surrendered the island, building still another fort on St. Joseph Island in the North Channel. But the story doesn't end here. In less than twenty years, the British would take Mackinac again.

When President James Madison declared war on Britain in June 1812, the British at Fort St. Joseph responded swiftly, taking Fort Mackinac with a single warning shot (see p.115). In recovering Fort Mackinac, Britain

gained control of the Upper Lakes. The War of 1812 ended with no con-
clusive victor. On Christmas Eve 1814, the two countries signed the Treaty
of Ghent which restored pre-war boundaries. On July 18, 1815, American
troops reclaimed Fort Mackinac and once again sent the British packing.

Mackinac's prominence as the key location in the Great Lakes fur trade
had continued throughout the 1700s. During the American period it was
largely controlled by John Jacob Astor's American Fur Company which was
headquartered on the island. Great Lakes furs were shipped from Mackinac
to New York City and distributed to hatters and merchants in Europe and
China. Astor's company thrived until the 1840s when it was crippled by a
national recession and by the rise of independent fur traders. The island
remained a shipping centre for the fur trade but fish became the chief
export, making Mackinac Island one of the earliest commercial fisheries on
the Great Lakes. The stench of fish entrails made the air in Mackinac
unpleasant. By the mid-1800s, the village council had outlawed dumping
fish guts on the streets.

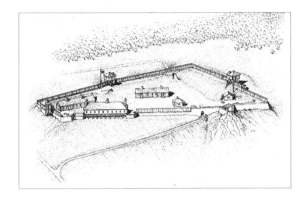

Fort Mackinac as it was originally constructed by the British in the early 1770s

The next decades brought sweeping changes to the Great Lakes. Michigan's population swelled from 175,000 in 1840 to 749,000 by 1860. By 1875, Mackinac's chief industry was tourism. Locals feared the island would be ruined by over-development. Spurred by concerned citizens, the federal government created Mackinac National Park, the country's second national park. The park included a larger portion of the island's interior. Two areas of the park along the east and west bluffs were also laid out for summer cottages. The soldiers from the Fort found renewed purpose as enforcers of the Park rules. Tourism also spurred on hotel construction, crowned by the completion of the Grand Hotel. The Grand transformed the island into the Midwest's most fashionable summer retreat. While opulent cottages were built, owners renovated older homes to keep up with the trends of the "Gilded Age."

In 1894 the War Department decided to shut down the old fort. Concerned Michigan leaders negotiated the tranfer of Mackinac National

Group in front of the fish merchant, Bromilow & Bates, Mackinac Island, 1870s

Cars were banned from Mackinac Island in 1898, so some tourists explored the island by bicycle.

Park to the state, resulting in the creation of Michigan's first state park. Today the park includes over eighty percent of the island's area. Numerous natural and historic attractions are preserved for the enjoyment of island visitors.

The splendid summer cottages, built in the late 1800s, still line the West and East bluffs. Historic buildings—such as Fort Mackinac, Biddle House (owned by fur trader Edward Biddle and one of Michigan's oldest surviving dwellings), Mission Church (1829) and American Fur Company structures—keep visitors in tune with the island's fascinating history. Mackinac Island State Park offers areas of solitude and stunning vistas. Cars were banned in 1898, and islanders carry out their daily business on horse and bicycle. Horse-drawn taxis chauffeur visitors to all the points of interest. Ferry service from both Mackinaw City and St. Ignace is provided by three commercial lines throughout the season.

MACKINAC ISLAND

The Surprise War

July 1812. Tensions with the British were running high. There were rumours that the President might declare war. And something was brewing at the British Fort St. Joseph 50 miles (80kms) away on St. Joseph Island. It was American militia captain Michael Dousman's mission to find out what was going on.

Dousman had paddled 15 miles from Mackinac when he noticed the familiar *Caledonia*, a sailing vessel of the North West Company. Slowly, hundreds of canoes and bateaux emerged bearing 400 Indians in war paint. Before he knew it, Dousman was surrounded. Aboard the *Caledonia*, Captain Dousman was amazed to learn he was a prisoner of war. America had declared war on Great Britain on June 18, 1812! Dousman did the calculation: that was 29 days ago. Just how long did the authorities intend to wait before informing Fort Mackinac it was at war?

With Dousman aboard, the *Caledonia* made her way to Mackinac Island, certain to take the American fort by surprise. St. Joseph's commander, Captain Roberts, and fur trader Robert Dickson approached the captive with a proposition: if Dousman gave his word not to alert the fort, they would allow him to evacuate the villagers who lived outside the garrison. It was a gesture of goodwill and Dousman accepted it.

The flotilla landed on the north side of the island by night. The British had constructed the fort in 1780 (and lost it to the U.S. after the Revolutionary War), so they knew its inherent weakness: the fort was built low, leaving the garrison vulnerable to attack from the high bluff behind. It was a weakness that would now work to their advantage.

Militia Captain Michael Dousman was captured by the British.

Dousman and a British soldier scrambled through the village, alerting the sleepy villagers and then herding them to safety. In the meantime, the Indian recruits and soldiers took their positions in the forest, while voyageurs hauled two six-pound cannons to the bluff behind the fort. They exploded the cannon toward the sleeping garrison. Confused, the Fort's soldiers tumbled into action. Messengers carried a summons of surrender to the fort's commander, American Lieutenant Porter Hanks. It was the first that Hanks had heard of his own country's declaration of war. Hanks assessed the situation: his sixty troops facing a British army of six hundred, its two cannons staring down upon the fort. It would be a massacre. Hanks surrendered without a fight. It was a key victory for the British. With Fort Mackinac and Fort Detroit on Lake St. Clair under their flag, the British would control the Upper Great Lakes, Michigan Territory, the Upper Mississippi and by extension, most of the western fur trade.

In a disastrous move, the Americans tried to reclaim the fort in July 1814. Under the command of Colonel George Crogan, five brigs delivered hundreds of American soldiers. Colonel Crogan botched his offensive by

The British knew Fort Mackinac's weakness and used it to their advantage.

copying the British attack and landing his troops at the north end of the island. Crossing the island, the Americans hit an ambush of between 140 and 250 British redcoats and 350 natives. Battered, they retreated to their ships.

Still, there was good news ahead for the Americans. On Christmas Eve of 1814, the Treaty of Ghent ended the War of 1812, restoring the pre-war boundaries. In 1815, U.S. troops returned to Fort Mackinac. Disappointed, the British withdrew for the second time from Mackinac Island. Because their fort on St. Joseph Island had been burned down in the war, the British went in search of a new island. (See Drummond Island p.169 for the continuing saga of the peripatetic British garrison.)

Today Fort Mackinac, with its commanding view of the Straits, is a popular tourist destination. All of the fort's original buildings, dating between 1781 and 1895 have been restored. Throughout the summer guided tours and reenactments such as cannon and rifle firings, programs of military music and an 1880s court martial are offered to visitors. Exhibits detail the fort's fascinating history, as well as the entire island story including the fur trade and the resort era.

In a disastrous move, Americans tried to regain the fort in July 1814.

MACKINAC ISLAND

The Grand Hotel in Grand Style

1890s. James Reddington Hayes had earned his nickname "The Comet." The fiery manager of the Grand Hotel raced through the crowd, grinning from ear to ear. Officers from the nearby Fort, dressed in their finest, nodded to the ladies as they strolled along the Grand's sprawling verandah. "The flirtation walk," as Hayes gleefully called it, was in full swing. "Well, let's see it," said Hayes to his assistant who was clutching a small printed card. Hayes threw back his head in laughter:

> This is to certify, that I, _____, the legally wedded wife of
> _____, do hereby permit my husband to go where he pleases and
> drink what he pleases, and I furthermore permit him to keep and enjoy
> the company of any lady or ladies he sees fit, as I know he is a good
> judge, and I want him to enjoy life, as soon he will be long
> time dead.

The card, to be distributed among couples, was in keeping with Hayes' outlandish style. He had a nose for the business, its changing trends and how to make the hotel a memorable experience for patrons. Hayes had turned the Grand Hotel into the premier Midwest resort. Patrons arrived by rail and steamer from Chicago, Detroit, Cleveland, Cincinnati, Louisville, Indianapolis, St. Louis and Kansas City. The secret to his success? "Give them an unforgettable experience." The Grand offered ballroom dances, horse shows, boxing matches, daily concerts on the verandah, shows in the Casino... Today

James Reddington Hayes was nicknamed the "The Comet."

Concerts were held on the Grand's famous verandah, and guests paraded its length in what was known as the "flirtation walk."

there was a special guest appearance by humourist, Mark Twain. Tonight's rage? Egyptian dancing girls.

"Bigger, bigger, bigger" had been Hayes' mantra for years. He convinced the Mackinac Hotel Company to add fifty extra rooms, even when other resorts were struggling to maintain capacity. And in 1897, Hayes began angling for a new clientele—the convention trade.

Then came the rain, two whole seasons of it. Articles in the magazine *Hotel* posted grim figures for the Grand: only 40 guests at season's open; only 214 guests for Fourth of July celebrations. Was the Comet fizzling? A deal was made to bring in Henry Weaver, the popular manager at the Planter's Hotel of St. Louis. The Company was relieved to have passed the hotel to a 'more manageable manager.' They were wrong.

"Weaver's threatening what?" exploded Francis Stockbridge, one of the Company's most vocal stockholders. "That's Blackmail!" Henry Weaver, the manager of the Grand Hotel from 1900-1918, would not have called it blackmail, but that is essentially what it was. The cash had not been rolling in during Weaver's lease of the hotel. To bring the business back around, Weaver wanted a larger stake. Half to be exact. And if the Mackinac Hotel Company wouldn't sell him half the stock, he would lock the hotel doors and leave it empty for the seven years until his lease expired! Amid shock and rage, the Mackinac Hotel Company complied.

Filled with renewed vigour, Henry Weaver proceeded to revive the Grand to its former splendour. His big plans required big money—$50,000—but he was unable to secure a loan. Soon, he could no longer conceal the worn furnishings and carpets and the clientele continued to decline. Anxious to be rid of the white elephant, the Company sold the remaining shares to Weaver between 1905 and 1910. That final season, Weaver took such a loss that he considered tearing down the Grand and selling off the lumber! Islanders were shocked. The Grand Hotel was a fixture of the island community and an essential part of the local economy. In 1911, they banded together to convince Weaver to save the structure—employees agreed to work for less money and local investors helped finance improvements until a new buyer could be found. Against all odds the Hotel remained afloat, even during the lean years of World War One. In 1918 the struggling venture was finally sold off.

Some say that the only good thing new owner Logan Ballard did for the Grand Hotel was to hire resourceful desk clerk, William Stewart Woodfill in 1919. Woodfill had a knack for the business and by 1924 the energetic Scot had risen to manager. Dedicated and impassioned about the Grand, Woodfill wrote in his diary: "I told him I just loved the work, and at the end of the season he could pay me anything he might think I was worth, or nothing at all." In 1925, Woodfill approached a bank headed by James L. Kraft of Kraft Cheese fame in order to raise the necessary capital to buy stock in the hotel. Aware the wooden fire hazard was too risky for investors, Woodfill brought images of the hotel shot through soft filters creating the effect that it was made of marble. The ploy succeeded and Woodfill became part owner in the hotel, only to sell his shares two years later at a handsome profit.

Ownership fell to the remaining partners—the disastrous duo of Joseph Ballard and Eugene La Chance. Neither had the talent to run a hotel. Ballard died as the Great Depression of the 1930s loomed. Now the Grand was a sinking ship without a captain. Although Woodfill left the Grand, his

Henry Weaver threatened to shut the hotel down for seven years unless he was given half the Hotel's stock.

William Stewart Woodfill began as desk clerk and within four years had moved up to management.

love for it had never waned. In 1933 he returned and purchased the hotel outright from government receivership, making sweeping changes. He reduced the daily rate to $3.00, the price in 1887! Woodfill enhanced the luxury, combining rooms and adding baths. He needed to register a minimum of 500 people every day throughout the season, and he knew that the key to his survival was to keep the Grand in the public eye.

In 1935, Woodfill claimed that the Grand housed "the longest piece of carpet ever made." Actually, the broadloom was made of pieces that were sewn together. He also started rumours of an impending visit from President Franklin D. Roosevelt, who would give a "fireside chat" on the Grand's renowned porch. He named guestrooms after famous people giving the impression that these celebrities had slept there. The Grand boasted of the "Longest Porch in the World! 880 Feet!" a claim accepted by Ripley's

Early tourists to Mackinac Island

The Grand Hotel, 1895

Believe It Or Not. But in the 1980s, a discrepancy of 252 feet, was found and the Grand's world record was withdrawn.

In 1951, Woodfill's nephew, Dan Musser joined the staff as a waiter and cashier. By, 1960 he had moved up to hotel president, and his wife Amelia had become treasurer. By then the hotel was in dire need of repairs and renovations, but the Mussers' vision for the hotel did not harmonize with Woodfill's: the plastics and vinyls Woodfill had ordered from Sears-Roebuck were not the appropriate décor for the historic hotel. It took until 1977 to convince Woodfill to redecorate. The Mussers contacted famous New York designer Carleton Varney, design consultant to the White House during the Carter administration.

Varney's design breathed new life into The Grand while preserving its classical-revivalist elegance. The hotel was changing, and the aging Woodfill, beset by respiratory problems, decided to move to Arizona. When Woodfill put the hotel up for sale, Musser raised the money to buy it. Dan Musser recalled that on that autumn day in 1978, the old man boarded his final ferry, not once looking back at the island hotel, his greatest passion since 1919.

Today the Grand Hotel is one of the finest surviving splendours of the Victorian era on the Great Lakes. (Much of the information for this story was gathered from John McCabe's *Grand Hotel: Mackinac Island*.)

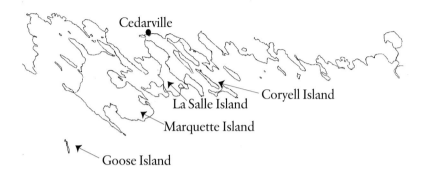

Cedarville

Coryell Island

La Salle Island

Marquette Island

Goose Island

LES CHENEAUX ARCHIPELAGO

The "Old Chimney," remains of Chief Shab-wa-way's home, c. 1912

Les Cheneaux, meaning "The Channels," is a series of narrow islands (carved by glaciers) and their many sheltering channels. Today Les Cheneaux is distinguished for the picturesque setting and beautiful historic cottages. Buyers began recognizing Les Cheneaux's potential as a haven for recreation in the 1870s. It was the beginning of an era. The Les Cheneaux Club was formed in 1888 by an emerging new class of businessmen and entrepreneurs. They built summer homes, many of them quite grand with multiple rooms for servants and guests. By the 1920s, many had large boathouses sheltering classic mahogany Chris-Craft. One of the finest cottages is perched on tiny Dollar Island, so named—as the legend goes—because its original purchase price was a single dollar. Many hotels were built in this same period, including the Elliot Hotel on La Salle Island and the Lakeside Hotel on Coryell Island.

An important site on Marquette Island is The Old Chimney, former ruins of Chief Shab-wa-way's former home. Chief of the Les Cheneaux native people, Shab-wa-way was among many native leaders who ceded most of northern Michigan to the U.S. in 1836, but he reserved the Les Cheneaux Islands for his people. Shab-wa-way died in his home on Marquette Island in 1872. The ruins were once a popular attraction. Today, a plaque marks where the house once stood. Saint Leger's Island played a significant role in the region's history. Around 1883, Michel Saint Leger squatted here, with the Indians' approval. A fisherman, Saint Leger eked out his living by guiding sport fishermen from the fort on Mackinac Island. His patrons included men who later founded the Les Cheneaux Club. Engage in the rich history of the region by visiting the Les Cheneaux Historical Association Museum, Cedarville, MI (906) 484-2821.

MARQUETTE ISLAND

The Les Cheneaux Club

Within thirty years of its establishment in 1888, the Les Cheneaux Club had a club house and 35 cottages, some appointed with fine furnishings, rugs and pianos. Club members were from prominent families from Chicago, Detroit, Kentucky, Nashville, Indianapolis, Cincinnati, and New York.

Between 1920 and 1940, the Rudd family lived year round at Marquette Island as the Club's caretakers, enjoying the tranquility of the Club during the winter, and the hectic, demanding days of summer. In the summer, there was mail to sort, and livestock to care for. The Rudds maintained the power plant, the two clay tennis courts and the grounds. They operated the private ferry to the golf course on the mainland. Every day, they collected the garbage by horse and wagon.

When daughter Uldene Rudd Leroy thought back to the Club and its clientele she remembered them through her childhood impressions,

The Les Cheneaux club grew into a cherished summer home for generations of people.

We children had the opportunity of meeting and knowing many famous and important people over the years, but we were not particularly impressed at the time. To us they were just summer people, all rather peculiar in their ways and not to be taken too seriously. Senators, well-known writers and editors, heads of huge corporations and even titled personages came and went.

In LeRoy's book, *Six on an Island,* she recalls the Club staff as an assortment of local residents and imports. Club House workers—many of whom were blacks from the South—often entertained the children, singing gospel songs on the dock during off hours. Mr. Rudd employed local Ojibwe for construction and grounds keeping. Bill, a grounds worker, had grown irritated by a member's barrage of questions. One day, she pointed to a rock painted with an orange X, inquiring what he knew about it. Bill could not resist pulling her leg. He told her it was an old sign painted by "his people" to show that the family living there was friendly to Indians. The woman darted from cottage to cottage, boasting of the great honour the "Indians" had bestowed upon her family. Bill then began noticing members checking outside their cottages for similar rocks. He spent the next few days sulking about with a brush and paint marking Xs on everyone's property.

Hotel Islington, 1904. Hotels on the islands and the mainland of the Les Cheneaux area attracted loyal patrons who returned summer after summer.

Once Rudd hired some Ojibwe men to chop firewood. He noticed a pair of deer antlers lying in the bush and picked them up. The natives looked at him with concern, congregated in a huddle, then they picked up their axes and walked away. Someone explained that the discovery of antlers meant that a death in the family was coming. Rudd hung the antlers in the wood shed. Two days later, the call came. He had to come immediately because his brother was dying.

In addition to the staff hired by the Club, members' brought an entourage of personal staff. One silk importer brought a Japanese servant. The Rudd girls marveled at his politeness. Whenever he picked up his employers he bowed backward all the way out the door. Evidently he sent many post cards home, but rarely did they show images of Les Cheneaux. He seemed to have a particular fascination with the Soo locks. No one thought anything of it, until the outbreak of WWII when his name began appearing in the newspaper. He was a high-ranking officer in the Japanese army.

LeRoy's book also remembers the Club's members. There were the quirky ones, like the woman who sent the Rudd girls little purses, each with a penny for Christmas. Two summers later she asked to see the purses, wanting to make sure they had saved their pennies. There were also members who distinguished themselves in the girls' eyes by their good humour and ability to laugh at the Rudd girls' pranks.

Over one hundred years since it began, the Les Cheneaux Club continues as a vibrant and historic summering community set among the picturesque Les Cheneaux Islands.

GOOSE & MACKINAC ISLANDS

The Adventures of Alexander Henry

He awoke at dawn beside the cold ashes of the fire. They had set up camp on the shore of Isle aux Outardes (Goose Island) one of Les Cheneaux, at the northern end of Lake Huron. The others were already readying the canoes. He hastily tucked in his shirt and tightened the colourful sash around his waist, intending to resemble a voyageur. Digging into his provisions, he found a lump of pork fat and smeared it over his face, next rubbing in a handful of dirt. These voyageur fellows paddled across a lot of water, but they rarely seemed to bathe. His disguise was nearly complete. He climbed into the canoe and pushed off with the others over the silent surface of the lake.

Fur trader Alexander Henry survived the attack on Fort Michilimackinac.

Several hours later he spotted in the distance three canoes, full of Indians. His heartbeat quickened. Would his disguise fool them again? Trying to paddle with the grace and speed of the voyageurs, he was convinced his awkwardness would show. His French friends called out cheerful greetings to the natives who returned the greetings and paddled on. It was a long moment before he recovered the rhythm of his paddle stroke.

The year was 1761. It was a bad time to be British in northern Michigan. Alexander Henry was an Englishman living in New Jersey who had been lured north by profits in the fur trade. He had been heading straight into the heart of Indian Territory just as the natives had declared war on the British.

In 1759, British General James Wolfe had defeated the French Lieutenant-General, Louis Joseph, Marquis de Montcalm on the Plains of Abraham in Quebec City. Many nations of the Upper Great Lakes had fought alongside the French. They had enjoyed a peaceful coexistence, sharing territory, and even calling the King of France their father. Within a year of the French defeat, New France had fallen to the English. The Treaty of Paris in 1763 transferred New France to British hands, ignoring the territorial arrangements the natives had had with France.

The betrayal only deepened the Indians dislike for the British. They seemed a people intent on taking over territory rather than sharing it. The

Chief Pontiac's eloquent oration incited natives to rise up against the British who were moving into Indian territory after France lost its North American territories to Great Britain.

British had no interest in supplying the natives with ammunition for hunting, as the French had done. Convinced of their superiority, the British looked on the Indians with contempt. Indian nations in Michigan Territory—the Seneca, Delaware, Shawnee, Miami, Ottawa, Sauk, Ojibwe and Mississauga—went to war against the British.

Paddling past the islands called Les Cheneaux, Alexander Henry's fear gave way to renewed optimism. Despite the danger he was heading into, he had not considered abandoning his fur trading plans. His French friends and disguise had worked so far. He was an observant, literate man, and kept a diary of everything that happened.

Late in the afternoon Henry and his French companions left Mackinac Island. They had beached before dark on the south shore of the Straits between Lake Huron and Lake Michigan. They made their way toward the fort there, Fort Michilimackinac, named after the Great Turtle. Within the fort's cedar stockade, thirty cabins housed French soldiers, fur traders and their families. Henry's friends were quick to find a house for him. Word soon spread among the French that an Englishman was in their midst, and the fort's inhabitants advised him to flee. But before he had time to react, sixty Oijbwe men arrived at Henry's door.

> They walked in single file, each with his tomahawk in one hand and scalping knife in the other. Their bodies were naked from the waist up... Their faces were painted with charcoal, worked up with grease... Some had feathers through their noses... The chief had in his countenance an indescribable mixture of good and evil...

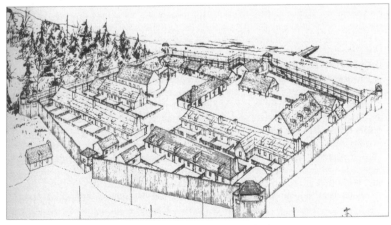

Depiction of Fort Michilimackinac as it was c. 1770

After an endless moment of confrontation, the chief said to Henry that the English must be a brave people, daring to come so fearlessly among their enemies. He continued,

> Although you have conquered the French, you have not yet conquered us! We are not your slaves. These lakes, these woods and mountains were left to us by our ancestors. They are our inheritance and we will part with them to none.

The Chief proceeded to declare the natives' intention to make war against the British, but then his speech took a surprising turn, "You do not come armed... You come in peace to trade with us... We shall regard you therefore as a brother." Acutely relieved, Henry's hand was still shaking as he smoked a pipe of peace with them.

Henry spent a very calm year at the fort. One day an Ojibwe named Wawatam came to visit him. He said that he'd had a dream inspired by the Great Spirit. It told him an Englishman was destined to enter his life and become his blood brother. Wawatam said that Henry was this man. If he were willing to accept the Indian's offer, he would always be one of Wawatam's family. Henry happily accepted.

Dramatic change came a year later when British troops took command of the fort. They let the French remain, hoping to take advantage of their friendship with the natives. A feeling of unrest grew every day. Indians, arriving in large numbers, camped outside the fort. Their mood seemed strangely jovial.

After a year, Henry's blood brother, Wawatam, appeared at his door again. Trying to conceal his anxiety, he urged the Englishman to go with him and his family to the Sault. The Indians camped outside had come demanding liquor, and he did not want Henry to suffer their drunkenness. Henry could not quite penetrate Wawatam's poetic Ojibwe phrases.

The next day, the fourth of June, was the British King's birthday. Two native groups started a game of lacrosse in the King's honour. The ball landed inside the fort. Indians entered on the pretext of retrieving it. War cries went up. From his window, Henry saw,

> a crowd of Indians furiously cutting down and scalping every Englishman they found... The dying were writhing and shrieking under the unsatiated knife and tomahawk, and from the bodies of some ripped open, their butchers were drinking their blood, scooped up in the hollow of joined hands and quaffed amid shouts of rage and victory.

Seeking refuge, Henry was turned away by a French family next door. A Pauni slave pulled him aside, took him upstairs and locked him in the garret. Before long Indians had entered the house, searching for British hiding there. Henry heard them on the stairs. He dove into a heap of birchbark pails in a dark corner. The key turned in the lock, and four natives entered, tomahawks in hand. His heart was pounding so loudly that he was sure that they would hear it. The darkness in that windowless space protected him. But only for the moment.

For the next seventy-two hours, Henry walked a fine and terrifying line between life and death. Captured, stripped, threatened, escaping death several times over, put into a canoe bound for Lake Michigan's Beaver Islands, captured on the way by another nation, then returned full circle to the fort, and delivered into Ojibwe hands. He was living in a nightmare.

The attack plan involved a game of lacrosse.

Rescued by his blood brother Wawatam, Henry's head was shaved and he was disguised as an Ojibwe.

At noon on the fourth day, sleepless, starving, wearing only a shirt, Henry was brought before the Ojibwe Chief. Suddenly, like a vision, his blood brother, Wawatam, appeared and pleaded eloquently for Henry's release. It was granted.

Henry had a brief respite with Wawatam's family, before they retreated to Michilimackinac Island, fearing the imminent return of vengeful British troops. Natives from other nations began to arrive to help with the island's defense. A lone Englishman would be easy prey. The chief of the Mackinac Island tribe recommended that Henry disguise himself. His head was shaved, and his face painted with bright colours. Silver bands encircled his arms, feathers decorated his head, and a scarlet blanket was draped around his shoulders. Young women gazed approvingly at the handsome newcomer.

Henry had been living as an Ojibwe for a year when he was discovered by another nation. Leaving his Indian life behind, he fled to the mainland, finally reaching safety at Sault Ste. Marie. He eventually found his way to Montreal, where he lived quietly as a merchant. He died in 1824, sixty years since he had lived with the Indians.

LAKE HURON'S GEORGIAN BAY

Manitoulin Island

Lonely Island

Fitzwilliam Island

Cove Island

Tobermory

GEORGIAN BAY

Cape Hurd

White Cloud
Island

Parry
Island

Parry
Sound

Wreck
Island

Christian
Island

Colpoy's
Bay

Wiarton

Mary Ward
Ledges

Penetanguishene

Ste.-Marie among
the Hurons

Owen Sound

Craigleith

Collingwood

Nottawasaga
Island

FITZWILLIAM ISLAND

"Horse Island"

The British garrison at Drummond Island was forced to relocate after the island became American territory.

"Horse Island," the fishermen's name for Fitzwilliam Island, dates back to the first shipwreck on Georgian Bay in 1828. In November of that year, further west along the North Channel, the British garrison at Drummond Island was preparing to move to Penetanguishene, in southern Georgian Bay. Months earlier, the International Boundary Commission had formally awarded Drummond Island to U.S., forcing the demoralized British troops to hand over their fort.

The brig *Duke of Wellington* and schooner *Alice Hackett* appeared as misty shadows through the sheets of falling snow. The ships would transfer the men and their families, but they could not carry everything that had been collected in seven years on Drummond Island. In rows and rows of houses, furniture and countless personal effects were abandoned. The American soldiers at Fort Mackinac would soon be circling like gulls.

The community of 91 soldiers, their families and various suppliers were ferried to the ships. First the *Wellington* set sail and then the *Hackett*, both packed to the rafters with everything from livestock to barrels of rum and whiskey. Below deck, the grim mood washed away as tavern keeper, Alex Fraser, tapped a barrel, fiddlers played and families sang. Angelina Lepine kept one hand on her daughter's back, as the eight-year-old balanced on a rum barrel. Her husband, Pierre, lifted a glass and gave her a silent toast. Soon Captain Hackett joined in the festivities. The Scotsman's tales became as rosy as his cheeks as he tossed the whiskey back. No one noticed when the wind came up.

The *Alice Hackett* was flung against the shoals off Fitzwilliam Island, hurling the passengers in all directions. The cries of trapped cows and horses pierced their ears. The pitch of night, the screaming wind, and the violent flapping of the sails added to the terror. Impaled on a rock, the ship listed so sharply that it was hard to crawl up to the lifeboat. A lantern held into the night revealed waves smashing against a nearby shore—they were not that far from land! It took several trips to ferry everyone ashore. Alex

The new garrison at Penetanguishene on Georgian Bay. When the Alice Hackett *failed to arrive a search crew set out.*

Fraser, determined not to lose the stock for his new tavern in Penetang, sought help tossing the barrels in the lake. The drinking continued on the mainland, this time to numb the chill. A shout went up as William Solomon's favourite horse, Louie, waded to shore.

It wasn't until dawn that Pierre Lepine realized his wife and child had not made it off the ship. Lepine and four others yanked the lifeboat back into the lake. As they approached the devastated vessel, they heard a moan in the submerged aft. What had he done?! Clinging to the railing, Lepine scrambled up the slanted deck where he found his wife and daughter bound to the mast, Angelina's long, raven hair tangled in her face. Both were weak from exposure. As they were carried off the ship, Angelina murmured, "We shouted and shouted but you couldn't hear, you couldn't hear."

It was several days before a rescue schooner arrived, with room for everything but Solomon's horse Louie. For years, passing Indians and fisherman observed the old steed wandering Fitzwilliam Island where it eventually died.

The wreck of the *Alice Hackett*, Georgian Bay's first shipwreck, was discovered in the 1860s by two fishermen. They hauled its 200-lb. cannon onto their sailboat, but the relic was lost when their boat capsized near Chantry Island. Captain Hackett's career was plagued by wrecks: between 1832 and 1835, he lost four more vessels, earning him the dubious Great Lakes record of having lost five ships in seven years. He retired from sailing in 1837 and became a lightkeeper.

Angelina and her child survived the stormy night by lashing themselves to the mast.

LONELY ISLAND

Robbing the Dead

September 14, 1882 was a heavy day in and around Georgian Bay. The steamer *Asia* had been lost in a hurricane, and with 122 passengers on board, nearly everyone in the region had lost a relative, friend or acquaintance. Little hope remained for their survival. Still, many signed up for the search, including Captain Richmond.

One hundred and twenty-two lives were lost on the Asia.

Richmond felt protective of the *Asia's* captain. He had heard rumours that the ship had been loaded down with extra passengers and livestock. Richmond was well acquainted with the pressure captains felt to make the year end quota. Still, Richmond had seen the barometer that day. He could not explain why *Asia* sailed straight into that storm.

Captain Richmond set course for isolated Lonely Island. The white lighthouse stood brightly on the cliff, set off by the autumn colours. The search crew landed and approached lightkeeper Dominic Solomon. The keeper assured Captain Richmond that no dead nor debris had drifted onto Lonely's shore. But Richmond was not convinced. Solomon appeared reticent and preoccupied as he fiddled with his fishing net. The crew set out to search the island while Richmond returned to interrogate the keeper. Before long, Solomon became flustered and confessed.

Yes, there had been a corpse, an unclothed woman so badly decayed he felt it best to bury her. The Captain wanted to see the grave, but Solomon stalled.

The crew returned having found a woman's body near the shore, covered with a board and still wearing a life preserver. Was this Solomon's idea of burial? Captain Richmond inspected the body, noting the impression of a necklace and a ring. Solomon eventually confessed to taking a pearl broach, $2.10 in silver, and a

Keeper's house, Lonely Island

gold watch. He returned the items—except the gold watch, already in for repair—swearing these were the only things he'd found. When one of Richmond's men arrived with an empty wallet recovered from the brush, Captain Richmond ordered an inspection of the lighthouse dwelling. He was horrified to find Solomon's stash: stools, chairs, axe-handles, a cabin door, a trunk, valise, block and tackle, a water tank, a pillow case, and a picture of a girl in a gilt frame. A local newspaper later reported that the discovery of three more life preservers with a "disagreeable smell pervading" led the search party to suspect more bodies were "secreted away."

On October 16, 1882, the Department of Marine and Fisheries announced an inquiry of the Lonely Island keeper's conduct. The Manitoulin Island newspaper defended Mr. Solomon, suggesting that his lack of regular com-

Lonely Island's second tower, erected 1907

munication with Manitoulin and the mainland kept him from reporting the bodies. Others retorted that his "isolation" had not delayed him from sending the stolen watch to be repaired. Ultimately, Solomon's behaviour went unpunished, and he stayed on as Lonely Island's keeper for three more years.

A teenaged girl and boy were the only two survivors of the *Asia*. They drifted for three days on a lifeboat along with seven dead passengers and crew. They landed on an island where they were discovered by an Ojibwe

Christy Ann Morrison

couple and returned to the town of Parry Sound. Christy Ann Morrison and Duncan Tinkis gave crucial testimony at the *Asia* inquiry, confirming that the hurricane—and not an unmarked shoal—had taken down the overloaded ship.

Four hundred and seventy lives were lost in shipping disasters on the Great Lakes between 1879 and 1882 alone. And unlike the *Asia*, many of these ships foundered because there were no charts marking the dangers in the lakes. The government finally responded to the pressure, building more lighthouses and undertaking a detailed hydrological survey of Georgian Bay's rocks, shoals and banks. The charts made from this survey are still used today.

COVE ISLAND

The Ghost of Captain Tripp

September 1881. A clock bobbing in the waves caught the fisherman's eye. His workmate reached in and scooped it from the lake. The hands had stopped at one o'clock. When the men returned to their home port at Collingwood, they showed the discovery around the dock. Someone recognized it from the schooner *Regina*. It belonged to Captain Amos Tripp, a local man with a sterling reputation— although many had joked privately that his schooner was a coffin ship. Why was Tripp's clock in the lake? The answer was already known miles up the lake, at the village of Lion's Head.

Lightkeeper George Currie found Captain Tripp's body on Cove Island.

The crew from the wrecked *Regina*— minus their captain—had arrived in Lion's Head having rowed 60 exhausting miles from Cove Island. It was only later, over whiskey, that some locals voiced suspicions. The victims' accounts seemed rehearsed, and full of contradictions. *The Toronto Globe* printed this version:

> ...At 10:30 p.m. we made a reef in the mainsail to clear the Cove Island light. Finding the vessel labouring heavily and making water fast, we bore up and ran for Cove Island beach. She made water so fast she got beyond control, and was sinking fast. The Captain gave order for the men to take boats to save their lives. All hands succeeded in reaching the boat except the Captain who was at the wheel. He caught the main boom and hung to it but the lifeboat being half full of water and having only one oar we were unable to render him any assistance. We then ran the yawl for Cape Hurd Passage. The Captain, when last seen, was clinging to the wreck and calling for assistance.

An official report suggested that both the captain and the vessel could have been saved had the ship been kept afloat a short while longer. People started to murmur "mutiny."

Days later, someone from Tobermory stopped at the Cove Island lighthouse to tell Keeper George Currie that the *Regina* had gone down in a gale. He told Currie that the ship's masts could be seen above the water. The keeper added a task to his routine—checking the shoreline for bodies. One corpse washed up thirteen days later. The uniform confirmed that it was Captain Amos Tripp. Currie wrapped him in an old sheet of canvas and buried him on the west side of the island.

The wreck of the *Regina* has never been recovered and divers continue their attempts to locate her. As for Tripp, his body was exhumed weeks after he was buried and transported home to Collingwood by the tug *Mathan*. Subsequent keepers at Cove Island believed that Tripp's ghost haunted the lighthouse—one even believed that Tripp lit the lamp on night when the keeper was off the island. If the captain haunts the island still, he must truly be a lonely ghost. The lighthouse—the last staffed lighthouse on the Great Lakes—has been automated since 1991.

Above) Cove Island light station was one of six stone Imperial Towers erected on Lake Huron between 1855-59.

L) Many schooners like the Regina *fell into disrepair when steamships replaced them in popularity.*

WHITE CLOUD ISLAND

The Jane Miller

November 25, 1881. People gathered along the shore of Colpoy's Bay, retelling Rod Cameron's strange story of the night before. Cameron had been watching the storm from his house when he had spotted the *Jane Miller's* murky silhouette behind the sheets of wet snow. Then, in the blink of an eye, she had vanished. Captains prepared their tugs to search for the missing steamer. The *Jane Miller* had left Owen Sound for Wiarton at 8 p.m., with a full load of wood, freight and anxious passengers. The captain had not been deterred by "a little snow." The *Jane Miller* was last seen at Big Bay.

Searchers headed out in the direction of Cameron's sighting. Eyes trained on the gray waters, they searched for smashed wood and other debris.

The Jane Miller *is Georgian Bay's only ghost ship.*

Meanwhile, local residents on White Cloud found remnants of the ship and crew: oars bearing her name, a broken flagstaff, a fire bucket rack, and a number of men's hats. These clues suggested she'd been hit by a succession of strong waves. When her cargo shifted, and she was unable to recover, she rolled over and plunged into the Bay. After the first discovery, another rescue group found a patch of oily water, seething and bubbling. The bottom was dragged. And dragged. And dragged again. In the end, they found nothing.

Colpoy's Bay. The final sighting of the Jane Miller *was from Rod Cameron's house.*

Twenty-six years later, in 1907, a group of hunters on White Cloud Island were enjoying the evening's campfire when they were startled by a noise. There it was again. A horrible cry, like a call for help, but muted, as though someone was trapped beneath the water. The next morning, the men were relieved to return home. En route to Colpoy's Bay, they sailed though a large patch of bubbles, a telltale sign of a shipwreck. Back on the mainland, they pointed out the shipwreck site. A local resident noted that the site was directly in line with Cameron's Point, where Rod Cameron had seen the *Jane Miller* disappear in 1881.

NOTTAWASAGA ISLAND LIGHTHOUSE

The Lightkeeper Who Saved 52 Lives

Lightkeeper George Collins pulled his lifeboat alongside the 120-ft. (36-m) *Mary Ward*. The steamer was stranded on the limestone reef within view of the Nottawasaga lighthouse. It was a serene November night in 1874, a blanket of stars reflecting on the calm waters of Georgian Bay. As he made his way to the pilothouse, Collins nodded politely to passengers who were strolling the deck. Songs and laughter mingled with the gentle breeze. The first mate thanked Collins for the offer of assistance but they had already sent for help.

The lightkeeper's intuition told him that the passengers should be brought ashore. At midnight, the wind shifted and the ship's rigging began to moan. The night watchman banged on the Captain's door. Within moments Captain Johnston sounded the whistle and called all hands. Back

at the lighthouse, George Collins could faintly heard the call above the growing wind. Looking at the sky he could see the cause of the alarm—a full scale November storm was about to be unleashed.

The storm hit, pushing breakers over the stern. Fearing the ship would be torn apart, the passengers refused to stay inside. Drenched and numbed from cold, they braced themselves against the railings. Eight panicked passengers launched a lifeboat, but the yawl flipped and was sucked under only yards from the steamer.

In his 32 years as light-keeper, George Collins saved 52 lives.

The tug *Mary Ann* had been dispatched when the steamer first foundered, but she turned back from the raging seas. The *Mary Ward* began to creak under the stress. The last lifeboat was prepared launch, but only six people dared get in.

Among them was Charles Campbell, "I will make it," he promised his pregnant wife. The lifeboat was flung into the waves that grew like mountains over the smooth limestone shelves. Within moments all six were drowned.

Collins paced the night away. There was nothing he could do. At dawn he observed the *Mary Ward's* condition from the tower-she was still holding on, barely. By afternoon he and his twenty-one-year-old son Charles risked launching the lifeboat for Collingwood. They reached the harbour, depleted and with only one oar. Collins convinced three fishermen that they had the strength and know-how to rescue the passengers of *Mary Ward*. They managed to grab the nine remaining passengers just minutes before the battered *Mary Ward* split apart, sliding down the ledges that still bear her name.

Later, under scrutiny, Captain Johnston of the *Mary Ward* claimed he had mistaken the light from a Craigleith tavern with Collingwood Harbour. It was a

The Mary Ward's *captain seemed to feel the grounded steamer and its passengers were in no imminent danger.*

hard claim to swallow when the Nottawasaga Lighthouse had been guiding his way. Among other accusations, it was alleged that Captain Johnston was drunk, and that the ship's compass was not working. The biggest mystery of all was why, with the barometer so low, he had let passengers and crew settle in for the night aboard the *Mary Ward*.

For their heroic rescue, George and Charles Collins and the fishermen were each awarded fifteen dollars. Collins was no stranger to such honours. It is estimated that Collins saved a staggering 52 lives in 31 years of service at Nottawasaga Light.

George Collins and his son rescued the surviving passengers and crew of the Mary Ward *moments before the ship split up.*

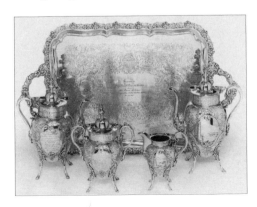

Silver tea service awarded to Collins in gratitude for saving four lives depicts the rescue scene and the lighthouse.

CHRISTIAN ISLAND

The Hurons' Final Refuge

The casual passerby would never even notice it. It was just remnants of a stone enclosure peeking out above the wild grass, shaded by a few trees. But, for the archaeologist about to start the dig, the site was anything but ordinary. As the soil was gingerly removed, a silent past revealed itself: a French copper coin dating from 1640; a French gun flint; Huron pottery. The 1965 excavation on Christian Island had unearthed the site of Ste. Marie II, the Jesuit fort built in 1649. The scientists bagged and catalogued each fragment. This was a major find.

The Huron story in this region began to unravel in the early 1600s, a time of mounting upheaval in the Great Lakes. Everything—the roads, homes, farms, and towns of much of southern Georgian Bay—was built on Indian land called Ouendake (When-day-kay), "people surrounded by water" or "the land separated by water." When French explorer Samuel de Champlain arrived on the shores of Ouendake in 1615, he was amazed to find 14,000 people—the Ouendat—living in 25 villages, surrounded by palisades. The French later dubbed the Ouendat people the Huron because some of the men shaved their head except for a bristly centre strip, reminding the French of boars heads (hures).

The Huron cultivated more than 20,000 acres of corn, beans, squash, and tobacco. They fished, hunted and traded. Using surplus corn and other commodities, they bartered with neighbouring nations such as the Petun, Neutral and Ojibwe for their pelts and dried fish. Huron was the language of trade.

It was Champlain's dream to establish a colony at Quebec. In order to support this dream, he wanted to set up an extensive network for the fur

Georgian Bay's Huron population numbered around 14,000 when French explorer, Samuel de Champlain arrived in 1615.

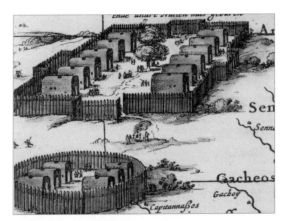

The Huron lived in palisaded villages as protection from the Iroquois.

The Huron bartered their surplus harvests with neighbouring nations.

trade, using Indian middlemen to collect furs from the other Indian nations. The well-respected Huron were the obvious choice, and a trade agreement was formalized in 1614. The Huron were soon to learn that the relationship was not confined only to trade.

Regarding the Huron, Champlain regretted "...that so many poor creatures should live and die without any knowledge of God." Hoping to bring their God to the Huron people, the Jesuits built Sainte-Marie-aux-pays-des-Hurons (Ste.-Marie among the Hurons) their primary mission in Huronia around 1639. It served as Jesuit headquarters, had a church, cemetery, hospital, and a pilgrimage site. Initially, the natives did not admire the Jesuits, or the Black Robes, as the Hurons called them. The priests depended on the Huron for survival, and they not only seemed weak and simple, but they were also a nuisance. Their beards provided a partial explanation, as the Huron believed facial hair impeded intelligence. While some Huron began to appreciate the priests' stoic dedication, and their earnest efforts to learn the Huron language and customs, others considered the

Ste. Marie mission on the Wye River was the Jesuit headquarters for the Great Lakes region.

In Huron tradition, before moving to a new village, communities would host the Feast of the Dead, a ceremony to honour their deceased. The dead were exhumed and reinterred in a mass grave as a symbol of the Huron community in life and death.

"Black Robes" sorcerers who brought grave illness. Contact proved deadly, as the Europeans carried diseases for which Indians had no immunity. In less than 50 years, epidemics had killed 5,000 Huron, mostly children and the elderly.

Between 1610 and 1618, the Iroquois—the Huron's enemy—was also decimated by disease and warfare. As the years went by, few Iroquois women were reaching childbearing age. Without drastic measures, the Iroquois population would certainly die out. In addition, the Iroquois supply of beaver pelts diminished, putting stress on their trade alliance with the Dutch. Not far away, the sedentary Huron had everything the Iroquois needed: a beaver rich territory and women, there for the taking. Starting in 1622-25, they began a deadly campaign. The Iroquois ambushed Huron canoes laden with furs and trade goods. For five years they blockaded the Ottawa River, the main Huron route to Montreal and Quebec. The Iroquois attacked Huron villages, slaughtered men and kidnapped women and children. Those who refused to integrate among their Iroquois captors were murdered. So began the Iroquois Wars,

The Iroquois began a campaign to push the Huron out of their territory and to kidnap their women and children. Jesuit priests were also murdered.

The Huron and Jesuits abandoned the Ste. Marie mission. They rafted parts of it to Christian Island and burned the rest to the ground.

a serious of small raids and battles involving thousands of warriors.

In 1646, the Iroquois gained the upper hand when the Dutch began freely supplying them with firearms. This put the Huron at a severe disadvantage. The French would only provide firearms to Catholic converts. In the war-ravaged Huronia, villages were burned and priests were killed. In 1649 the Huron teetered on collapse. Father Paul Ragueneau wrote, "...so crushed are our Hurons by disaster, that most of them have been forced to change their abodes... and now we, stationed at the front, must defend ourselves with our own strength, our own courage, and our own numbers."

The mission at Ste. Marie became a hospice for the wounded and the dying. Terrified Huron descended upon the mission until

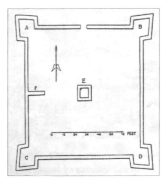

Rendering of Fort Ste. Marie II after archaeological excavations. The fort was erected on Christian Island to protect the Jesuits and Huron from Iroquois attacks.

Huron Chiefs at Loretteville, late 1800s

numbers had reached the thousands. By 1649, the Ste. Marie mission was certain to be the Iroquois' next target. Many Huron people fled the region, joining other Indian nations. But one group chose to stay and fight. Three hundred Huron families fled to Christian Island, entreating the priests to join them. In mid-June 1649, priests, French labourers and soldiers dismantled Ste. Marie, bringing it by raft to Christian Island. The remaining fort was set ablaze, according to the Jesuit Relations, "for fear that our enemies only too wicked, should profane the sacred place, and derive from it an advantage..."

There was no time to lose. In order to withstand a siege, the Second Sainte Marie had to be built, the forest cleared, and food gathered. Devastated Huron arrived en masse as news spread of the new refuge, until numbers soared to around 3,000. A summer drought killed the corn crop, forcing the people to subsist on roots and some fruit and fish. Winter brought a miserable famine in the Huron village. The refuge had become a prison stalked by starvation and disease. The Iroquois were waiting on the mainland and some even came on to the Island to continue the slaughter. By spring, the 3,000 Huron who had come to Christian Island a year before had dwindled to 300. The survivors believed that their only hope was to disperse. In 1651, the few who remained burned Ste. Marie II, and left Christian Island little more than a graveyard. Many had already accompanied the priests to the St. Lawrence region where descendants of the

Christian Island group still live in Loretteville. Of their departure, Father Ragueneau wrote, "It was not without tears that we left the country which possessed our hearts and engaged our hopes; and which reddened with the glorious blood of our brethren promised us a like happiness. But yet, self must be forgotten and God left for God's sake."

In 1856, more than 200 years after Sainte Marie II was abandoned, a Jesuit, Father Felix Martin, visited the site, finding seven feet walls (they were originally fourteen feet high), a masonry cistern, and traces of a moat around the fort. Relic hunters apparently plundered the site in 1902-3, stealing the stone for house foundations and docks. Over sixty years later, in 1965, an archaeological team excavated the site, finding more artifacts. Even more recently, many graves were discovered between the Huron village and Ste. Marie II. Metal fragments—hinges, a lock plate with keyhole, and a kettle handle—were found at the fort. Old logs had been preserved in the fresh water well and looked like they had been just cut down. Some burned items, such as glass and brass nuggets, may be remnants of that terrible June day in 1650 when the Huron and priests set fire to their fort, and left Christian Island and Huronia forever.

To learn more about the Huron people of Georgian Bay visit the Huronia Museum and the recreated Huron/Ouendat Village in Midland (705) 526-2844; www.georgianbaytourism.on.ca/huronmus.html Also of interest in Midland are the recreated Ste.-Marie among the Hurons mission (705) 526-7838 and the Martyrs' Shrine (705) 526-3788.

WRECK ISLAND

The Premonition

November 1879. As Eliza plunged into the raging water, a piercing shock rushed through her. Then, as she struggled to pull off her woolen coat, a crashing wave submerged her. She resurfaced to find she'd been turned towards the sinking ship. The kerosene lamps inside the ship lit up the foaming peaks, and she could see people bobbing helpless in the waves. "Where is Douglass?" she scanned the water, panicked, just as she was gripped by the suction of the 120-foot side-wheeler as it plunged into the lake. Kicking desperately, Eliza exploded to the surface, with a loud gasp...

Dr. Doupe awoke with a start. His bride, Eliza, was sitting up in their berth, breathing hard, one hand clutching her nightgown at her chest. It was some time before she spoke, "It was so real."

The next day, Eliza strolled along the deck wrapped in her long black woolen coat. She leaned against the railing, watching new passengers come

The Waubuno docked at this wharf on the night of the storm. Those passengers who spent the night in the nearby Globe Hotel were the fortunate ones.

aboard, clinging to their hats as the wind blew up. She was still troubled by the dream. "Why don't we have breakfast in Collingwood?" Dr. Doupe smiled, joining his wife and taking her hand. He hoped it might ease Eliza's mind to take her briefly into town. He had been supportive, but now he wanted her to lay the dream to rest. "Eliza, it was just a nightmare." "No," she insisted, "It was like nothing I have experienced."

During breakfast, Eliza attempted to find out if the ship would be delayed due to bad weather. When they returned to the ship, Douglass was troubled to find his wife talking about her fears. An older woman showered Eliza with sympathy, while another woman comforted her by insisting "Captain Burkett has an excellent record of fourteen years." Someone, amused by Eliza's fears, fanned them by explaining that the ship's name "Waubuno" meant black magic in Ojibwe. Once they were alone again, Eliza turned to her husband, "I want to leave the ship." Douglass nodded but made no reply. Elizabeth knew that nothing would come of her request.

Elizabeth and Douglass settled in for a stormy night. They were wakened by the ship's whistle. Mrs. Doupe urged her husband to investigate, and she

The ill-fated Waubuno

was not far behind. Smoke billowed from the stack. Men were loosening the lines, preparing to sail.

When Eliza returned to the berth she quickly stuffed their clothes into the trunk. "Get the purser, we're leaving." "But our belongings," Douglass responded. They were on their way to set up his new practice in McKeller Village and the *Waubuno* was conveying all their household possessions. So it was that around four in the morning, with the wind howling, and with the Doupes on board, the *Waubuno* vanished into the black predawn chill. No one on the steamer was ever seen again.

In the days that followed November 21, 1879, little light was shed on the ship's disappearance. There had been twenty-four on board when the ship headed out in the heavy snow. The Christian Island lightkeeper noted in his log, "stiff wind from the nor'west but ship seems to riding well with full cargo." A small vessel taking shelter at Hope Island lighthouse noticed the *Waubuno* rolling in the heavy seas, with no signs of turning back. Around noon, two loggers on the Moon River thought they heard the faint

Just off Wreck Island lies the hull of the Waubuno.

signal of a steamer in distress. The *Magnetewan* arrived in Parry Sound two days later and had not seen the *Waubuno*. *Mittie Grew*, the Parry Sound Lumber Company's tug, was sent to look for her.

The tug captain shifted his gaze back and forth from the water to his chart. What had possessed the Captain to head out that stormy morning, and with so many of his passengers still asleep at the Globe Hotel in town? Thankful for the discourtesy, these abandoned people recounted the story of a young bride who had had a premonition of the *Waubuno's* fate.

The *Mittie Grew* searched and searched. Then, off the islands in the South Channel, the tug finally came across debris—a paddlebox, some freight, shattered pieces of the Doupe's furniture, and a crushed lifeboat. By the end of the day, the search party had located all of the *Waubuno's* life preservers, but had found no bodies.

The following spring, a man named Pendonquot discovered the *Waubuno's* upturned hull just off Wreck Island, 7 miles (11.2 kms) off its course, where it is visible today. A theory developed that Captain Burkett, seeking shelter, hit a shoal just southwest of the Haystack Rocks and dropped anchor. The stormy seas capsized the vessel, trapping the passengers and crew. The hull ripped away from the passenger deck and floated to Wreck Island. The missing portion of the *Waubuno* was never found. The ship's anchor is now displayed at Waubuno Park in Parry Sound. (Please respect the privacy of nearby cottagers.)

PARRY ISLAND

Stolen by a Lumber Tycoon

James Beatty sat back, the chair creaking as his weight settled. He gave the newspaper a sharp flick before scanning the headlines. BOOTH TO SET UP RAILWAY ON PARRY ISLAND. He read it again, stunned. Now the scoundrel has done it to us, he thought, he's really done it.

The Booth referred to in the headline was lumber tycoon, John Rudolphus Booth. A humble mill owner in 1857, he gradually came to control the most extensive timber limits in Canada. He also became the premier lumber manufacturer for the American and British markets. He bought strategically into railway interests, piecing together rail access to the ice-free Atlantic ports. By 1883, Booth was eyeing the lucrative grain trade, for which he needed a Great Lakes port and a railway. His keen eye focused right on the village of Parry Sound on Georgian Bay.

Parry Sound residents were ecstatic. Seeing potential in their harbour, Booth bought into the troubled Parry Sound Colonization Railway. A ribbon

of steel would connect Parry Sound to Booth's thriving rail network, transforming the town into the western terminus from the Atlantic Ocean!
Residents imagined Parry Sound Harbour packed with grain laden ships.
Massive elevators transforming the skyline. Jobs for everyone. An economic boom. A dazzling future.

As railway construction began at a furious pace, the town ignored the
first signs of trouble. Booth was always in Ottawa, and rarely available for
important meetings. One might suspect he was avoiding them. Then came
the day that Parry Sound landowners named
their price for the railway lands. Booth
feigned outrage at the inflated figure, making his exit from Parry Sound. The town
was stunned. "He'll be back," they
quipped. "He needs our harbour and our
land." But, in fact, Booth needed nothing.
He may have already made other plans.

It had not taken long for Booth
to find a better port. It was about
7 kms (4 miles) south on Parry
Island, and it was Canada's
largest natural freshwater harbour. Historians allege that
Booth never intended to do
business with Parry
Sound. He simply used the
early partnership to gain

*John Rudolphus Booth (above) was negotiating with the town of Parry Sound to
link the community to his established rail line. Such a connection would have
made Parry Sound's harbour the western rail terminus from the Atlantic Ocean.*

Depot Harbour. The homes with peaked roofs were for managers.

government subsidies. At first the Ojibwe living on the Island considered the news preposterous. Impossible. But Booth knew something the Ojibwe didn't—a piece of legislation that permitted the appropriation of native land for rail purposes. In 1895, the Ojibwe who lived on the 314-acre Parry Island were forced to sell a right of way for 9 dollars an acre. Booth was in business. Parry Sound was not.

In 1896-97, Booth amalgamated his interests in the Parry Sound Colonization Railway with the Ottawa Arnprior Railway, creating the shortest route to the Atlantic Ocean via Montreal. Depot Harbour on Parry Island was the western terminus. In 1899, Booth made the new Ottawa-Arnprior-Parry Sound line part of his Canada Transit Company, which also operated seven ships. That year, Booth bought up another 110-acres on Parry Island and created an on-site community to service the ships, coal dock, water tower, freight sheds, railway roundhouse and station, powerhouse, and two towering grain elevators. The company town of Depot Harbour was born.

Although dry, Depot Harbour was the liveliest place around. One hundred and three families soon settled into small, square company-owned

Workers at Depot Harbour spoke many different European languages.

houses. Management enjoyed the finer, peaked-roof, tongue and groove buildings. The bunkhouse was for single men, and there was a 110-room hotel for transients. Depot Harbour had all of the amenities of a community: three churches, two stores, a post office, a butcher shop, and barber shop. By 1911, its 650 people—English, Irish, German and eleven other European backgrounds—gave Depot Harbour its reputation as a

Parry Island Ojibwe. Booth appropriated Ojibwe lands on Parry Island for a railway right of way.

friendly town. By 1926, the base population had grown to 1,600 and in summer, it was bursting at the seams with 3,000 residents.

During the boom years of 1910 to 1928, Depot Harbour was a hive of activity. Ships jostled at the wharf, heading for ports both east and west, carrying tons of flour, grain, feed, packaged freight, and manufactured goods. Warehouses were filled with the aroma of spices, silks for the East, wool from Australia, and manufactured goods from Chicago for Woolworth's five and dime. Passenger trains arrived daily from Ottawa. Many Parry Island Ojibwe took local jobs, while some, dressed in traditional costume, greeted tourists, selling their traditional crafts. Like any company town, Depot Harbour's strength depended on the company that built it. Soon the biggest port on Georgian Bay would be the biggest ghost town.

The stage was set in 1904. Booth sold the Canada Atlantic Transit Railway

Warehouses were filled with goods from all over the world

During WWII, cordite stored in a Depot Harbour elevator caught fire creating a massive explosion.

to the Grand Trunk Railway, which, in turn, was amalgamated with the Canadian National Railway (CNR) in 1923. The blows came swiftly. When the CNR refused to mend a vital bridge, Depot Harbour was no longer the shortest route to the Atlantic. The Great Depression destroyed the grain trade and Depot Harbour's massive elevators fell into disuse. Unemployment caused an exodus.

Then came the death blow. During World War II, one of Depot's grain elevators was used to store explosive cordite. The elevator caught fire, triggering a fireworks display that was talked about for generations. The flame was so bright that onlookers in Parry Sound could read by it at midnight. The intense heat melted and warped the steel rails like plastic. The dreams and hard work of the people who put Depot Harbour on the map were lost in those ferocious flames.

A coal company tried to operate in Depot Harbour, but closed down in 1951. The CNR sold many of the buildings to cottagers who hauled them away in pieces. What remained was torn down or left to the elements.

In 1987, the appropriated land was transferred to the Department of Indian and Northern Affairs. The island's Ojibwe people renamed Parry Island Wausauksing, its original name. Today permission to explore the remains of Depot Harbour can be obtained from the Band Office. Where ships once lined up three deep, the concrete wharves remain. Trees grow in the roundhouse, its roof long ago collapsed. House foundations are small indentations in the thick grass. The concrete steps that once led to the Roman Catholic church now stand alone. The town is disappearing almost as fast as it was built.

The fire was so powerful it melted and warped the steel rails.

THE NORTH CHANNEL

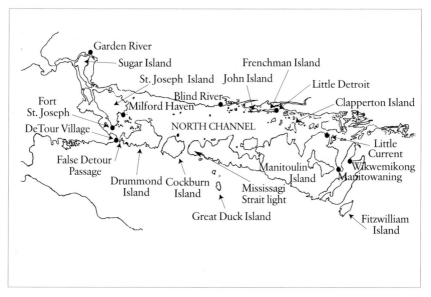

Garden River
Sugar Island
St. Joseph Island   John Island
Frenchman Island
Little Detroit
Fort
St. Joseph
Blind River
Milford Haven
Clapperton Island
DeTour Village
NORTH CHANNEL
Little
Current
False Detour
Passage
Wikwemikong
Manitoulin
Island
Manitowaning
Drummond
Island
Cockburn
Island
Mississagi
Strait light
Great Duck Island
Fitzwilliam
Island

MANITOULIN ISLAND

The Failed Experiment

By the 1830s, governments in Canada and the United States began a campaign to move native people from their traditional lands onto reservations. In 1836 Manitoulin natives signed a treaty opening up their island to all of the Indians of Upper Canada (Ontario).

In late November of 1838, Manitoulin Island natives discovered thirty white people living—nearly starving—on their island. They were Indian Agent Thomas G. Anderson, and his entourage including a nurse, missionary, doctor, schoolmaster, servants, and families. They were there to establish a centre of government and education on Manitowaning Bay, but their winter provisions never reached them. The Ojibwe

Thomas G. Anderson

Manitowaning, 1845. Here Thomas Anderson created a centre of government and education for the natives of Manitoulin Island. It proved to be short lived.

rescued them, bringing fish, partridges, rabbits, venison and maple sugar and teaching the settlers winter survival skills like ice fishing. Ironically, it had been Anderson's mission to teach the natives trades and farming so they could abandon the very traditions that had saved his life.

Anderson persisted and within five years, his community—called The Establishment—had grown to 55 buildings including homes, a store, a mission, stables and a smithy. It was a short-lived success. By 1858, only 22 buildings remained and the educational programs had failed. And shortly after, in the 1860s, the government returned its gaze to Manitoulin. They wanted it back. The pressure was on to open the sparsely-populated 100-mile island to general settlement. But how could they convince the Indians to give up Manitoulin? They needed a smooth talker, and a smooth operator. Enter Superintendent of Indian affairs, William McDougall.

Francis Assiginack remains a controversial figure in the Island's history. He persuaded many natives to give up their land on Manitoulin Island.

McDougall knew his enemy: the village of Wikwemikong. With 600 residents, Wikwemikong represented 60 percent of the island's population. And all of Wikwemikong was against him. Established in 1833 around a Roman Catholic mission, it was Manitoulin's oldest permanent community. McDougall needed to divide and conquer. He needed an ally from within.

He found that ally in native interpreter and orator Assiginack (Blackbird), renowned for having once spellbound an audience from dawn until dusk. Assiginack remains a contentious figure in Manitoulin history. On one hand, he was a proud man who fought the ill treatment of his people. On the other hand, it

In the 1862 treaty, forty percent of the Island's Indian population gave away 80% of the land. The village of Wikwemikong (depicted here) held out.

was through his influence that Manitouliners gave away their island.

McDougall met with chiefs from outside Wikwemikong. With Assiginack's help, McDougall convinced them to accept one hundred acres per family, with fifty acres for single men. All land-sale moneys—after surveys were paid—would be placed in a fund for their future use. One chief at a time, he persuaded the remaining 40 percent of Manitoulin's population.

October 6, 1862. The treaty signed, McDougall had convinced 40 percent of the population to give away 80 percent of the land. The majority of the population, who lived in Wikwemikong, was now subject to a treaty it had not signed. To add to the tension, the government began to interfere in other areas. New restrictions on the sale of Indian firewood created a black-market trade that brought unwanted liquor into the community. Then the government tried to restrict Indian fishing to rivers and bays.

There was trouble brewing and Commissioner of Fisheries, William Gibbard was assigned to squelch it. Gibbard arrived on Manitoulin thinking he could set policies that would erase years of local tradition. He tried to reassign a native

Traditional Indian ring games, Wikwemikong.

When the government began imposing new restrictions, anger and tension mounted in Wikwemikong.

fishing ground in Wikwemikong to a settler named Proulx. But as soon as Gibbard left, Manitoulin natives forced Proulx off the water. This was Wikwemikong after all, and it had not been ceded.

For Gibbard, it was time to assert his power. He returned in a month with 22 revolver-wielding constables. Gibbard's group marched to the home of Reverend Jean-Pierre Choné. Four hundred natives, a black flag held high, surrounded the house. Gibbard ordered a Wikwemikong Chief's arrest. Indians closed in. Someone leapt out of the crowd, raising a truncheon above the Sergeant. Constable Dan Callaghan pressed a pistol against the offending Ojibwe. It was a stand off. Wikwemikong citizens watched as their Chief was handcuffed. Outraged by the strong-arm tactics, the priest began to incite the mob to violence. He was grabbed and handcuffed. Rage seethed through the crowd. The school bell was rung to signal attack, and hand to hand combat ensued. Since Gibbard's men were outnumbered—and Gibbard had been told the Indians would sacrifice their lives for Father Choné—a truce was called. Offending parties would be taken to Quebec to settle their grievances officially.

Gibbard was last seen in July 1863, returning to Manitoulin on the steamer *Ploughboy*. He never arrived. Gibbard's corpse was pulled out of the lake near Little Current, a deep gash in his forehead. He had been carrying two thousand dollars in treaty payments. Was he robbed? Murdered? The money was later recovered from the ship's safe. Only Gibbard's wallet—and the porter and bartender—were missing. A chief and priest were arrested but no charges were laid.

Today, the Wikwemikong Indian reserve is the only "unceded" reserve in Canada. Over 3,000 people of Odawa (Ottawa), Ojibwe (Chippewa), and Potawatomi descent live on these 105,000 acres. The community is proud of its heritage. It is now a vital centre for Indian culture and medicine. Each August, dancers and drummers from all across North America participate in Wiky's international pow wow. In addition, the reserve is host to a contemporary native music festival and to the vibrant De-ba-jeh-mu-jig Theatre.

*William Gibbard
was last seen on the
steamer* Ploughboy.
*His corpse was
later pulled out of
the water near
Manitoulin Island.
A chief and a priest
were arrested for
his murder.*

FRENCHMAN ISLAND

The Iroquois Wars

Frenchman Island, on the beautiful North Channel, has a fascinating history. It is here that the Ojibwe and Odawa peoples battled the deadly Iroquois to keep their home. By the mid-1600s, fur in the St. Lawrence and Lower Lakes was so depleted that the Iroquois began a fierce campaign to take over the Upper Great Lakes, still rich with beaver. The Iroquois population was also being threatened by disease. Beginning in southern Georgian Bay, the Iroquois waged wars—ranging from small skirmishes to full-scale battles—nearly annihilating the Huron people in their large, settled villages. Not only were the Iroquois heavily armed (compliments of the Dutch and British), but their marauding also spread disease in epidemic proportion. With southern Georgian Bay in enemy hands, the Odawa and Ojibwe feared their region would be next. They were right.

*Traditional Ojibwe
dance. After the
Iroquois had deci-
mated the Huron
they began invading
Ojibwe territory.*

European depiction of Iroquois brutality. The Ojibwe rightly feared that the Iroquois Wars would spread into their territory. Armed only with traditional weapons, they would have to rely on ingenuity to survive.

To the Iroquois' surprise, the Ojibwe were not the easy targets the Huron had been. The Ojibwe were skilled hunters, used to living on the move. Armed only with stone tomahawks, bow and arrow, and clubs, the Ojibwe would not be conquered. An Ojibwe elder prophesied the first attack, allowing the Ojibwe to devise a good defense, and catch the Iroquois off guard. Meanwhile, the Iroquois ignored one of their elders' disturbing premonitions. Blinded by success, they dismissed the prophecy as foolishness. Armed with their guns and skill, they had nothing to fear from the Ojibwe.

Ojibwe canoes were sighted. The Iroquois mobilized for attack, grabbing weapons and launching canoes. With stealth, they paddled toward a group of women in canoes, unaware that they were simply playing into the Ojibwe's trap. The women, acting as decoys, sped off. The Iroquois picked up their pace thinking the women would lead them straight to the encampment. As the Iroquois canoes crowded into a narrow channel, a war cry cracked the stillness. Rocks hailed down from all sides. The Iroquois swiftly met their deaths.

The few warriors who managed to escape the initial ambush, were brought down in a second, further up the channel at Landry Point. After the attacks, the Ojibwe hauled the bodies onto the island. For years to come, it is said that tormented Iroquois souls could be heard wandering Frenchman Island.

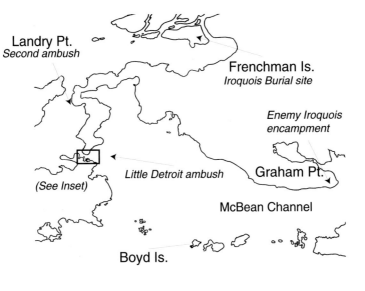

CLAPPERTON ISLAND

Trials of a Lighthouse Family

Benjamin Baker left the light-house for a game of cards and never returned.

The story of Clapperton Island light-house is the story of the Bakers, believed to be the longest serving lightkeepers on the Canadian Great Lakes. Three genera-tions operated Clapperton light from 1875 to 1962. Their 88-year-legacy began with the enigmatic Benjamin Baker. Educated and enterprising, Baker ran the lighthouse as well as a successful farm. But in September 1894, Baker disappeared, with scarcely a trace.

Henry hadn't really noticed his father's boat until it had sailed past the lighthouse. But then fear hit him like an anvil. Only the dog was visible on board. Henry rowed out to meet the boat, finding no clues but his father's wallet and a bottle of whiskey. From that day on, Henry tended the light. At thirty years old, he was the second Baker on Clapperton.

The police concluded that Benjamin had stumbled into the water. After all he had been returning from the mainland, where Baker typically enjoyed a night of liquor and card playing. But his sons, Henry and George, were not convinced. The empty wallet mystified them. Benjamin had lived a long time far from the convenience of a bank— he would never have played until he ran out of money. Unable to prompt an investigation, Henry and George Baker went on with their lives, and with their unanswered questions.

One day, Henry's wife Jenny developed an excruciating toothache. Her husband proffered a nip of whiskey to help soothe the pain. The Bakers weren't big drinkers, and so, the whiskey bottle had sat on the shelf for years, forgotten. Jenny poured an ounce and swished it in her mouth. She was overcome instantly

Baker's wallet was found in his drifting sailboat.

Clapperton Island lighthouse was tended by the Baker family for 88 years.

by an agonizing pain. Was the bottle poisoned? Years later Benjamin Baker's great grandson, Norman Lloyd, speculated, "The feeling was the bottle had been doped up somehow. Now, had he been lucky at the table and someone drugged his bottle, rolled him and in the act, he was killed and body disposed of and the boat set adrift...We'll never know."

Henry's son, William Baker, was named the next Clapperton keeper when Henry Baker was killed in a lighthouse accident when he was 82. In fact, Bill received notice of his appointment tacked to the government's letter of condolence for his father's death. Bill kept the light for sixteen years, retiring in 1962. Today the only evidence of the Baker's long sojourn on Clapperton is their nineteenth-century log house and barn, visible from the air amid the overgrown fields. As for the old lighthouse, it was rolled down the rocks and towed to Spanish, a town along the North Shore. It got stuck on a sandbar where it sat until the water level dropped enough for it to be retrieved. A metal beacon occupies its former site.

Henry Baker was 82 when he was killed in a lighthouse accident.

JOHN ISLAND

Misadventures of a Stolen Mill

April 1, 1889—April Fool's Day. The sheriff's boat rammed through slabs of floating ice. The sheriff fixed his gaze upon the thieves' getaway tug, now lying trapped in ice. In tow and piled high were a disassembled lumber mill and its contents. He raised his shotgun.

There had been rumours all around DeTour, but the villagers had not supposed that the lumber mill was completely broke. No one had guessed that Chicago creditors had posted the guard there to keep watch over the business. Only the mill's owners, the Moiles Brothers, could have fashioned such a daring plan, a plan the town would talk about for years.

The town was busy with election day. The tug *Tom Dowling* slipped into the dock unnoticed. Fifty men filed out quietly, and made their way up to the mill. "New season ahead of us-time we give the place a good overhaul!" was enough to allay the guard's suspicion. Good cheer pervaded, and the guard accepted a few shots of whiskey, as the team went about "tightening" the bolts.

Once the walls and machinery were loosened, the Moiles brothers played their ace. Knowing that the guard's wife was pregnant, the conspirators announced she was in labour. The watchman raced off, abandoning the post. The Moiles wasted no time. They severed the town's phone line, dismantled the mill and loaded it onto the waiting tug. They left nothing but the real estate.

The town was finally alerted, but it was too late to stop them. Someone made it to the next town and sent the call out to the Sheriff in Sault Ste. Marie, Michigan. "DeTour's mill has been stolen!" At first, it sounded like a prank to him. After all, it was April Fool's Day. Within hours, the Sheriff and his deputies were verging upon the Tom Dowling, firmly lodged in ice. According to John Nevill's book, *Wanderings*, the Sheriff was about to board when one of the Moiles brothers shouted, "the boat and her tow is in

John Island harbour

Workers' homes were built along sand roads.

Canadian waters and you can't touch her. The first men among you who tries to set foot on any of these vessels gets a bullet through the head!" Unsure about the border, the sheriff bid retreat.

The thieves waited for nightfall before skulking back toward DeTour without their running lights. They tried a new route, grinding through the frozen water of False DeTour Passage, but they became stuck again between Drummond and Cockburn Islands. Exasperated, the fugitives might have mutinied had they been closer to land. At long last, they spotted the *Pathfinder*, another tug. The captain was happy to assist the Moiles' cold and anxious crew. Working as a team, they broke through to John Island. The *Pathfinder* went on her way, an unwitting accomplice to the crime.

The stolen mill was rebuilt on John Island and a lively community sprung up around it. The mill operation was never a great success, but the small village was spirited, its great dances, excellent poker and baseball games known for miles around. It all came to an end one Saturday night in April, 1918. While the villagers were dancing, a fire blazed, burning the mill to the ground. In an echo of thirty years before, workers dismantled most of the surviving buildings and shipped them to the mainland. They followed soon after.

Today John Island is home to a YMCA camp. Traces of the Moiles' mill and community can still be found. The main sand road was once lined with employees' homes. Wildflowers bloom on the baseball field, reputed to be one of the oldest ball diamonds in the province. Large dock pilings extend into Moiles Harbour and hundreds of rotting planks from the extensive pier and railway are visible underwater. At the mill site, only a massive, crumbling stone wall survived the fire of 1918. The wall housed the sawdust burner and encloses a pit 30 feet (9m) deep.

ST. JOSEPH ISLAND

Fort St. Joseph—The Military Siberia of Upper Canada

The following stories, in this order, offer a chronological understanding of the War of 1812 on the Great Lakes: St. Joseph Island, Mackinac Island, Drummond Island, Fitzwilliam Island. Additional 1812 history: South Bass Island-Battle of Put-in-Bay.

July 12, 1812. British Captain Charles Roberts stopped pacing, long enough to take stock of the fort and his hodge-podge garrison. After service in India and Ceylon, he was not sure this appointment was a promotion. Nicknamed the "Military Siberia of Upper Canada," St. Joseph was the furthest west in the serpentine string of forts that began on the St. Lawrence River. It was the end of the line.

Often shortchanged on provisions, Captain Roberts also felt he'd been shortchanged on soldiers. His army consisted of forty older men, only fit for garrison duty. Desertion—even when seriously punished—was a common problem, especially in winter. It was already twenty-four days since America had declared war on Britain. Captain Roberts was awaiting orders to attack the American Fort Mackinac. Lying in the narrows between Lakes Huron and Michigan, Mackinac Island would give Britain control of the Upper Lakes. In the meantime, Captain Roberts feared an American attack. His fort was not even fortified—the partial log palisade had never been repaired after it collapsed in a windstorm.

The tension was mounting. In addition to Captain Roberts' men, over 400 Indians, and 160 voyageurs had gathered to fight the Americans. Fur trader Robert Dickson himself brought a force of 123 natives. Everything was ready—all Roberts needed was the chance to strike while he could still count on an element of surprise. Roberts spied a canoe coming toward him. The winded voyageur approached with an official message. "Brock wants us to hold off on hostilities! If he waits much longer he won't have an army." There was nothing Roberts could do.

But three days later, a messenger brought more ambiguous orders from General Brock, which Roberts chose to interpret as approval to attack Fort Mackinac. Led by the fife and drum, the troops marched to the wharf and boarded the *Caledonia*, the North West Company sailing vessel Roberts had commandeered. The small armada was an impressive sight. British regulars in scarlet red coats were in position around the Caledonia's two cannons. Ten bateaux were each filled with 160 voyageurs, decked out in colourful sashes. Seventy canoes carried hundreds of Indians adorned in war paint and feathers, and led by notable chiefs such as Grizzly Bear, Black Wolf, The Teal, and One-eyed Decorah.

Fort St. Joseph was the end of the line for British military provisions

They landed in the middle of the night on the northwest side of Mackinac Island, at a spot now known as British Landing. The Americans, unaware of the outbreak of war, were taken completely by surprise and surrendered without a fight (see Mackinac Island p.115).

Now that the British garrison was installed at the more strategic Fort Mackinac, Fort St. Joseph was completely vulnerable. In 1814, American soldiers retaliated by burning all of Fort St. Joseph's garrison buildings except for the residences. Today, at the excavated Fort St. Joseph, a museum displays military artifacts, uniforms and weapons from the 1800s. St. Joseph Island is accessible by bridge from the North Shore.

ST. JOSEPH ISLAND

The Polygamist of Milford Haven

In June 1848, eminent biologist Louis Agassiz and his research team were en route to Lake Superior when a sudden storm threatened their canoes. As Agassiz's team set up camp on the shores of St. Joseph Island, a dishevelled man emerged from the bush and introduced himself as Major William Kingdom Rains. Intrigued by this charming man and his incongruous appearance, the scientist could not resist the invitation to visit Rains' home.

Rains led Agassiz to a crude dwelling in a freshly-cleared field. Agassiz was astounded to find floor to ceiling books on every wall with classical

Major William Kingdom Rains obtained a charter to colonize St. Joseph Island.

volumes in French, Italian and Greek. His host spoke poetically and passionately about politics, science and literature, even flattering Agassiz by being well-versed in his work. The rumpled Major then brought out a portrait of himself dressed in full British army regalia. The Major confided proudly that he was once considered the best-dressed man in the regiment. The scientist was dumfounded. How had this man of learning and position come to live here?

Tired of the military, Major Rains had retired at the age of 36. In 1830, he left his estranged wife in England, and sailed to Canada with Frances Doubleday and her sister Eliza. The three settled on Lake Simcoe until Major Rains obtained a charter to colonize St. Joseph Island. Full of optimism, Rains and a few other founding families arrived at St. Joseph in 1835. They named the settlement Milford Haven, and erected a store and sawmill, hoping for an influx of English settlers. To their disappointment, few settlers came. Rains lost a fortune and fell out with his business partners.

Rains, Frances, and Eliza relocated to what is now called Rains Point. Between them, Frances and Eliza bore twenty-five of Rains' children, and from all accounts, the families were perfectly contented. Many of the children became well-known in the region, respected for their various enterprises.

Indians arriving for the present-giving ceremony at Drummond Island

DRUMMOND ISLAND

Fort Drummond

The snow crunched beneath his boots as British Lieutenant Colonel Robert McDouall trudged home. The years of anger, frustration and disappointment had taken their toll. Some days he felt Fort Drummond was a blight on his military career. McDouall looked up at the rows of white-washed log houses belonging to his soldiers. He had no one to blame. After losing Fort Mackinac after the war, he had chosen to build a new fort for his soldiers on Drummond Island. An eccentric society evolved, a melting pot of cultures—Indian, French, English, German and Spanish.

Commandant McDouall's house at Fort Drummond. He left the garrison disillusioned with the British command's neglect of the military garrison.

Drummond Island graveyard

The community outside Fort Drummond was made up largely of voyageurs and fur traders. Speaking French and Indian, they helped bridge communications among the nations on the island. The community also had a civilian population of farmers, shopkeepers and trades people. Many soldiers and citizens were married to native women.

From the start, Fort Drummond did not really have a role to play. Tensions with the United States were finally at rest after the War of 1812, and Great Britain's interest in the fort had waned. Britain reduced funds for the gift giving ceremony to the Indians, an annual event that had helped maintain ties between the British and the local Indian nations. As a sense of purpose fell away, idleness and discontent crept in. Strict regulations were not enough to curb the use of liquor. To alleviate the boredom, one commandant sent for gamblers, who arrived along with a group of "professional women." But the women drove the soldiers to distraction, and soon the whole lot was sent back to Detroit.

With McDouall himself disillusioned by Britain's neglect, it was difficult to discipline his soldiers. Official mail was known to arrive almost a year late. This was a thorn in the Lieutenant's side. His superiors had failed to inform him that the War of 1812 was over and he had continued to wage aggressive action five months after peace. The problem with provisions—the lack of lime juice, in particular—also plagued McDouall. In the spring of 1816, with five men dead and many others sick from scurvy, McDouall resigned from service at Fort Drummond.

A series of commanders and regiments came and went, and eventually the soldiers at Fort Drummond were reduced by half. When author John Bigsby arrived on the island around 1819 he wrote, "The friendly and intelligent gentlemen of the garrison had little to do save read, hunt for fossils, fish, shoot, cut down trees and plant trees. Their military duties took up little of their time."

Bigsby's book, *The Shoe and the Canoe*, recounts a story that has become part of local folklore. Frustrated by the confining winter, five soldiers planned to slip away from Fort Drummond at night, and make their way into the United States to assume new lives. According to accounts, the commandant was so enraged to find them gone that he nailed a notice on the barracks doors offering $20 for each soldier—dead or alive. Word of the notice reached the Indian village, and according to Samuel F. Cook's *Drummond Island, the Story of the British Occupation 1815-1828*, the bounty produced gruesome results,

> The post commandant had not yet taken his morning coffee when in walked two Indian athletes covered with frost, their breaths coming quickly, and their eyes eager and ferocious. Advancing to the centre of the room, each unfastened from his girdle a human head that had dangled there and, placing it on the table, demanded the reward for the deserters. The commissary was quickly summoned and soon the bearers of the heads were washing away all thought of the blood they had treacherously spilled for money in copious libation of the King's rum.

Bigsby also wrote of the desertion and its tragic failure in *The Shoe and the Canoe*,

Natives from both sides of the border found work on Sugar Island which had become an important refueling depot for steamers on the St. Mary's River.

While I was there, an order came from Quebec to the post, forbidding the employment of Indians in capturing deserters; for during the proceeding summer five soldiers started early in the morning across the strait to the American main, and made by the Indian path for Michilimackinac...The commandant sent half-a-dozen Indians after them, who in a couple of days returned with the men's heads in a bag.

In 1828, the International Boundary Commission gave Drummond Island to the United States, signalling the end of Fort Drummond. Uprooted once again, the remaining ninety-one soldiers, their families and other civilians moved to Penetanguishene, on the southern end of Georgian Bay. The abandoned fort eventually crumbled to the ground, and its ruins were lost in the limestone quarry that is still in operation there today.

SUGAR ISLAND

The World Hears of Sugar Island

Michigan's Sugar Island is situated in the idyllic St. Marys River that flows out of Lake Superior. Straddling the Canada/U.S. border, Sugar Island was connected to both countries. In the 1840s, it was home to a mixed population of Indians, Scots, English, French Canadians and

Refueling depot and store at Church's Landing

Americans. The economy was largely agricultural. The local hay was of such fine quality that much of it was shipped to thoroughbred stables in Kentucky.

Sugar Island's population happily served two markets until the turn of the century. Albert Larmie sent his grandson by dogsled to sell wool in Canada, where it fetched forty more cents a pound. Bernie Arbic's *Sugar Island Sampler* tells of "Mooney" Sebastian, who was intercepted by two U.S. customs officers on his return to Sugar Island with a boatload of supplies. The officers admonished Sebastian for crossing in daylight. This easy-going attitude gave one Sugar Islander an unusual idea.

In 1943, delegates from fifty nations met to hammer out a charter for the United Nations (U.N.), an international body to replace the failed League of Nations. An international committee was to select a site for the U.N.'s headquarters from a list of twenty-two North American cities, including Chicago, Miami, Philadelphia, New York, Quebec City and Vancouver. Published in newspapers around the world, one entry puzzled readers: Sugar Island, Michigan.

Sugar Island's bid was the brainchild of former Michigan governor, the flamboyant, eighty-five year old Chase Osborn. Osborn owned property on Sugar Island. He also saw the 55,000-mile, unfortified Canada/U.S. border as a powerful symbol of the U.N.'s objective. To Osborn, the American's peaceful acquisition of Sugar Island in the 1842 Webster-Ashburton Treaty was a perfect example of the U.N.'s pledge "to settle international disputes by peaceful means, to refrain from the threat or use of force." It was in this context that Osborn began to promote Sugar Island as international Island. Despite Osborn's determined lobby, the U.N. chose a site on the East River in New York City.

Osborn's vision of Sugar Island as United Nations headquarters

Garden Island
High Island
Hog Island
Waugoshance Point
Gull Island
Beaver Island
Washington Island
North Fox Island
Chambers Island
South Fox Island
Green Bay
North Manitou Island
South Manitou Island
Manitou Passage
Traverse City
Door Peninsula
Benton Harbour
Chicago

LAKE MICHIGAN

4

LAKE MICHIGAN ISLANDS

Of Dunes and Beach

Rimmed by startling cornflower blue waters, the islands and shores of Lake Michigan are renowned for their expansive sand beaches and dunes. The stories from Lake Michigan's islands show strong individualists drawn by the separate and sheltered spaces that the islands offered, away

Schooner fighting through Manitou Passage in one of Michigan's notorious storms. In the distance are the bluffs from Sleeping Bear Dunes.

from the chaos of the outside world. Here immigrants fleeing economic hardship and political instability in their homelands set a foothold in a new land. Islands provided a haven from religious persecution for a few charismatic leaders who established insular societies in which they proclaimed themselves king. Island living offered a restorative peace for denizens as diverse as hermits and millionaires.

Lake Michigan has two archipelagos. On the west side of the lake are the islands split off from the rocky spine of the Door Peninsula. The largest of 42 islands are Washington Island and Rock Island, separated from the mainland by the treacherous passage called Death's Door. Tourism is popular on these islands which are known for their charm and their quaint towns.

The second archipelago, along Lake Michigan's northeast shore, has three clusters of islands. The largest of these islands are North and South Manitou, North and South Fox, and the Beaver Group including Beaver, High and Garden Islands. Except for Beaver, these islands see less tourism, and some, such as Garden Island, are a haven for those in search of some island solitude.

CHAMBERS ISLAND

Chambers' Ghost

It was the spring of 1976. Joel Blahnick arrived on Chambers Island to take up his duties as lighthouse keeper. Abandoned for over twenty years, the old stone lighthouse needed a fair bit of work. Joel and his nine-year-old son spent the first day sweeping and clearing, dusting and fixing. By nightfall, they were good and tired. They curled up in the bedroom at the foot of the tower's spiral staircase.

A strange heavy sound pushed its way into Joel's sleep, pulling him awake. There it was again. He wasn't dreaming. He sat up and listened closely. It was the sound of footsteps coming down the great, long staircase. The hair bristled on his neck. The footsteps reached the bottom of the stairs, hesitated and then proceeded down the hallway. The steps continued through the living room, down the steps into the kitchen and then out the kitchen door. It was several hours before Joel could get back to sleep.

The next night Joel lay down to sleep, his eyes wide with worry that the sound would return. But it did not. For the remainder of the season, Joel's nights were peaceful. But on the first night of the next spring, the heavy steps returned. The strange visit recurred on the first night of spring for the

Chambers Island lighthouse

next ten years. Joel brought family and friends who verified they heard and felt it too. It became a sort of invisible friend, especially when it began to play tricks, borrowing items that would later reappear in unlikely locations. A screwdriver disappeared from a windowsill and turned up beneath a pillow.

1987 was Joel's eleventh summer. A group of nuns from a local Catholic retreat came to tour the stone tower, and learned about the playful ghost. One of the sisters crossed to the southwest side and put her hands hard against the tower wall. She focussed her energy in prayer to release the spirit. Since then, the footsteps and all signs of the ghost have disappeared.

Joel believes the spirit was that of Lewis Williams, the first and longest serving keeper at the Chambers' Light. Beginning in 1868, Williams, his wife and their eleven children lived there every summer for twenty-two years.

ST. MARTIN ISLAND LIGHTHOUSE

Green Light

The isolated island of St. Martin is a small, two-hundred-acre piece of rock. The lighthouse keeper's children travelled the ten miles across the water to Washington Island school. One day when they were half way to the mainland, a quick and brutal storm blew up. The boat flipped over, and their father watched, helpless, as his children's flailing arms vanished in the waves. The keeper fell into deep despair. Passing ships often saw the green

St. Martin Island lighthouse

light from his lantern glowing on the shore as he searched in vain for the lost bodies of his children.

One night in the midst of a terrible gale, the lighthouse lamp went out because the distracted keeper had forgotten to trim the wick. With no light as a guide, a schooner hit a shoal just offshore. Waves crashed hard against the hull, smashing the schooner to pieces. Clinging to the wreckage, the crew was swept ashore on St. Martin Island.

Through the night, the crew spotted a small green light glowing warmly on the shore. Drenched and cold, the crewmen followed the beacon as it moved along the beach. They pursued it as it flickered and floated, weaving through the trees.

Pushing through the dark and pelting rain, the men came to the lightkeeper's house in a clearing. The door ajar, the men entered to find a keeper's lantern glowing brightly on the table. The keeper's oilskins hung dry on a peg nearby. The lightkeeper himself lay still on the bed. Stone cold dead.

PLUM ISLAND

TREACHEROUS DEATH'S DOOR

French explorers translated Porte des Morts—"Death's Door"—from the Potawatomi name, earned when this treacherous six-mile channel between the Door Peninsula and Plum Island claimed the lives of an Indian war party. Since then its strong currents and large waves have kept its reputation going strong. Plum Island lighthouse and lifesaving station were built to improve shipping safety and to curb the shipwrecks at Death's Door.

Plum Island light station

Shipwreck off Plum Island

Plum Island lightsaving station was put into operation in 1896.
Inset) Lightsaving crew

Plum Island lifesaving crew

WASHINGTON ISLAND

The Icelanders

Iceland. For Americans living on the Wisconsin shore of Lake Michigan a hundred years ago, Iceland conjured visions of an icy, barren tundra. When they learned Icelanders had come to live nearby on Washington Island, the Americans imagined stocky people with long raven hair, dressed in animal skins and accustomed to the Arctic way of life.

Many of the people of Washington Island came from the desolate town of Eyrarbakki, Iceland.

The first Icelanders to arrive were tall and thin and dressed in rough cotton clothes, looking very much the average pioneer. But the high level of education of this group of Icelanders made them stand apart. On passage from Liverpool, a sailor asked Icelander Pall Thorlaksson, if he would write him a letter of recommendation so that he could offer his services to immigrants as a guide. Thorlaksson penned him several—in Danish, English, German, French, Latin and Greek! But in America the exotic myth of the Icelander persisted and led to exaggerated predictions.

According to *The Door County Advocate*, 25,000 immigrants Icelanders were expected, but only about a hundred Icelanders arrived

between 1870 and 1880. The newspaper also reported the Icelanders' delight with their new home. This was borne out, at least to some degree, in the Icelanders' own accounts. In his first letter home, Jon Gislason described the easy life on Washington Island. "This place is one of the best for poor people to come to...

The Icelanders on Washington Island represent the first permanently settled Icelandic community in the United States.

Children on Washington Island

Washington Island had its share of shipwrecks.

Arni Gudmundsen was one of the educated Icelanders who came to Washington Island.

There is no lazy and idle man in Iceland, no matter how many children he has got, who cannot live a good life here." Gislason described the food that was served to them by the Irish and Danish living on the island. "...Pancakes with syrup, pork and beans, fried pork and potatoes and white bread, and 12 to 14 cups of coffee a day. It's customary here to fill the cup as soon as it is empty." To the Icelanders, such food was the stuff of dreams. Volcanic eruptions had ravaged their homeland so that neither trees nor grain would grow.

The Icelanders had been lured to America—and in particular to Washington Island—by the golden promises of William Wickmann, a Dane who had lived in Iceland and emigrated to Wisconsin. Wickmann wrote back to Iceland that "the waters of Lake Michigan are a bottomless mine of gold for the fisherman. Land can be had for homesteading and you can let your hogs run wild and catch them in the fall, fat." The reality was leaner. By the late 19th century, the Great Lakes' fish stocks had declined

The Icelandic immigrants had to be taught how to fell trees.

dramatically. What's more, the Icelanders who came were not predominantly fishermen. Those who did fish, had fished the sea, which is quite different from lake fishing.

The only other way to make a living was to cut trees, sell wood and clear the land for farming. The island was covered with forest, but most of the Icelanders had barely even seen a tree, let alone chopped one down. They struggled to adapt, earning ten cents for each felled tree and five cents for stripping cedar bark for telegraph poles.

Selling tan bark became one of the ways Icelanders scratched out a living on the island.

Jackson Harbor on Washington Island with Rock Island in the distance

Winter was an even bigger challenge. Conditions were far harsher than back home, since the Icelanders had lived in the more temperate, southern part of their country, and not in the Arctic Circle as was reputed. "I don't remember it ever being as cold in Iceland as it was here around Christmas," wrote Arni Gudmundsen on January 20, 1873. "It was minus 30 at least. We feel it in bed at night, because the house we are living in really ought to be called a shed, like most of the houses on the island." Boredom made the winter even more severe. According to Gudmundsen there was "little communication with the mainland, except when someone walks to land, which is seldom because it's a long way over the ice."

By the mid-1870s, Norwegian, Danish and Icelandic immigrants had replaced the New Yorkers and New Englanders in local office. With its rudimentary houses, and rough roads linking isolated homesteads, the community still lacked critical amenities. "There is no doctor in this out-of-the-way place," wrote Arni Gudmundsen with dismay. "We have just learned of the death of the woman next door. She was in labour for almost a week, and suffered horribly. A good doctor could surely have saved her."

Over a decade passed before Arni persuaded a doctor—his younger brother, Thordur—to move to Washington Island in 1885. Thordur's impact was enormous. Money didn't mean that much to him. After trudging many miles to see a patient, he would often say, "Ach! Just give me a good dinner and we'll call it square." At one point, friends noted his coat was in tatters. They got together and bought him a new one.

Word of his dedication and generosity spread far beyond the island. For many, Dr. Thordur Gudmundsen's loving spirit became a symbol of the island, the oldest Icelandic settlement in the United States. And in the American imagination, Gudmundsen's generosity became a mythic trait of the Icelanders as a people.

Washington Island—named for a schooner that was forced into a lengthy stay by a storm—offers visitors galleries, full-service marinas, swimming, shops, lodging and a golf course. The cedar buildings of the Jacobson Museum date to the 1930s and now display native artifacts. Ferry service runs year round to Washington Island: (920) 847-2546. Washington Island Chamber of Commerce: (920) 847-2179.

Crude homesteads of Irish fishermen

ROCK ISLAND

The Millionaire's Dream

By 1910, Rock Island's only community—a tiny fishing village—was deserted. Earlier that year, a millionaire had cruised by the island. Liking what he saw, he bought the entire island except for the area owned by the U.S. Coast Guard for the lighthouse. He imagined the dense forest transformed into an elegant estate of lawns, exotic plants, greenhouses and stone buildings designed in the style of the Vikings. Within twenty years he had realized his dream.

Hjortur Thordarson was not born into a life of ease. Things were so tough in his native Iceland that his family emigrated to the U.S. in 1873. When his father died soon afterwards, his mother found work on a farm in Wisconsin with her children. Not much later, they trekked to cheap land in North Dakota and started their own farm. School did not offer Hjortur very much. A teacher who couldn't pronounce Hjortur's name changed it to Chester. Very few books had come his way. One was an Icelandic text on physics. He learned it by heart.

At eighteen, he quit the farm and took a job in Chicago at an electrical firm. Soon he had started his own company repairing motors and before long he was manufacturing his own electrical inventions. At the 1904 World's Fair in St. Louis, Hjortur won a gold medal for a million-volt transformer, the first device of its kind. His fame grew, and he became a wealthy man.

A visit to the Icelandic community on Washington Island kindled a connection with his roots, and a desire for his own island property. He and his wife discovered Rock Island only ten minutes away by boat.

Hjortur's resources, ideas and energy seemed limitless. Clearing the land, he built large living and dining quarters for his workmen. Stone cottages and a generous lodge housed his family and guests. All the dwellings had roofs of terra cotta tile. A splendid greenhouse rose on the great sweep of lawn that sloped down to the water. Flowerbeds bore bronze plaques

Above) Hjortur (Chester)
Thordarson in his library
Right) Thordarson and one of his
many inventions

The Great Hall housed Thordarson's library, the country's largest private collection of Icelandic literature.

engraved with poetry. The thirty-acre, groomed estate was elegantly fenced to protect exotic plants from deer. On a bluff to the east, a stone cottage discreetly housed an immense water tower. On higher ground, a great cedar gateway framed the view across the lake to Washington Island.

Most impressive of all was a stone boathouse on which the Great Hall was built. Inspired by ancient Viking halls, it was the centrepiece of Hjortur's vision. From the water, high arched windows enhanced its commanding presence. Inside was as vast and lofty as a castle, with stone parapets, an immense fireplace, Viking buffalo horn chandeliers, and heavy wood furniture carved with scenes from Norse mythology. The walls were completely lined with books—25,000 books—the country's largest private collection of Icelandic literature. Hjortur Thordarson also loved Rock Island's natural beauty, and after 1930 he preserved the rest of the island as a nature sanctuary.

After his death in 1945, Hjortur's heirs refused to sell. Finally and after much negotiation, in 1964, they sold to the state of Wisconsin. Today Rock Island is a state park, its original wildness intact. Thordarson's Viking Hall houses Indian artifacts dating back to 1678, one of Thordarson's inventions, and his original Icelandic carved oak furniture. Scholars consult the tremendous book collection (now at the University of Wisconsin, Madison). And Hjortur Thordarson's ashes have been laid to rest on the island he so loved.

A short ferry ride from Washington Island, Rock Island State Park has 10 miles (16kms) of hiking trails. No cars or bicycles are permitted on the island. Only a short hike away is the Potawatomie Lighthouse built in 1836. The Rock Island ferry from Washington Island is seasonal: (414) 847-2252. Camping and Park information: (920) 847-2235. In winter, call: (920) 746-2890.

SOUTH MANITOU TO HOG ISLAND

It is a contested fact that the islands off Lake Michigan's northeast shore are a related strand. Many scientists believe North and South Manitou were once connected to the shore at Leelanau County; and that North Fox Island is a sibling of the Beaver group (Beaver, High, Garden Island etc.), which long ago was part of the Waugoshance Peninsula. Some argue that South Fox's remote location proves it was always an island. Carved out by the glaciers, it was once three times its present 3,300-acre size.

By 1672, the islands were noted on Jesuit maps. In 1679, French explorer, Sieur de la Salle wrote about his shipping passage through the archipelago, "Those [islands] in the lake of the Illinois [Michigan] are a hazard on account of the sandbars which lie off them." As shipping increased, the safe waters between the mainland and the islands (Manitou, Fox and Beaver) became know as Manitou Passage.

La Salle's ship, the Griffon. *La Salle was one of the first to document the hazardous shipping passage through the islands.*

NORTH and SOUTH MANITOU

Manitou Bears

Manitou is an Ojibwe word that encompasses the idea of Spirit. A native legend tells how the North and South Manitou Islands came to be. One summer, a forest fire raged along the shore of what is now Wisconsin. Desperate to escape, a mother bear and her two cubs swam all day towards the distant eastern shore.

It was evening before the mother bear, exhausted, felt her claws scrape against the pebbles of a beach. When she turned to help her cubs to safety, they were nowhere to be seen. She scanned the water anxiously. Lacking their mother's stamina, the cubs had been swallowed by the lake. Disconsolate, the mother laid down to wait for them. After days of fruitless vigil, death took her too.

The Great Spirit, Kitchi Manitou, honoured the mother's love and loyalty by raising a great ridge of sand along the shore where she had waited. Then two islands appeared, floating on the lake in the places where the cubs were lost.

SOUTH MANITOU

Cholera: Spirits of an Immigrant Ship

Thousands of immigrants—lured westward by the promise of a better life—were crammed into ships that steamed past the Manitous in the mid-1830s. Located in the shipping route between Chicago and the Straits of Mackinac, South Manitou had become an important place to refuel their ravenous wood furnaces. One foggy summer's night, seized by desperation, a ship's captain loaded wood, and left a gruesome offering on the sandy shore.

Congested Detroit Harbour in 1837. Steaming past the Manitous in the mid-1830s were ships crammed with thousands of immigrants lured west by the promise of a better life.

South Manitou refueling station was crucial as the island had the only harbour deep enough to accommodate large ships in the region.

In the preceding days, the captain's vessel had become a floating hell. Irish and German immigrants crowded every foot of deck and hold. The numbers were so great that cleanliness was hopeless. The drinking water became tainted. Dysentery developed, then thirst, vomiting, cramps, and seizures. Crew members whispered "cholera", as they attended to the dying. Soon the ship was choked with corpses.

The Captain's need to purge the ship mounted to desperation. Out of the dark loomed South Manitou, shrouded in fog. It was a grim solution. The ship tucked into the harbour to be refueled. In the dead of night, with harbour master and cove dwellers fast asleep, the captain and crew hauled the corpses from the ship. The fog muffled the groans of the dying, dragged along beside the dead. Armed with spades, the captain and his crew reached the woods at the edge of the beach and began to dig with fervour. Before long, the dead lay in a wide, shallow grave, together with those who were not quite dead, their feeble protests silenced by a shroud of sand.

The legacy of cholera is also linked to the Crescent Bay Cemetery that lies close to the harbour. Some of the bodies interred there were removed

After dozens of wrecks and pleas from mariners, the U.S. government finally built a lifesaving station on South Manitou in 1902.

from ships due to typhoid and cholera. This was also a graveyard for those who were washed ashore from shipwrecks.

South Manitou became the first pioneer homestead on the islands of the Peninsula's western shoreline. The settlers were primarily German immigrants. George Johann Hutzler, the first to establish a permanent residence here, had suffered his own tragedy with cholera, losing his eldest son on a hellish, three-month crossing to America. Arriving on the island around 1853, Hutzler discovered a hive of activity—because of South Manitou's refuelling depot, it was not unusual to see sixty ships anchored in Crescent Bay. Hutzler was soon cutting wood for the depot. The family then began a cattle and grain farm.

Today South Manitou is a National Park. Hiking trails lead to the historic farms, lighthouse, and breathtaking sand beaches and dunes. Ferry service leaves from Leland, MI. For information: Sleeping Bear National Lakeshore (616) 326-5134.

SOUTH FOX ISLAND

Hunger at the Zapf Logging Camp

It was the long winter of 1923 on South Fox Island and Ed Horn was hungry. It was not a hunger he had ever known before. It gnawed at his belly, pushing him to desperation. He was not alone in his pain. At the Zapf logging camp, they had started out the winter with a fair store of supplies, but by February, the workers had become so starved for meat that they had butchered the work ox. Then there were only beans and potatoes left. By March, food had dwindled to almost nothing. With his hopeful declarations they would make it through to spring, Foreman Nels Ask was either in denial or he was shielding the others from the truth.

It was early April. Ed Horn stood on the shoreline staring at the ice mounds buckling on the frozen lake. Over the last weeks, the lake had thawed and broken up, only to freeze again a few days later. There was no guarantee this ice could hold a man. Fighting the hunger in his gut, Ed looked out to the horizon. It was 22 long miles (35kms) to the mainland. His mind fixed on a plan. It was crazy, he told himself. But no crazier than doing nothing while they starved to death. He talked two others into joining him. Carl Cooper and Ellis Ayers were just as hungry and just as desperate.

In the predawn of Monday, April 15, the three men started to scale the icy crags on hands and feet, dragging an ax, a pole, a pair of oars and a small skiff. After several hours they reached sparkling open water and nudged their boat in. So far, so good. Before long they hit more ice. The sharp floes scraped and pierced their skiff, and it began to fill with water.

They reached solid ice again just as their skiff was swallowed up. Down went the oars, the ax, the pole. Cooper stepped onto a patch of ice too thin to hold him and he went crashing through. Horrified, the others watched him clawing at the ice, while he kicked hard to propel himself. Stubborn and strong, Cooper managed to haul himself from the icy water. Soaked and numb, he kept on moving. They continued over solid ice, making better time without the boat to drag. For several hours they trudged on silently, wondering what they would do if they met open water.

The sun was both friend and foe. It warmed them, but it also glinted off the ice, burning faces, and melting the frozen surface into an unnerving mush. The darkness brought a chilling wind as they reached a stretch of ice that was riddled with cracks. To their horror, the cracks began to swell and open, black water gushing around each icy slab. Before they knew it, each man stood alone on his own ice raft. There was nothing left to do but jump from floe to floe.

For hours they tracked the motion of the floes, and timed their leaps—one misstep and the icy lake would swallow them. Fatigue crept in like a shadow. Ed Horn's mind was plagued by an inner voice that warned his plan would bring them all to death. Soon his legs refused to take another step and he was lying on an icy slab, drifting barely conscious into the night.

The dawn woke him to the stark truth of his floating prison. A hundred yards away he saw a dark mound on another floe. To his great relief, the others had huddled on the same piece of ice and it hadn't drifted far from his. Off into the distance, he could not believe what he was seeing. A long, thin, gray band on the horizon. He squeezed closed his weary eyes and

Panic set in at the logging camp as the winter food supply dwindled.

Like South Fox, most Great Lakes islands have been logged. Because felling was a winter job it was essential that supplies be delivered before the winter freeze up.

opened them again. It was still there. Land.

It took the three men another whole day and night. By nine o'clock on Wednesday morning, they had dragged themselves ashore and fell exhausted on the stony beach. A fisherman found them and took them to the nearby town of Northport. The town was abuzz with the imminent starvation on South Fox Island. A man called Gilman Dane proposed to send a plane full of supplies to the ten remaining workers at the Zapf Camp. The fact that there was no airstrip on the island didn't seem to matter. Concerned citizens rounded up a thousand pounds of food. They'd get it to them somehow.

Once Ed Horn had rested up, he paid a visit to the Zapf Head Office in Traverse City, MI to tell his story. The superintendent there, Mr. McAlvay, was incredulous. He told reporters at the Traverse City Record-Eagle that the story of starving employees was "quite puzzling."

When the plane full of food landed on the slushy ice off South Fox, it broke through. The two on board were pulled ashore. But the supplies could not be reached. Several more planes attempted the mission. A plane from Chicago, a government mail plane, and two Army planes. They all failed.

Finally on Sunday, April 23, they pulled out all the stops. Rescuers brought the *Bull of the Woods* into action. Also known as the *Ann Arbor Car Ferry No.5*, this 360-foot (108 m) ship was an icebreaker, the biggest of its kind in the world. Nothing could prevent success this time. The starving islanders watched in amazement as the *Bull* neared the shore. Ed Horn was on deck, staring down in wonder as great heaving slabs of the ice he'd struggled on, bowed before the ship. The ship parted ice twenty inches thick, leaving a black channel in its wake.

Before long, the Zapf workers were on board and the ferry steamed back to the mainland. When the *Bull's* captain questioned foreman Ask about their lack of food, Ask continued to deny that they had almost starved. But just a look at the gaunt faces of the loggers was enough to undermine his word. The camp cook piped up, "You don't get hungry on the kind of food we had. You get faint... I heard there were 800 bushels of potatoes at Nels Ask's place, but I never saw any of them."

South and North Fox Islands share a human history like all the islands of the Michigan Archipelago: fur trade, fishing, lumbering farming and lightkeeping. Today the Foxes are privately owned.

HIGH ISLAND

House of David Cult

For a time, Utopia existed on an island called High, in northern Lake Michigan. Healthy, smiling men and women worked hard in the hot sun, the breeze catching their hair which swung free over their shoulders. They brought in vegetables, bumper crops of cabbages, corn, carrots, potatoes and beans. The men cut down timber and hauled it to the saw and shingle mills. They built a blacksmith shop and a bakery, sturdy homes, and a schooner called the *Rosa Belle*.

Although fish were plentiful, the people of High Island did not partake. They were completely vegetarian. They had an abiding respect for nature and coexisted peacefully with the natives on the island. They also believed they were a chosen people—who were granted a life span of a thousand years—and that only they would survive the coming cataclysm.

The charismatic "King Ben" Purnell

Founded in 1912, the Utopian

The High Island school was comprised of natives and children from the House of David. As couples practiced celibacy until the "new millennium" these children were born before the parents joined the cult.

community on High Island was a colony of the House of David, a sect begun in 1903 in Benton Harbor, on the southeastern shore of Lake Michigan. The High Islanders supplied produce and timber for the sect's community in Benton Harbor, and for its leader, Benjamin Purnell. When he arrived in Benton Harbor, King Ben Purnell was forty-two. He had all of the fiery charisma that had earned him his title. He drew people to him with his intense gaze, and deep honey-toned voice. He had a red mustache and goatee, and his hair tumbled past his shoulders. He wore a jaunty, wide-brimmed white hat, gold chains around his neck and a tasteful, tailored suit. Purnell was irresistible. Especially to women, who were Purnell's secret obsession. His climb to kingship had been

King Ben purchased the bankrupt mill on High Island to ensure a lumber supply for his community at Benton Harbor.

Young boy showing off the new crop

long and steep. Born in the hills of Kentucky in 1861, he married in his late teens, deserted his wife and child, and then married his future queen, Mary Stollard. He and Mary moved about, staying poor at odd jobs. Then he laid hands on a book that would change his life.

The Flying Roller was book of sermons, published in 1888 by James J. Jazreel, a religious zealot in the Cult of the Seven Messengers. Founded almost a century before by an Englishwoman turned prophet, this was a cult of evangelical latter-day Israelites that, by the 1810s, had drawn 100,000 followers. It offered the vision of a New Jerusalem and adhered to a strict code of morality. When its prophet, the First Messenger, passed on to join the heavenly host, a succeeding line of Messengers sprang forward to spread the Word.

After one failed attempt to have himself proclaimed a Messenger, Ben and his wife Mary trudged from place to place selling *The Flying Roller*, writing a new book, *The Star of Bethlehem*, and gathering a handful of

House of David members did not believe in cutting their hair. Some even strung hair locks of highly-respected members on their belts.

followers. Then in 1902, a devoted fan gave Ben $1,200 to publish his book. He was becoming a true prophet in the eyes of devotees.

In March 1903, Ben and Mary Purnell took up residence in Benton Harbor, persuading the local group of House of David followers that they had brought the seeds of the New Jerusalem. Believers soon flocked to the new kingdom, surrendering all their worldly gains to King Ben. The King became a wealthy man. Meanwhile 140,000 devotees dressed in the simple garb of poverty and ate a modest vegetarian diet. They upheld a strict code of behaviour, which included chastity, even for the married members.

King Ben soon climbed to great commercial heights. A Coney Island-style amusement park at Benton Harbor lured hundreds of thousands of visitors from nearby Chicago. The King assembled a baseball team that toured the country, drawing sellout crowds that cheered their shutout scores and marvelled at their long, flowing hair. And in a humbler business move, Purnell bought the failed High Island lumber company.

And so began the House of David's colony on High Island, established in 1912. Its 130 members were friendly, hard working and well-liked by their neighbours. The community looked like a shantytown. Its most curious building was the eight-sided "House of Virgins" where the women slept under guard. An extensive pier was built to ship wood and produce back to Benton Harbor.

While High Islanders lived a simple life, their King's self-indulgence knew no limit, his desire for wealth only eclipsed by his sexual desire for young girls. Ben's devotees handed over their girl children. To doubt him was to be damned. "I felt I was going right into the gates of Paradise," one

House of David members believed they could live to a thousand years of age.

teenage true believer testified later, having submitted to a "cleansing of her blood" through repeated sexual intercourse.

Ben's wife, Queen Mary, was well aware of his nubile harem and viewed his orgies with calm acceptance. But eventually, the exploitation of the girls became public and the scandal flowed.

Beginning in 1910, a series of morality charges was levied against Purnell. For sixteen years he went in and out of hiding while the law searched tirelessly for him.

The moment of truth finally came in 1926. On a tip from a former harem member, the police burst into his hideaway. They found Purnell, a skinny old man, wearing nothing but underwear and a nightcap. Purnell, now sixty-five, was herded off to a summer of interrogation filling thousands of pages with graphic testimony. Declaring the King and his cult to be a public nuisance, the judge ordered the colony's dissolution. Undone by the ordeal, and ill for several years, Ben Purnell died on December 16, 1927.

Neither the judge's order nor King Ben's demise could destroy the colony. It split into two rival groups, launched sensible business ventures and continued to thrive. But in a post-Ben battle for the cult's leadership, a judge—vying for the job—took the island over. The tight colony rebelled and fell apart, spelling the end of a curious but enterprising time on High Island. The High Island colonists were gone by 1940. In Benton Harbor, as recently as the late 1970s, a few elderly, long-haired members could still be seen ambling through the abandoned amusement park.

Today High Island is part of the Beaver Island State Wildlife Research Area. The entire island is open to recreational camping and hiking, except for two areas protecting the nesting grounds of birds. The only buildings on the island belong to the Department of Natural Resources. Nature has nearly obliterated all traces of the homes belonging to House of David members. The 200 acres that the members cultivated have now grown over.

No one knows where the House of David buried its dead. Death before a thousand years of age, or before the new millennium, was interpreted as a weakness of faith, and proof of a sinful life. It is said that members would shamefully bury these fallen souls in unmarked graves in the woods. Others suggest that some of the smaller local islands were used to hide away the bodies.

To get to High Island, take the ferry to Beaver Island and then hire a local resident to take you over. You are best to arrange this before you leave for Beaver Island. One way to make arrangements is by browsing www.beaverisland.net

Ojibwe family working the land on High Island. Natives and cult members co-existed peacefully on the island.

GARDEN ISLAND

When Bishop Baraga came to the region in 1831, Indians were living on Miniss Kitigan (Garden Island) and Beaver Island. In the late 1830s, the Indian population was large enough to attract a trading post on Beaver Island. (It is likely that whiskey was a prime commodity as the site of the post on Beaver Island con-

tinues to be known as Whiskey Point.)

Nicknamed "cornshockers," Ojibwe islanders had planted corn and squash here for generations. Garden Islanders also earned their income from trapping, and from selling dried fish, maple syrup, and balsam oil for its medicinal properties.

Garden Island log home, early 1900s

The Ojibwe cemetery is the best-preserved link to the island's past, and is still in operation.

Danish families such as the Larsons and Jensens settled the north shore at the turn of the twentieth century and fished the surrounding waters. Garden Island had a church, school, lumber mill, and post office. Only the partial walls of about 7 to 10 of their cabins remain.

Garden Island fishermen. Garden Islanders did good business with fish they dried on Gull Island. Dried fish was used as currency.

Native spirit houses in the cemetery. The homesteader's cemetery is in a different location.

Other islanders called the natives "corn-shockers" for their gardens of corn.

Abandoned homesteads on Garden Island

BEAVER ISLAND

King Strang the Island Ruler

It was the summer of 1850. The stars, shining on the island in Lake Michigan, twinkled from the King's tin crown. The King sat upon a throne padded with moss. Before him in the roofless temple made of logs, four hundred select guests shouted, "Long live James, King of Zion!"

Before his royal ascent, King James Jesse Strang had been a farmer, a teacher, lawyer, editor, and prophet. He was a consummate charlatan, charismatic and persuasive. Barely five foot three, he often wore a stove-pipe hat and a bushy, auburn beard. He claimed that his bulging forehead harboured the prophetic powers that burned through his intense, dark eyes.

Strang grew up in New York State in the 1820s and 30s, acutely grandiose even then. He wrote on his

The self-proclaimed king, James Jesse Strang

nineteenth birthday, "I am yet no more than a common farmer. 'Tis too bad. I ought to have been... a Brigadier General before this time if I am ever to rival Caesar or Napoleon which I have sworn to." In 1843, Strang and his young wife and child moved to Burlington, Wisconsin. He became involved with the Mormons at Nauvoo in western Illinois, and was soon proclaimed a Latter Day Saint. When Mormon leader Joseph Smith was killed by a mob of dissenters, Strang claimed he had been appointed the supreme ruler of the Saints on earth.

Smith's followers splintered into twenty

THE

BOOK OF THE LAW

OF

THE LORD,

BEING A TRANSLATION FROM THE EGYPTIAN OF THE LAW GIVEN TO MOSES IN SINAI, WITH NUMEROUS AND VALUABLE NOTES.

PRINTED BY COMMAND OF THE KING,

AT THE ROYAL PRESS,

SAINT JAMES,

A. R. VI.

"Printed By Command of the King." Strang took his role of monarch and religious leader seriously, printing this "Book of the Law" for his followers.

The lighthouse on Beaver Island is built on Whiskey Point, named for a former fur trader's operation.

groups. Those who rallied behind Brigham Young travelled west to Utah. And with his powers of persuasion, Strang, too, commanded some attention. As his grandson later said, "like a prospector who has finally struck it rich, [Strang] knew he had found his El Dorado, a listening audience." He won the leadership in Illinois.

With prophetic conviction, Strang wooed his disciples to the site of a new holy city, to be named Voree, Garden of Paradise, which soon fell casualty to competing factions, economic problems and to hostile neighbours. In a revelation, Strang saw the Holy Land relocated to the northern end of Lake Michigan, on Big Beaver Island, one of a cluster of islands called the Beavers. Thirteen fertile miles long and six timbered miles wide, with beautiful white sand beaches, and a fine harbour full of fish, Beaver Island was nothing short of paradise. No matter that Irish-Catholic fishermen had already settled a small piece of it.

By 1849, fifty Mormon families had settled the town of Saint James, around the shore of

Irish-Catholic fishermen were not pleased with the influx of Mormons to Beaver.

The town of St. James on Paradise Bay, Beaver Island was the heart of "God's Kingdom on earth."

Paradise Bay. Strang soon had another vision, one so radical that at first he kept it to himself. God wanted him to be crowned king, to rule over Beaver Island, God's Kingdom on earth. God also required him to put aside monogamy, and set a new example by marrying a second wife.

But beneath the heavenly decree was its earthly explanation: on one of

Elvira Field became Strang's second wife

his proselytizing forays, Strang had met an attractive—irresistible to him—young woman. Elvira Field was modest, devout, bright, charming, and all of seventeen. Strang shared his vision with his second in command, a failed stage actor named George Adams. Strang sent him as emissary to Miss Field. Enhanced with dramatic flourish, Adams revealed to Elvira her divine selection as the queen of God's Kingdom on earth. Seduced by Adams' presentation, Elvira agreed to embrace her role and was secretly spirited away. A year later, she was still missing from her parents' home.

On July 13, 1849, Elvira married Strang in a bedchamber somewhere in Michigan. Rather than returning home immediately for the coronation, Strang devised a daring ruse. Cutting off Elvira's long hair, he dressed her in a man's suit, transforming her into Charles J. Douglas, his nephew and new secretary. At first, his wife and four children back home suspected nothing. But as Strang and "Charley" honeymooned up and down the East Coast, drumming up converts, they left a wake of whispers about Charley's "anatomical peculiarities."

L) Strang—who had attracted con-verts with his stand against polygamy—anticipated a negative reaction from followers and his cur-rent wife to his second marriage.
R) Charles Douglas

The following spring, bolstered by a host of new believers, Strang returned to Beaver Island, set for his coronation. Despite Strang's charisma, the ranks of the disillusioned swelled. The residents of the region and of nearby Mackinac Island resented this "chosen people" who wooed away friends, neighbours and family. The strongest protest was from local fish-ermen, whose land and waters had been invaded by these "clannish and ornery Mormon marauders." Indeed, the Beaver Island Mormons pros-pered by selling fish and timber to passing ships. St. James had replaced

Tensions began to escalate between the Strangites and non-Strangites.

Mackinac Island as the main refueling stop. Strang's followers had claimed the whole island for their own. Before long, the cries grew hostile: "the only good Mormon was a dead Mormon."

Defectors' tales of torture, theft and fraud hit the front page, finally arriving on the desk of the President in Washington. He sent the warship, *Michigan*, to appre-

The captain of the US Navy's ship the Michigan lured Strang to the dock where Strang's followers ambushed him.

hend Strang, and convey him to Detroit to face indictment. The King's trial lasted a month. With his trademark eloquence, Strang portrayed himself as the victim of religious persecution. He was acquitted.

Looking for a bulwark against local hostility, Strang ran as a Democrat for the Michigan State legislature. His bloc of 2,600 loyal Mormon voters

Ruth Ann and Thomas Bedford. Strang's end came at the hand of his own followers.

ensured the seat for him. While in office, he passed a bill making Beaver Island a separate county. He also declared his intention to rule all of northern Michigan, creating new Mormon communities on the mainland, and sometimes ousting existing residents at gunpoint. Despite angry resistance, Strang and his followers continued unimpeded. The King expanded the royal household, taking in more wives and fathering more children.

Strang's harshly autocratic rule finally led to his undoing. In one petty ruling, Strang decided that women should wear loose smocks with long pantaloons underneath, a style later popularized by the feminist, Amelia Bloomer. When Ruth Ann Bedford refused, her husband, Thomas, was given thirty-nine lashes with a willow switch. Seething with indignation, Bedford decided that King Strang had reigned long enough. Buoyed by other radicals, he and another rebel, Alexander Wentworth, plotted their leader's death. On June 16, 1856, they ambushed Strang and fired on him. He crumpled to the ground, alive but hit several times. His assassins beat him with their pistols before escaping on the U.S. navy ship *Michigan*, which was

Strangites like this couple were herded on ships and forced off Beaver Island.

anchored in the bay. Bedford and Wentworth were whisked away on the ship and released shortly after, never charged for their crime. King Strang breathed his last on July 9, 1856, six years after his coronation. It is still uncertain if the *Michigan's* role indicates a government conspiracy in Strang's assassination.

Leaderless and lost, the Beaver Island residents were attacked by drunken vigilantes from Mackinac Island and the mainland. And although some Mormons were well-liked by the community and stayed on at Beaver for many years, most were forced from the island, dropped along the shores of Lake Michigan to start their lives anew.

The Mormon Print Shop is the only substantial evidence of the Mormon epoch on Beaver Island. Historians and archeologists have yet to find a graveyard of the Strangite population. The occasional Strangite still visits, curious about the legacy the Mormons left behind. Today, the Print Shop houses the Beaver Island Historical Society and Museum, displaying the full range of Beaver Island history, including the Mormon era. Other museums include the Protar Home and the Marine Museum. Beaver Island offers beaches, swimming, hiking, camping and two lighthouses. The islanders are friendly, and the rural setting and town have not been over-commercialized. Ferry information: Beaver Island Boat Company (616) 547-2311 or (888) 446-4095. For motels, camping and activities call the Beaver Island Chamber of Commerce (616) 448-2505. Website is: beaverisland.net

Beaver Island harbour

BEAVER ISLAND
Who Was Protar, Really?

March 3, 1925. Dr. Palmer jumped off the wagon and rushed into Protar's rough-hewn log cabin, neighbour Patrick Bonner closely behind. While the Doctor took the old man's pulse, Pat stood at the end of the bed in dismay. "We're too late," he mumbled looking at Protar's still face, framed by his unruly beard. It was true. Dr. Palmer sat down at the dead man's table and reminisced about him. Patrick Bonner looked around the small cabin. He felt guilty for invading Protar's privacy, but he felt compelled to know. Just who was Protar, anyway? This strange man had appeared on Beaver Island in 1893 and had never left. He refused to discuss his past. He had money but lived like hermit. He hated visitors, but was always ready to help anyone who was ill.

Pat Bonner stared at the old man's books: a German-English Medical book; a book on Buddhist teachings; Goethe, Schiller; Tolstoy; and volumes of plays, philosophy and poetry. In Protar's diary, Bonner found only descriptions of the weather. He picked up a small Lutheran prayer book and found the name Johann Jacob Friederich Wilhelm Parrot (1791-1841) inked inside the cover. "Parrot!" said Bonnar out loud, a smile of realization spreading across his face. Parrot was an anagram for Protar, the name the dead man had assumed on Beaver Island. Was this a clue to the dead man's mysterious past?

After Protar's death, the islanders could only piece together parts of Protar's past. On Beaver Island, he treated the sick—tallying 17 per month for thirty years—and never charged a fee. He lived simply in his log cabin, growing vegetables, making apple cider vinegar and sauerkraut, and tending chickens, goats and horses. He never shaved, or cut his hair. He bathed in

While he didn't like to be called a doctor, for no pay, Protar treated more than 2,000 patients during his thirty years on the island.

Protar lived as a hermit and refused to discuss his family or his own past.

a barrel on his porch. While neighbours sometimes helped him out, none could claim him as an intimate. It seemed he had only one friend in the world, Dr. Bernhardi from Rock Island.

Protar's mystery was finally—and mostly—solved in the 1970s. Antje Price, a member of the Beaver Island Historical Society, gathered all his books and writings, and interviewed the people who had known him. It was Price's hope to uncover the mystery of Protar's life before he arrived on Beaver Island. The main hurdle was Protar himself who had gone to great lengths to conceal his past and his identity.

Price learned that Protar/Parrot came from a Russian family of prominent scientists, professors and intellectuals. Protar/Parrot's grandfather studied economics, mathematics, and physics in Germany. He was a member of the Imperial Academy of Science in St. Petersburg and contributed to theories in osmosis, dialysis, and galvanic electricity. Protar's father was knighted for his scientific explorations, most impressively he was the first to the summit of Mount Ararat in 1829.

Perhaps the greatest clue to Protar's character was his break from the family's scientific tradition, choosing a career in the arts. His father's prayer book revealed Protar's date of birth as 1837; marriage to wife Louise on October 12, 1868 and then Louise's death on June 22, 1872. In the 1860s, Protar was an actor and stage manager in a German and English acting troop that had resettled in America from Europe. Around 1882, Protar became the editor and publisher of the German paper *Volks Zeitung* on Rock Island, where his friend from Europe, Dr. Carl Bernhardi, also lived.

In 1892, Protar was a passenger on a steamer when the ship sought shelter on Beaver Island. He was so enchanted by the island that he concluded his vacation there. He discovered an abandoned cabin, built in the late 1850s by an Irish family who had used logs abandoned by Mormons after their "expulsion." Within two years he had sold his newspaper and was living a simple life on Beaver.

At their last meeting before his death, Protar and his friend, Dr. Bernhardi sensed it was the last time they would meet. Cryptically Protar asked if his good friend would know Protar's moment of death. The doctor assured him that he would. Protar died March 3, 1925. His friend, Dr. Bernhardi died the very same day.

Having gathered all the evidence she could find, Antje Price drafted an article entitled "F. Protar: The Heaven-Sent Friend" which concludes,

Protar home on Beaver Island from 1892-1925

He deliberately sought a world unlike the urban, cultured, literate one he had known before, one to which he could belong and contribute but where he could also find the solitude he needed to come to terms with his inner self... He could be and often was gruff and forbidding. This was not, as has sometimes been assumed, because he feared detection by some external political force, but because the focus of his existence, of his whole being, was on the inner man. All his efforts were devoted to the battle raging within him. He was by all accounts, including his own, a troubled, struggling, unfinished man.

According to Price, Protar had requested a simple funeral: a sturdy bag, a heavy stone, and to be dropped in the lake between High and Beaver Islands. Because Michigan law prohibits this kind of burial, Protar was laid to rest on his property. A collection was raised to erect a bronze plaque bearing his likeness. The Beaver Island Historical Society maintains Protar's memorial and his home.

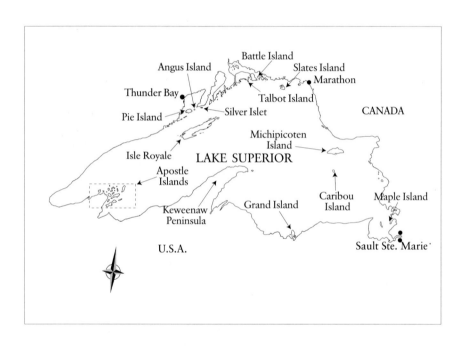

Battle Island

Angus Island

Slates Island
Marathon

Thunder Bay

Talbot Island

CANADA

Pie Island
Silver Islet

Michipicoten
Island

Isle Royale

LAKE SUPERIOR

Apostle
Islands

Maple Island

Caribou
Island

Keweenaw
Peninsula

Grand Island

U.S.A.

Sault Ste. Marie

5

LAKE SUPERIOR ISLANDS

The Mythic Giant

The largest of the inland seas, Lake Superior is the greatest expanse of freshwater in the world. Early French explorers, amazed by its enormity, thought it was certainly the sea route to China. Covering a total surface area of over 31,700 square miles (82,100 square kilometres), and as deep as 440 yards (400 metres), its size and power are daunting. An autumn storm on Superior with its towering waves and gale-force winds can defeat the most experienced sailor and sink the most seaworthy ship. Yet the lake has many other guises: in the spring it can cloak itself in thick fog for weeks; on tranquil August days, it can be flat and beguilingly calm.

Many Superior islands are remote and mysterious places often isolated from the mainland by great distances and treacherous waters. Not surprisingly, a rich mythology has developed around them... mysterious floating islands, islands of golden sands, islands made of copper, imaginary islands....

Sculpted sandstone and sand beaches give Superior's south shore its distinctive beauty. On the islands, sometimes these are found in dramatic formations. The remarkable caves rimming Devils Island have been carved by thousands of years of

Majestic Pie Island

Devils Island Caves

waves. Grand Island's majestic 200-foot cliffs rise in sedimentary bands of rich earthen hues.

Born of volcanic fire, scraped down to Precambrian Shield bedrock by the glaciers, the islands along Superior's wild North Shore are tough and rugged, surviving Superior's constant pounding. Towering flat-topped cliffs at Pie Island plunge sheer toward the water, the shoreline of the Slates appears as a rock sculpture garden, and the gnarled lava ridges and reefs of Isle Royale are a virtual blueprint of the glaciers' paths. The rock holds mineral treasures, like copper on Isle Royale, and silver on Silver Islet, that have attracted miners for thousands of years.

The history of the region is filled with tales of endurance in the face of the lake's great power. There are stories of lighthouse keepers and shipwrecks, silver miners and hermits and their efforts to survive. Today this wild and little-populated region is one of the most breathtaking on the Great Lakes, and many of its islands are still sought out by those who seek nature in its rawest form.

GRAND ISLAND

The largest island on the southern shore of Lake Superior, Grand Island sits in Munising Bay, the largest natural harbour between Sault Ste. Marie and Marquette. Grand Island offered the Ojibwe a bounty of food, as well as a place rich in history and legend. They named the island Kitchi Miniss, "Great Island." But in 1836, the Ojibwe people turned over the island and parts of the mainland to the United States, in return for promises of cash, education, medical care, tools and other supplies. The band continued to live on Grand Island until 1873, when the majority moved to the mainland.

In 1901, William Mather, the wealthy owner of the Cleveland-Cliffs Iron

Company, bought most of the island and built a resort. Establishing a wildlife preserve and nicknaming the island "my little Yellowstone," he imported deer, ruffed grouse, caribou from Newfoundland, Ontario moose, Swedish game birds, Belgian hares, and reindeer. Only the elk and moose thrived here. Unfortunately, when Mather died in 1951, the Iron Company jumped in and began harvesting the large trees—pine, hemlock, cedar, beech and maple. The company put Grand Island up for sale in the 1980s and the Trust for Public Land bought it and resold it to the U.S. government.

Grand Island's north shore cliffs

The Island is now a National Recreation Area within the Hiawatha National Forest, a huge protected forest in the central and eastern part of the Upper Peninsula of Michigan that reaches the shores of three Great Lakes. The island's spectacular 200-foot cliffs are made of sedimentary bands of sandstone dating back over 500 million years. Visitors can sea kayak, bike, hike, camp, or take boat tours that include East Channel lighthouse, one of the oldest lighthouses on Lake Superior, and the shipwreck *Burmuda*. During the summer, a 2 1/2 hour sightseeing bus tour visits the beautiful forests and lakes of the island's interior and scenic vistas along the shores. The Grand Island Ferry leaves from Munising, MI (906) 387-3503 or (906) 387-2433. Hiawatha National Forest Visitor Center in Munising: (906) 387-3700.

Two lighthouses were constructed on Grand to serve the increased shipping along the south shore. (This was partly due to the booming iron industry, and the establishment of an iron furnace on Munising Bay.) The North Light, built in 1867, is the highest lighthouse above sea level in the world at about 817 feet. It replaced an older tower built in the 1850s. The wooden East Channel Lighthouse was built on Grand in 1867 and abandoned in 1913. Today both lighthouses are privately owned. These waters are clearly treacherous, judging by the number of ships that have wrecked around Grand, even after the lighthouses were built—the Schooner *Merchant* in 1847, the schooner *Dreadnaught* in 1870, the wooden freighter *Henry B. Smith* in 1913, and the schooner *Burmuda* in 1870.

GRAND ISLAND

Abraham Williams and the Ojibwe

When Chief Monomonee of the Grand Island Ojibwe met Abraham Williams at Sault Ste. Marie, MI in 1840, he sensed he'd met a good man. Grand Island had long been a summer paradise for the Ojibwe people. White fur traders had come and gone. But Williams was different. He

would be the first white man to take up residence on Grand Island, at Chief Monomonee's invitation.

Abraham Williams was an enterprising man from Vermont. He had sold his home and, with his wife and seven children, moved north to the Sault. But the Sault had all the excesses of a frontier town with two billiard halls, as many card tables as houses, and thousands of gallons of liquor. Williams soon decided it was not the place to raise a family. Chief Menomonee's invitation to settle on Grand Island, 100 miles away, was fortuitous and welcome.

Abraham Williams

The sixty Ojibwe of Grand Island were industrious. In spring they launched their maple sugar operation, producing over 3,000 pounds of syrup used in cooking and as medicine. In summer, they caught fish in the bay and cultivated over 30 acres of corn and potatoes. Williams' daughter, Anna, recalled that in winter they also trapped, "mostly otter and beaver and mink. The squaws made the traps. One old squaw caught two hundred mink in hers." They were also known for their impressive attire: wool jackets, leggings, hats decorated with bright ribbons and embroidered with beads. The elder, Tarhe the Crane, wore a blue broadcloth

Grand Island Ojibwe were known for their flamboyant dress.

frock-coat, a ruffled chintz shirt, and a palm leaf hat bound with bright red and yellow French calico.

Williams built his first of several houses with a great open fireplace. He went on to build a row of cottages, a warehouse, a cooperage and a smithy. He was a fine carpenter, mason, and blacksmith. He made irons for the fire, hinges, locks, and latches shaped like a stem and leaf. As he mended the Ojibwe's well-used tools, hoes and pots, Williams' tiny empire grew. He ran a fishery, sold timber to passing ships, and made Grand Island one of the most active stopping points on Lake Superior.

Williams family settlement

He also saw his chance to sell Ojibwe furs for his own profit. "Father always dealt fairly with the Indians. They were surprised that he should pay them so much," Anna remembered. "He paid them mostly in provisions, sometimes part money." He also paid them in whiskey, an illegal practice at the time. Competing traders who bought furs from natives complained bitterly about Williams but no one ever interfered with his whiskey trade.

The Ojibwe and Williams prospered together. Williams' death in 1873 marked the end of an era for the Grand Island band. Most moved to the mainland in search of other opportunities.

The site of the former Indian village, called Gete Odena (Ancient Village), is no longer visible, but it was located near the dock at Williams Landing. Two of Williams' homes are used as private cottages. The Forest Service has a series of panels in a small visitor shelter at Williams' Landing that interpret the island and its history.

GRAND ISLAND

Oriole *Flight*

Andrew Fleming was a cook on board the *Oriole* when the three-masted schooner set sail from Marquette, Michigan, one summer's evening in 1862. The sun was a red ball in the sky as the ship left the south shore of Lake Superior with thirteen people aboard. Fleming served up bread and cheese and cool drinks.

Toward midnight, when the captain and his wife retired, fog crept in and curled around the ship. Four of the crew kept watch while another four dozed in the forecastle. Cook Fleming headed for his berth noting the signal lamps glowing through the mist. The light from the Grand Island lighthouse came into view. Comforted, he climbed into his berth and fell asleep.

A ghastly sound of breaking wood scraped him awake. Within moments he was in the water, floundering amid chaotic screaming, splintered wood and flotsam. He seized a piece of the cabin and clung to it. Peering across the water he could not believe his eyes: the *Oriole* gliding away into the mist in ghostly full sail. But she had no stern. It had been sliced away, right through the cabin where he had been sleeping.

Amazed, Fleming also saw the grey hull of a massive steamer pushing

The Oriole's *captain went to sleep after catching sight of the Grand Island lighthouse.*

through the fog. He yelled wildly for help, but the steamer vanished. He clutched at the piece of wood. He heard a lone voice cry out in the night. It grew faint, and then all was silent.

When morning came, Fleming found the ship's stern floating nearby with the lifeboat still attached. For the next forty hours he drifted in it, oarless, exposed to the sun. Meanwhile, the steamer *Illinois* had pulled into Marquette harbour, her bow shattered from keel to upper deck. Her captain said they'd hit an unknown schooner that had run directly toward them in the fog off Grand Island. He explained the fog whistle was not blowing because the fog was intermittent. The steamer had veered off striking the schooner's stern. The *Illinois'* passengers had heard screams in the water, and were aghast when the steamer didn't stop to rescue the victims.

The captain claimed he had sped off toward harbour with the safety of his passengers in mind. Once he realized there was no fear of sinking, it seemed too late to return to the scene of the accident. Besides, the mate on watch at the time had reported that the schooner "appeared not much injured." The day after the *Illinois* came into port, a brigantine found the *Oriole's* sole survivor drifting in the lifeboat, and brought him back to Marquette. Fleming's sad tale exposed the *Illinois* captain's callousness, and deepened local bitterness towards him.

Days later and miles away, the captain of the *Plover* observed the ghostly *Oriole*, fully rigged, and still floating.

TWENTY TWO APOSTLES

Twenty-two strikingly beautiful islands—the Apostles—fan out into south-western Lake Superior from the tip of Bayfield Peninsula, Wisconsin. Formed when the last glacier of the Ice Age scoured the sandstone bedrock, the islands have been further sculpted by thousands of years of waves. Along the islands' exposed northern coastlines, the red-brown sandstone has been carved into elaborate caves, while the protected southern shores have become fine sandy beaches.

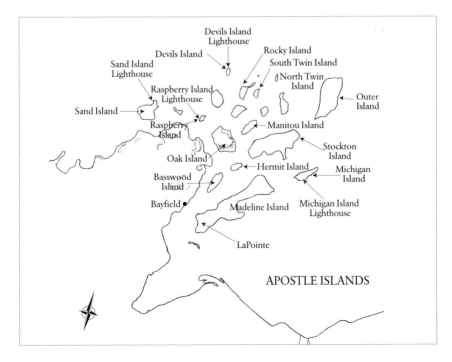

Once home to Ojibwe and Sioux, the islands were christened the Apostles by Jesuit missionaries in the 1600s. Their shores gained prominence during the fur trade and later thrived with commercial fishing, logging, farming, and brownstone quarrying. Six light stations were built on the islands between 1857 and 1901. Today the Apostle Islands Cruise Service offers excursions to lighthouses, sea caves, abandoned quarries, and the Manitou fish camp, a preserved fishing camp from the 1930s and '40s. Hiking, camping, canoeing, kayaking, scuba diving and excellent sport fishing are all preferred activities at the Apostle Islands National Lakeshore. Apostle Island National Lakeshore, Bayfield, WI (715) 779-3397. Web site: www.nps.gov/apis

MICHIGAN ISLAND LIGHTHOUSE

Waiting in Terror

For Chicago-raised Anna Carlson, it was a trial to live in a location as remote as Michigan Island lighthouse in the late nineteenth century, "I was always afraid to be alone on the island... the stark loneliness of it was appalling." One winter's day in 1891, Anna was left alone at the lighthouse with her three small children, while her husband, Robert (the lightkeeper), his brother and the dogs went ice fishing. Robert promised Anna they would be back by evening.

The weather worsened, night fell and the men did not return. The next day, chores kept Anna from her terror. Getting milk for her two-year-old child and nine-month-old twins meant dealing with the cow, her husband's job. Afraid the cow would kick her, Anna axed a hole through the stall, and milked her through the opening.

Her chores finished, Anna returned to the house to wait. She waited all through the second day and night. "On the third day I could stand it no longer... I fell to the floor, screaming. I screamed at the top of my voice, until I was exhausted... I think if I had not screamed I would have lost my mind."

Believing her husband dead, Anna now began to face the fact that she and her children were trapped there on the island. In

Anna Carlson, a city girl, recalled being alone at the lighthouse, "On the third day I could stand it no longer... I screamed at the top of my voice, until I was exhausted."

fact, her husband Robert was alive and suffering his own miserable ordeal. The wind had picked up unexpectedly, breaking up the ice where the men were fishing. Trapped on a small floe, their bodies became sails for the gale-force wind. For hours their ice-raft drifted on the black frigid water. Night came, and mercifully they were blown toward Madeline Island where the floes collided against the shore. The men jumped from floe to floe with desperate effort. By the time they reached land, the dogs' paws were bleeding.

They found a fisherman's shanty and built a fire, boiling up some flour and water, their only nourishment for three days. Carlson paced the beach, tormented with worry about his wife and children. On the third day he came across an old boat. They did their best to patch and caulk it and then rowed and dragged it home, eight stormy miles across the ice. They had been missing for four days. Badly frost bitten, it took the men two weeks to recover. The Carlsons never spent another winter on the island.

The Apostles' first lighthouse, the conical stone white-washed structure, was completed on Michigan Island in 1857. This lighthouse had originally been intended for Long Island, but the site was changed to Michigan Island at the last minute. A lighthouse was put into use on Long Island the following year, and the Michigan Island light discontinued until 1869 when it was put back into use. In 1929, a 112-foot steel skeleton tower was erected near the first Michigan Island light to address the inadequacy of its beam. (This second tower was moved from its original location at Schooner's Ledge on the Delaware River.)

R)Lightkeeper Robert Carlson was trapped on ice floes for days. L) The Carlson children

Above) The first Michigan Island light-house was erected in 1857. It had originally been intended for Long Island.

Above) Anna & Robert Carlson and their grown children
Left) The higher second tower was added in 1929 to make the beam more visible to ships.

MADELINE ISLAND

From the Voice of the Shell

On Madeline Island, with its rich stands of birch, aspen, balsam and spruce, a large Ojibwe village once thrived. In fact, in Ojibwe history, Madeline Island is one of the most important islands on Lake Superior. Hundreds of years ago, the Ojibwe lived by the "Saltwater Sea" in the St. Lawrence region. Following the directions of a sacred Megis shell (cowrie shell), they began a slow pilgrimage west to the Great Lakes. Here they split into three groups: the Ottawa inhabited Manitoulin Island in the Lake Huron region; the Potawatomi, the Southern Michigan region; and the Lake Superior Ojibwe, the Superior region. The shell guided the Ojibwe (or Chippewa) to Bawating, where the rapids flowed from Lake Superior, and whitefish were abundant. Today Bawating is the twin cities of Sault Ste. Marie, where massive locks have carved away much of these rapids.

Around 1490, once again following the Megis, a group travelled west from Bawating along Superior's southern shore, eventually settling on Madeline Island, and on the mainland. There were long years of war with the Ojibwe's enemies, the Fox and Sioux, over disputed territory. For over one hundred years, Madeline Island was a refuge from these mainland wars. But the community on Madeline Island also suffered its own internal threats.

Windigo, a giant skeletal spectre, roamed through the Ojibwe winter creating terror in its wake. Windigo was a horrifying sight with sunken eyes and bones protruding though ash-grey flesh, rotting lips tattered by its gnashing teeth. On the verge of perpetual starvation, it craved human flesh and blood. To the Ojibwe, Windigo represented the horror of starvation, a real possibility in any severe winter.

A sacred conch shell guided the Ojibwe to the Great Lakes from the "Salt Sea."

*John & Susan
Johnston*

One particularly brutal winter brought Windigo to Madeline Island. The daemon possessed a number of respected healers from the powerful healing society, the Midéwiwin. Under Windigo's power, these shamans began to terrorize the people, killing their children. The victims' souls had begun to haunt the island when someone finally killed these possessed men. From 1620, the Ojibwe stayed clear of Madeline Island.

The first French fur traders entered the Superior region in the late 1600s. Superior's first trading post was built on Madeline Island around 1693. The island was known as La Pointe. The post proved lucrative, drawing many Ojibwe back to their ancestral home. But the French post met its end abruptly in 1761 when a voyageur murdered the clerk and his family over the winter, and angry fur traders ransacked the post.

After the Seven Years' War, the 1763 Treaty of Paris handed over vast tracts of North American territory from the French to the British. The Lake Superior natives had been strongly allied with the French, and did not welcome or trust British traders. One of the first newcomers to La Pointe Island was Belfast émigré, John Johnston. He came as a greenhorn fur trader, and had a rough start when his five hired voyageurs stole his boat, fishing net and supplies. But Wabojeeg, the sympathetic chief of the La Pointe band, sheltered Johnston for the winter and during those months, Johnston and the chief's daughter, Susan (Oshauguscodaywayqua), fell in love. Wabojeeg refused to sanction the marriage, having seen too many transient traders abandon their Indian brides. The Chief told Johnston to return to Montreal. Wabojeeg would bless the union only if Johnston returned to La Pointe still committed to his daughter. When Johnston finally returned, he and Susan began a long and successful life together at Sault Ste. Marie, MI.

Superior's southern coast became American territory at the end of the Revolutionary War (1776-1783). The American Fur Company played an important role on Madeline Island until the mid-1800s. Around 1830, the Company moved the post and surrounding village to where the town of La

Treaty payments at La Pointe

Pointe is today. There was a mission north of the old French Fort for a time, but in 1854, most of the Ojibwe moved to the Red Cliff and Bad River Reservations on the mainland.

For a fascinating view of the changing eras of Madeline Island's history, from its early years to twentieth century tourism, visit the Madeline Island Historical Museum (715) 747-2415, (madeline@win.bright.net). Island ferries leave from Bayfield (715) 747-2051.

SOUTH TWIN AND ROCKY ISLANDS

Fishing Stations

Over the Norwegian fisherman's tool shed hung a sign, "JA VI HAR DET GODT EN AMERIKA (Yes, we have it good in America). AND IT COULD BE BETTER." ...and new immi-grant, Lenus Jacobson, was in a hurry to make it better.

Jacobsen was in the second wave of about 185,000 Norwegians who arrived in the U.S. in the late 1800s. Many of these young men were leaving a bleak coastal life. The newcomers were called "fishermen without boats" and many, like Jacobson, assisted fishermen, living in small shacks and eating with the fishermen and their families.

Lenus Jacobson was one of the Norwegian immi-grants who settled at the Apostles. Fishermen hired immigrants like Jacobson as assistants.

Lenus Jacobson shocked fellow fishermen by purchasing South Twin Island and charging them rent. Taking on airs, he also began donning a suit for the fish tug's arrival at South Twin.

Early morning, rain or shine, they headed out in sailboats (which were later fitted with engines). Independent fishermen could sell their fish to the highest bidder. Those who were "tied up to Booth" could only sell to Booth Fisheries, the most powerful fish company on the Great Lakes. (Alfred Booth extended credit to fishermen who, in order to repay their debts, had to sell their fish to Booth.)

The fishermen at South Twin knew each other well. They had simple rules. They always fished in the same area. If a man moved on, that area was free for the taking. Up until 1931, the Island's owners, the Willeys, allowed the men to squat on their land. Then everything changed.

Landlord of South Twin, Lenus Jacobson

Booth Fisheries head office in Duluth. Alfred Booth controlled the commercial fishing industry on the Great Lakes. Note the sign for Booth's mail steamer, the H.R. Dixon. *The* Dixon *is a now a shipwreck off Michipicoten Island.*

Lenus Jacobson put on his best suit, boarded the train for Minneapolis, and headed straight for the home of Samuel and Marie Willey. $975.00 later and Jacobson was the sole owner of South Twin. He started charging rents. It is said that in one year the yearly rent jumped from $25 to $300. Jacobson began to take on airs. He even wore a suit when the Booth tug came to pick up the fish. Jacobson's behaviour was too much to swallow. The fishermen left for Rocky Island, leaving Lenus Jacobson alone on South Twin.

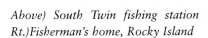

Above) South Twin fishing station
Rt.)Fisherman's home, Rocky Island

DEVILS ISLAND

The embankment of caves and vaulted chambers along Devils Island's shore is an extraordinary sight, at once powerful and terribly fragile. Sculpted from reddish brown bands of coloured sandstone, the web of caves is filled with emerald green water. Large waves roll in with strange, moaning sounds. The specific origin of the island's name is unknown, but other islands along the lake's eastern shore, such as Devil's Warehouse and Devil's Chair, had Ojibwe associations with the half human, half manitou, Nanaboozho. Nanaboozho was sent by the Creator to teach the Ojibwe how to live well. Like all humans, he learned as he went along. He was known to be foolish and silly, yet he gave the Ojbwe revered gifts such as the pipe of peace and fire. It is believed that Devils Island may also have been an important Ojibwe site.

Top) Devils Island light-house
Left) Sandstone caves of Devils Island

HERMIT ISLAND

The Enigma of a Recluse

"Some sad, overwhelming secret clouded his life, and it died with him," begins an 1891 tale about Wilson, the hermit of Hermit Island. Virtually nothing is known for sure about the recluse who hid himself away on this island in Lake Superior. His name may not have been Wilson at all. All that is really known of the Hermit Island hermit is speculation, for indeed, he was the object of untold speculation.

"He came from no one knew where," one account proclaimed, while another specified, "He was born in 1792, in Canada of Scottish parents." It's likely he lived on Hermit Island toward the mid-19th century, about the time that pioneers, immigrants and adventurers were making their way westward.

Because mystery demands a man who is larger than life, Wilson was portrayed an adventurer (1953): "Wilson went into the wilderness whenever he felt like it. He lived with the Indians, fought them, and took part in various wars until his name became a terror to some of the western tribes. He learned every trick of woodcraft, warfare and frontier survival."

Most of the accounts agree that Wilson was a fur trader who roamed the wilds all the way to the Pacific. And most of the versions focus his story on the anguish of lost love. "One day a friend found him sleeping beside his cabin," claimed the 1891 account. "Out of his dreams he awoke, and in an agonizing cry he uttered one word... 'Estelle!'"

The identity of his "lost love" deepens the mystery. In one tale, at the age of 18 "he ran away from home, deserting a young French girl he was to have married." In another, "he had a wife and daughter at L'Anse, in upper Michigan, who he took out to the Columbia River and there deserted. Later, repenting of this cruelty, he sought to reclaim them and found they had been murdered."

Purchased by developers in 1909, plans were made to turn the island into a cottage resort with a commerical orchard and forest reserve. Wilson would not have been pleased.

Desertion. A murdered wife and daughter. In the 1953 account, he loses his true love to someone else:

> Even in the midst of adventure, thoughts of his Canadian home, of his aged parents, and of the girl he had deserted so heartlessly must have preyed on his mind... He must see them again... It took two years... When he walked up the path to his parents' house there were no familiar faces to greet him. His mother and father were dead. His deserted sweetheart...had married a well-to-do farmer and was the mother of a large family. ...[His parents] left what property they had for him... It was a large sum of gold.

Gold. Wilson surely had gold when he hid away on Hermit Island, "Gossip said he had a treasure of gold hidden there... At times curious Indians wanted to get into his living place to search... Wilson frightened them away with a loaded rifle and ill-omened shouts..."

In summer, Wilson tended a vegetable garden. His only company was his dogs and chickens. In winter he made barrels and sold them to fishermen. Once or twice a year he headed to the mainland for supplies. Some say he paid with Mexican silver dollars. He bought a good horde of whiskey.

The death of the hermit was as mysterious as his life. It may have been linked with rumours of a hidden treasure, as the 1891 account hints: "He died in terrible agony and his story died with him. The Indians found him, and they also found buried underneath the fireplace over 300 Mexican silver dollars." Another version is more specific: "He had undoubtedly been murdered... evidently by parties in search of his wealth. There was evidence of a violent death struggle, crude furniture broken, the trunk empty, money bags missing."

All that is ultimately known is that a sad recluse lived and died on Hermit Island. Not even his cabin remains.

APOSTLES & BROWNSTONE QUARRYING

By 1870, the brownstone industry on Apostle Islands was flourishing. Brownstone buildings were all the rage, as growing cities and towns imitated the New York City fashion. The stone had become a symbol of modernity, permanence and dignity, and the invention of steam cutting meant that middle-class row house owners could now afford it.

Apostle Islands stone was submitted to the Smithsonian Institute for testing. Excellent laboratory results won the quarry on Basswood Island the contract to supply the new courthouse in Milwaukee with brownstone. It is

New Yorker Frederick Prentice began Excelsior Quarry on Hermit Island. The consummate promoter, in 1892 he spent about $80,000 to cut the world's largest brownstone obelisk (109 feet high) for the Chicago World's Fair. (Unfortunately, shipping costs were too high and the obelisk was never sent.)

listed on the National Register of Historic Places in recognition of this distinction. Quarries active on the Apostle Islands between 1869 and 1898 include: Superior Brownstone Co., Strong French and Co. Quarry, Bass Island Brownstone Co. (Basswood Island); Excelsior Brownstone Co. (Hermit Island), and Ashland Brownstone Co. (Stockton Island). The industry died out around 1893, as attention turned to steel and concrete.

As a gift to his new wife, Frederick Prentice built an opulent cedar bark cottage on Hermit Island. In 1892, a newspaper columnist wrote, "...entirely veneered in cedar bark... coquettish balconies are all entwined with the rustic beauty of cedar limbs... the [fireplace] mantels are of brownstone, handsomely and artistically carved to represent the limbs of a tree." (Sadly, the story goes that Prentice's wife was not thrilled with the rustic charm.) Nothing survives of the building.

The Bass Island Brownstone Company quarry on Basswood employed 100 men during peak season, and about 25 over the winter. The winter proved too isolating for Swedish immigrants who often crossed the ice to Bayfield. The Bayfield newspaper reported their toasting to each other's health: "numerous exclamations of yaverly, labona, Stockholm, and King Georgia" suggested the "salubrious effect of John Barleycorn." By spring, the same newspaper was through pondering their exotic toasts, listing instead their drunken brawls.

Quarry managers learned that hiring families kept workers content in isolated conditions. On Basswood Island, many of the women worked as cooks. The first baby was born at the quarry in December 1871.

RASPBERRY ISLAND LIGHTHOUSE

How Francis Jacker Got His Assistant

As keeper of the Raspberry Island light, Francis Jacker had implored his boss for an assistant. The government expected—unofficially of course—that wives would work for free. Jacker refused. His wife did not belong "on this godforsaken island." On September 13, 1887, being alone on the light almost cost Jacker his job. And his life.

The day dawned dark and moody. A squall was coming. Concerned for his sailboat, Jacker made his way down the clay bank below the lighthouse, cursing the dock that was completely unprotected. He had to sail the boat to the safety of the boathouse nearly a mile to the west.

As he readied the boat, the wind picked up. He hoisted the sail and the gusts blew him hard in the opposite direction. Then the centreboard jammed. Unable to control the boat, he flew out of control across the water. As large swells threatened to engulf his tiny craft, Jacker started to panic. The gale was blowing him straight toward the rocky tip of Oak Island. Would the island save him? Or would he be dashed to bits upon the rocks?

Luck was on his side. As he was blown toward the island, the boat foundered on a small reef. Jacker was tossed into the pounding surf and pummeled onto the sandy shore. The lake water gushed from his lungs, and gasping for air, Jacker somehow struggled to his feet. Oak Island was

Raspberry Island fog plant

Francis Jacker, lightkeeper at Raspberry light in 1887, nearly lost his job when he was swept away from his post during a storm.

deserted. He huddled by some overhanging rocks, looking out into the storm. Night came on, and Jacker was suddenly aware that there was no one at the lighthouse. The tower loomed dark against the black sky, and Jacker feared a shipping disaster.

The next day Mrs. Jacker caught a tugboat to the island, only to find no sign of her husband, and no sailboat. She spent that day in terror. At night she lit the lighthouse lamp, but she could not operate the revolving mechanism. The keeper, marooned on Oak Island, was relieved to see the lighthouse glow but his anxiety remained. Raspberry was a rotating light. If fog rolled in, a fixed light could confuse a mariner.

On the morning of the third day, Jacker came down to the beach, hoping he might spot a passing boat. The tugboat had gone searching for Jacker on the islands, and it wasn't long before the captain spied him standing forlorn on the beach.

Having left the lighthouse dark almost cost Jacker his job. But his wife's quick action and his own suffering put his boss in a lenient mood. He agreed at last that the job was too much for one person. Jacker finally got his assistant.

The lighthouse was built to service the increased shipping to the city of Bayfield resulting from the new locks at Sault Ste. Marie. Completed in 1863 (and extensively remodelled in 1906) the white clapboard structure is now preserved by the National Park Service as part of the Apostle Islands National Lakeshore. Rangers provide guided tours of the light station during the summer.

SAND ISLAND LIGHTHOUSE

The Ship that Ripped in Two

The sturdy *Sevona* had hauled ore through the rough waters of the Great Lakes for over a decade without mishap. But, in 1904, new owner, James McBrier, wanted more. He ordered the big ship to be made bigger still. It was cut in half, and a new seventy-three foot mid-section was added, making it an impressive 373 feet long. On September 1, 1905, it steamed away from Allouez, Wisconsin, into the swells of Lake Superior, the pride of the McBrier fleet. It was pride before the fall.

On board the *Sevona* were a crew of twenty-four, and two young women, guests of Captain Donald McDonald. Below were tons of iron ore. Miss Kate Spencer and Miss Lillian Jones leaned against the deck rail, delighting in the surge of the freighter as it pushed out into open water. At dinner, Miss Spencer sipped red wine from her crystal goblet as she took in the elegance of the oak-panelled, sky-lit dining room. She smiled appreciatively at the captain, enjoying the surprising luxury of what was, after all, a freighter.

At 9 p.m. Miss Spencer and Miss Jones bid the captain good night. Returning to their cabins, they had to

Made of local brownstone, the impressive Sand Island lighthouse was completed in 1881. It was automated in 1921 with the installation of an acetylene light operated by an automatic timer. Today the light is preserved by the Apostle Islands National Lakeshore and is open to the public in the summer.

hold their long skirts down as they billowed up in the strong wind. By midnight the gale was crashing waves over the bow.

The rain started pounding at 2 a.m. Captain McDonald figured they were nearing the Apostles, and veered southeast in hopes of sheltering there. According to Miss Spencer's later account, the captain woke the young women, asking them "to put breakable stuff in a secure place as when the boat put about she would toss badly."

Only a few miles away on Sand Island, lighthouse keeper Emmanuel Luick intently scanned the dark rough seas for signs of distress. By 4 a.m. the storm had grown worse and the bow was taking on water. The Captain ordered sailors to rig a lifeline and to take the women aft, closer to the lifeboats. The women pulled themselves along through waist-high surf and took refuge in the dining room.

Close to 6 a.m. the captain strained to see the lights of either Sand or Raspberry Islands through sheets of rain, but only darkness greeted him. Atop his lighthouse Emmanuel Luick signalled to the blind, careening ship. With a sickening shudder, another and finally a third ghastly crunch, the *Sevona* came to a halt on the shoal off Sand Island.

Suddenly at rest amid the chaos of the storm, Captain McDonald assessed the devastation. The rocks had ripped a huge hole in the bow. But what was worse, the ship had cracked in two. The captain and six of his crew were cut off from the others on the stern. And they were cut off from the lifeboats. Foaming breakers surged around the jagged edges of the severed ship. Struggling to be heard above the roar, the captain hollered orders through a megaphone to those stranded astern.

In September 1905, the Sevona *hit a shoal*

Chief Engineer William Phillipi took charge of the stern. He pulled the women from the lifeboat and returned them to the dining room below deck, where they huddled together watching the water rise inch by inch. Shards of glass came showering upon them as the surf smashed through the skylight. As Miss Spencer pulled back from the cascade, she felt the wall bulge at her back. She pulled away in terror as the wood paneling gave way to a great geyser of water.

The Sevona *broke in two, separating the crew.*

On the bow, a sailor blew the whistle in a futile call for help. Emmanuel Luick looked on helplessly as flares shot into the air in a final desperate signal. As water flooded into the gaping hull, Captain McDonald and the six men stranded on the bow worked frantically to build a raft from hatch covers and doors.

Sand Island light-keeper Emmanuel Luick and his wife Oramill. Luick stood in the tower and helplessly watched the Sevona's *crew struggle for their lives.*

Emmanuel Luick

In the *Sevona's* stern, "everything seemed to be breaking at once," recalled Kate Spencer. "By order of the Chief Engineer we took to the small boat again. One by one we piled in, leaving six men behind us. I never heard such a heart-rending cry as came from those six: 'For God's sake, don't leave us!'" Chief Engineer Phillipi ushered those six into the second lifeboat, and both were lowered into the giant seas. They bobbed along as helplessly as corks. A one-armed crewman in the second boat pulled off his cap, bailing obsessively. His life seemed to hinge upon that motion.

Minutes rolled into hours. The wind seized the first boat and drove it toward the Wisconsin mainland. Cliffs and sharp rocks threatened overhead. Finally picked up in the surge of giant breakers, the boat was hurled upon the sand. Safe at last. The second boat landed on the beach at Sand Island. The lifeboat passengers had barely clambered out onto the sand when the next wave hit the beach and smashed the boat to bits.

Former Lieutenant Governor of Wisconsin, Samuel Fifield, built the Sevona Memorial Cottage on Sand Island from timber salvaged from the wreck. The cottage is still standing.

Sand Island group

On the mainland, a farmer directed the eleven survivors of the first boat to the closest shelter, a lumberman's cabin two miles away. Concerned about the captain and six men left on the *Sevona's* bow, Phillipi and the lumberman set out to find help in Bayfield, the nearest town. The road was so strewn with uprooted trees that it took almost all day to get there. Once in Bayfield, Phillipi found fifteen men to assist him in the rescue. A tug took them through the gale-force winds to the disaster site. As they neared the reef, to Phillipi's sinking horror, all that he could see was the twisted length of stern. The bow of the *Sevona* had vanished, without a sign of captain, crew, or raft.

Only Emmanuel Luick at the Sand Island lighthouse had seen their fate. He had watched breathless as the men climbed onto their raft, just as the bow gave way into the seas. Smashed by massive waves, the seven clung to their raft as it was pushed toward Sand Island. It looked like they might make it. But the raft could not withstand the power of the breakers. Luick watched aghast as the raft was hammered into pieces. All seven men were washed under to their deaths.

It took almost a week for the battered bodies to wash ashore. Captain McDonald's pockets no longer held the $1,500 he'd been carrying for ship's business. The money was believed lost in the storm until wads of water-soaked bills started turning up in Bayfield stores and pubs. Three shady spendthrifts were arrested for stealing money from a dead man.

Today the remains of the *Sevona* lie in depths between 20-25 ft. (6-7.5m). The prime features are twisted stern and the strewn cargo of iron ore. Interestingly, underwater archaeological investigations in the early 1990s showed that the boat did not break apart at the joint where the vessel was lengthened, as had been commonly speculated. It is one of eight wrecks that the islands offer diving enthusiasts.

ISLE ROYALE

If Lake Superior is the shape of a wolf head, then Isle Royale forms its eye. This is a unique, 45-mile-long (72-km) island archipelago of relatively untouched wilderness. Fringed by chains of tiny islands, its fiord-like bays, ridges and valleys were formed over a billion years ago when the mid-continent of North America was ripped apart and vast quantities of volcanic material gushed to the surface. After about 200 million years of intermittent volcanism, the massive scar that stretches from Lake Superior into eastern Kansas was gradually covered by sediment.

Isle Royale shares the same mineral composition as the great thumb of Precambrian rock on the Keweenaw Peninsula, the region containing the largest deposits of pure copper in the world. During the Ice Ages, glaciers exposed the ore by scraping away the surrounding bedrock. As early as 2500 B.C., aboriginal peoples used stone hammers to mine the copper veins. At Isle Royale's Minong Edge lie the archeological remains of thousands of these open pit mines. In historic times, Isle Royale has seen many groups pass through: Ojibwe, miners, trappers, loggers, fishermen and lighthouse keepers and their families.

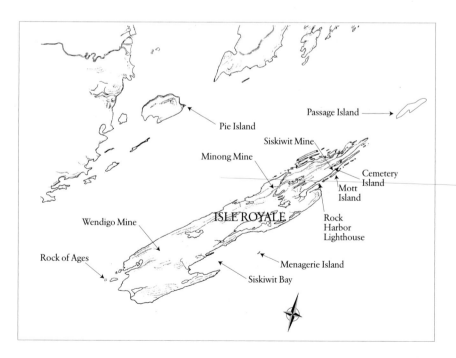

Steamer South American *with some of the 1,000 guests for the official dedication of* Isle Royale National Park, August 1946

Today Isle Royale National Park protects and preserves this wilderness environment, including moose, beaver and wolves. Visitors can enjoy hiking on this enormous island, the second largest on the Great Lakes. The park offers camping, sport fishing, kayaking, canoeing and scuba diving. For those wishing a more relaxed stay, the Rock Harbor Lodge perched on the edge of the lake, offers a magnificent view of Superior. Ferries to Isle Royale leave from Grand Portage, Copper Harbor and Houghton, Michigan. Isle Royale National Park, Houghton, MI: (906) 482-0984. Rock Harbor Lodge—summer: (906) 337-4993. Winter: (502) 773-2191.

ROCK OF AGES LIGHTHOUSE

Rescuing the Steamer Cox

Rock of Ages, cleft for me,
Let me hide myself in thee.

On the night of May 27, 1933, the steamship, *George M. Cox*, pushed its way through thick fog on the frigid waters of Lake Superior. The passengers on this maiden voyage were bound for the Chicago World's Fair. At 6:20 p.m., in the midst of an elegant dinner, a sudden crash brought china and crystal smashing to the floor. So began the chaos and the terror.

Rock of Ages is a tiny but treacherous reef that rises out of the water 3 miles (5 kms) west of Lake Superior's Isle Royale. In the late 1800s, its jagged shores claimed the sidewheeler, *Cumberland*, and the steam barge, *Henry Chisholm*. A lighthouse was critical. Soaring an impressive ten storeys, Rock of Ages lighthouse is an engineering feat. In order to withstand 30-foot waves, walls at the base of the tower are four and a half feet

thick. Imported from France, the lens for the light was more than nine feet tall, the largest on the Great Lakes.

These features were comforting for those on the water. As for the lightkeepers... "What a place! What a life for a man!" exclaimed keeper John Soldenski when he was first dropped off at Rock of Ages in 1931. The barren rock was barely wide enough for him to stretch his legs. But the tower's 120-foot spiral staircase provided plenty of exercise. (The former keeper had fallen to his death on these same stairs only months earlier.)

Lightkeeper John Soldenski watched from the lanternroom as the Cox *maintained its deadly course.*

The 300-foot-long George M. Cox *had a ballroom and was to have featured live bands with showgirls. After the* Cox *foundered, 120 passengers and crew spent the night crammed on the spiral steps of Rock of Ages lighthouse.*

At the time of Soldenski's posting, Rock of Ages was considered too bleak and remote for keepers' wives. By 1933 Soldenski persuaded the U.S. Lighthouse Service to permit his wife to join him. On the night of May 27, 1933, both he and his wife were in the lanternroom. As they anxiously surveyed the fog blanketed beneath the beam of light, they were praying for the ship gliding toward them.

The *George M. Cox* (formerly the *Puritan*) was built in 1901, about the same time as the Rock of Ages lighthouse. In 1932, entrepreneur George M. Cox refurbished—and renamed—the vessel. His plan was to ferry customers from Fort William on Lake Superior to the "Century of Progress Exposition," opening in Chicago the following year. "We have spared no effort to provide the last word in comfort, luxury, service and entertainment," Cox proclaimed to the dockside crowd in Houghton, Michigan, on the eve of the maiden voyage.

The ship's new coat of white paint gleamed in the sun. The horn blew. The crowd cheered. A plume of smoke trailed from the stack as the *Cox* pulled away from the dock. Lake Superior was serene that afternoon in

On the tiny shoal, a two-storey foundation was drilled into solid rock to allow Rock of Ages lighthouse to withstand storm waves as high as 30 feet.

May. But as the *Cox* neared Isle Royale, thick grey tendrils of mist entwined themselves around the ship. As the dinner hour approached, Captain George M. Johnson ordered that the fog whistle be sounded every sixty seconds. For more than an hour, he tried to get his bearings, watching anxiously for the Rock of Ages light to guide them through the reefs.

Atop the Rock of Ages lighthouse, John Soldenski and his wife watched transfixed. Under a strange blue sky, two steamer masts pierced the low-lying fog and headed toward the rock. Soldenski frantically blasted the foghorn, but the boat kept to her deadly course.

Aboard the *Cox*, Captain Johnson strained to hear the lighthouse whistle. But it was too late. Not yet aware of the impending danger, passengers sat down to a fine dinner. At 6:20 p.m. the *Cox* hit the Rock of Ages, throwing dishes and passengers in all directions. "I saw a heavy buffet table slide across the floor and crash into other tables," the ship's nurse, Adeline Keeling, later reported.

Within minutes of the crunch against the reef, Soldenski had his motor launch roaring into the fog. By the time he reached the doomed vessel, passengers and crew had rushed starboard high out of the water. Many were being lowered in lifeboats from the port side. Soldenski towed the boats, and it was not long before everyone on board had been safely pulled ashore. The Rock of Ages light had never had so many guests, cramped one per step spiraling up the lighthouse staircase.

The lightkeeper transported four seriously injured passengers to a freighter that had responded to the *Cox's* S.O.S. Within twenty-four hours all the other survivors were back on mainland, resting in Houghton's best hotel. The *Cox's* captain and first mate were found guilty of reckless navigation and stripped of their licences.

A salvage crew found the entire hull that was torn out by the reef. Remarkably, the *George M. Cox* perched there for months until an October storm took her to the bottom of the lake. The wreck of the *George M. Cox* has become one of the most popular scuba diving sites on Lake Superior. She lies less than a mile from the wrecks *Cumberland* and *Chisholm* in depths of 15-85 ft. (4.5-25m).

MENAGERIE ISLAND LIGHTHOUSE

The Malone Family

Off the south shore of Isle Royale, a ridge rises above of the pounding waves. It is Menagerie Island, desolate, treeless, with shallow reefs that make it virtually inaccessible. The island once had a dock, but the stormy power of Lake Superior washed it away. Today, a small boat can land here when the weather is calm. Coast Guard boats occasionally come by to service the Isle Royale lighthouse.

In 1875, Will Stevens was the island's first keeper. Although he had been provided with a spacious stone house and a good stock of provisions, Stevens could not endure the lonely rigours of the job and he soon vacated the post.

In the late 1800s, the island was home to a veritable human menagerie—the offspring of Julia and John Henry Malone, the keepers of the light. When he transferred to Menagerie Island, John Malone had been keeping the lighthouse at Portage Entry on the Keweenaw Peninsula. When he moved to Menagerie in 1878, Malone was 33 and single. His boss at the U.S. Lighthouse Service preferred to employ a married man on

Julia and John Malone encircled by the eleven children they raised on Menagerie Island. The boys were named after lighthouse inspectors.

such an isolated post. So Malone sailed into the port of Hancock, Michigan, looking for a wife.

"Mrs. Malone came here today," Malone's logbook states on July 25, 1880. His new wife, Julia Shea, was all of twenty when she took up residence on Menagerie, the first of thirty-two summers on the windswept island. Her strong mettle would soon be tested.

Within a year, Julia gave birth to a son. Over the next fifteen years, the Malones had three girls and eight boys who lived to adulthood and they spent every summer together on the tiny rock. One of the sailors aboard the lighthouse tender said, "There was a new little face behind the rocks every spring."

In the spring, John Henry Malone he began storing up enough food to see them through the season. They also ate Lake Superior whitefish and trout, salted and fresh. And there were the eggs gathered from the rocks. "The sea gulls commenced laying their eggs," Malone wrote on May 13, 1885. Over the next ten days, they had gathered over a thousand eggs, eating many, and selling the rest to sailors to supplement their annual income of $620. "Lighthouse keepers eat gull eggs scrambled, with onions," recounted a local sailor. "You can't eat gull eggs plain. Onions kill the taste." Onions wouldn't grow on the rock, so the Malones bought them with the money from the eggs.

Winter brought pounding storms waves, coating the island in thick layers of shimmering ice. The rocks became strange creatures, blue silver in the winter light. Then the snow fell in great billows and drifts. The wintery days were measured out in coal. Coal fires kept the family warm. Filling the coal scuttle. Lifting the heavy iron cover on the stove top. Watching the shiny black lumps rattle down to join the glowing embers below. These were central daily events in the Malones' housebound world. Confinement made the house—and Julia Malone's patience—shrink day by day.

The end of the season was a trial: "The island looks like an iceberg aground," wrote John as early as November 16, 1884. "We have to cut the ice off the walkways every day to be sure we can launch our boat." They left to spend the winter of 1884 in Duluth. For many years to follow, they wintered in Superior, Wisconsin. But every spring the family returned, usually toting a new baby. Sterling. Folger. Reed. They named their boys after lighthouse inspectors.

In 1910, at the age of sixty-five and after 32 years of tending the Menagerie light, John Malone was transferred to a lighthouse near Detroit. He was paid $68 less per year at his new post. His son, John Albert, took over as keeper on Menagerie. The light was automated in 1914 and the last Malone left the island for good.

Menagerie Island lighthouse

ISLE ROYALE

Survival

On a bright clear morning in November 1874, the MacGuire brothers set out in a sailboat from the Keweenaw Peninsula on the southern shore. They had planned to sail past Isle Royale seventy miles to the new Canadian town of Port Arthur. It was an ambitious course for the late fall season.

After hours of smooth sailing, black clouds scudded across the sky from the northwest. Soon a blizzard raged, waves cresting in the boat. Blinded by the swirling snow, the brothers could no longer navigate and they travelled aimlessly until dawn. Suddenly a massive wave crushed the boat against the rocks. Strangely, the same wave also brought salvation. The elder MacGuire was standing in the boat when the breaker hit, lifting him into the air and then landing him gently on the shore. His younger brother rode the crest of another wave and, at the last moment, was pulled from the water by his brother.

Port Arthur was a rough and tumble town in 1870, but the brothers risked their lives to visit it.

Elder MacGuire carried his brother, chilled and in a state of shock, into the shelter of the woods. Luck had kept a box of matches dry. Soon the two brothers were lying on a bed of cedar and balsam boughs, before a roaring fire. The morning dawned clear and cold on Isle Royale. Leaving his younger brother by the fire, MacGuire hiked around the island and stumbled on an abandoned miner's camp. There he found a fireplace, some tools, a few tallow candles, and a bag of beans, food enough to buoy them. His younger brother was so seized up with rheumatism, MacGuire had to carry him to the camp. Boiled beans seasoned with melted candles, it seemed like manna from heaven. But his brother's recovery would take many weeks more and a lot more food.

Wendigo mine, c. 1870. Lost on Isle Royale in winter the brothers searched end-lessly for one of the Island's mining settlements.

MacGuire used thin strips of basswood bark to make snares, and soon the two brothers were feasting on rabbit.

That night snow fell. And the next. Before long a dense white blanket buried the cabin. They were going to need snowshoes. Elder MacGuire fashioned webs of wood fibers, lacing them to frames made of bent basswood branches. When his brother was strong enough, they strapped the frames onto their boots and travelled over snow that was now three feet deep. But the hell had just begun. They followed a whistle for a long time before they realized it was coming from the far off Canadian shore. They trekked the other way, trying to overcome their disappointment. Their pace was slow. The younger brother's strength faded frequently, forcing them to set up camp and rest for days.

One morning sitting by the fire, they heard the distant shrill of another whistle. They followed it, and lost it again, for days. Determined to find the whistle's source—and their salvation—they tramped for weeks through the dark woods. Their matches long since gone, a live coal in hemlock bark, kept them alive. As weeks turned to months, they lived on rabbits and melted snow.

One day in early February, they saw signs of civilization. Cut trees. A beaten trail. The whistle became clearer. The trail took them to the shore of Siskiwit Bay and to a house, smoke coming from its chimney. Their knock was answered by the manager of the Island Mine warehouse who stared at them like they were ghosts, with their straggly beards, gaunt, frost-bitten faces and tattered clothes.

Soon they were sitting by a blazing fire, mugs of hot grog in their hands, while the elder MacGuire mesmerized their host with details of their tale. Before too long, the brothers were working at the Island Mine waiting out the rest of the winter.

MOTT ISLAND

The Ordeal

In the winter of 1843, together Charlie and Angelique Mott suffered an ordeal that only Angelique lived to tell. In July of that year, Charlie and Angelique were hired to protect a copper claim by camping on tiny Mott Island, off the shore of Isle Royale. Dropped off on the lonely shore, they were promised supplies in a few weeks. And to be picked up in October when their job was done.

In the meantime, provisions were sparse: a barrel of flour, six pounds of rancid butter and a few beans. They fished with a net and a canoe. September came, with no sign of a supply boat. Their net broke and a storm swept away their canoe. October and then November passed and still not a soul appeared. Not a scrap of food was left. December brought the snow. The lake froze. They lost hope of rescue.

In a newpaper interview she gave in 1845, Angelique conveyed the anguish that they felt: "Nothing seemed left to us but sickness, starvation and death itself. All we could do was eat bark and roots and bitter berries that only seemed to make the hunger worse. Hunger is an awful thing. It eats you up so inside, and you feel so all gone, as if you must go crazy...."

Charlie grew weaker and lost heart. Around Christmas, crazed with fever, he seized a knife, and wheeled on his wife. He growled that he must

Angelique built this style of birch bark hut during her dreadful winter.

kill a sheep, that he must have something to eat. For hours Angelique watched him like a hawk, finally wresting the knife from him. Then the fever passed: "I saw him sink away and dry up until there was nothing left of him but skin and bones. At last he died so easily that I couldn't tell just when the breath did leave his body."

Angelique now struggled to survive alone, her husband's body beside her in the hut. "How could I bury him when the ground was frozen as hard as a rock? I could not bear to throw him out into the snow. For three days I remained with him in the hut, and it seemed almost like company, but I was afraid if I kept up the fire he would spoil." She decided to build a second lodge and leave him in the hut.

Occasionally Angelique visited her husband's frozen body. It was then she met her greatest fear. "The hunger raged so in my veins that I was tempted, oh how terribly I was tempted, to take Charlie and make soup of him...." At one point in her fight she saw rabbit tracks outside the hut. Tearing out a lock of her hair, she made a snare. The first rabbit trapped, Angelique was so hungry that she ripped off its skin and ate it raw.

Rabbits, faith, and an astonishing will to survive brought her through the endless winter. One morning in May she heard the firing of a gun. She almost fainted. On shaky legs, she ran to the shore. There was the man who had abandoned them ten months before. She led him to the hut where Charlie's body lay. "He saw that Charlie was dead... that I had not killed him but that he had died of starvation... He began to cry and to try to explain things... I thought his own conscience ought to punish him more than I could do."

MOTT ISLAND

The Plight of the Algoma

November 7, 1885, was a day both of triumph and tragedy for the Canadian Pacific Railway (CPR). The last spike of the transcontinental line was driven in British Columbia, marking the completion of an immense enterprise. And on that day, the *Algoma*, one of the CPR's impressive ocean-going steamships, foundered off Isle Royale.

The *Algoma* had been on the Great Lakes only a year. The ship's design was state-of-the-art, and could carry over 1,000 passengers. She had six watertight compartments, and was considered unsinkable. The *Algoma* was built in Scotland and sailed to Canada where she had to be cut in two to pass through the canals west of Montreal. In a strange twist of fate, she was once again cut in two, but this time by the force of Lake Superior.

The state-of-the-art Algoma *could accommodate over 1,000 passengers. Built in Scotland, she sailed to Canada where she was temporarily cut in two in order to pass through the canals west of Montreal.*

On Thursday November 5, the *Algoma* headed up Georgian Bay from Owen Sound, Ontario under a bright sky. It was late in the season so there were only a handful of passengers on board. Passing through the Soo locks Friday afternoon, Captain Moore was unfazed by the sudden shift in weather. Apart from the rain and sleet, gale-force tail winds were serving the ship well. Sails full, the ship was making record time.

By midnight they were fifty miles from Port Arthur. The rain changed to heavy snow, whipping against the ship so forcefully that Captain Moore was blinded. Fearing the rocks of Isle Royale, he lowered all but one small sail and steered the ship to open water. At 4:30 a.m. the stern struck rock. With a shuddering crunch, the rudder crumpled and the captain lost control. Huge waves pounded the ship, crushing most of the lifeboats. Captain Moore rushed through the ship ordering the steam valves open to prevent explosion. He rigged a rope along the deck, rushing the passengers along the lifeline to the stern.

One of the survivors, William McArthur, of Meaford, Ontario, was assisting the captain in the crisis: "Captain Moore alone remained cool and steady and showed just what a man he was. I was working beside him when a great sea burst brought the cabin crashing down on top of him. Captain Moore was pinned to the deck and fearfully hurt...."

McArthur and a few others struggled to free the captain and haul him to the stern. Heaving the 1,773-ton ship into the air, the huge waves then dropped it with tremendous force onto the rocks. The captain knew the *Algoma* would break in two. As McArthur described it, many were "swept away like feathers into the sea, crying vainly for help." Others hurled themselves into the water, hoping to reach shore, and were soon pummeled against the rocks. Those in the stern crouched together.

At 6 a.m. the ship broke in two. The front section plunged bow first into the lake and disappeared. The dozen survivors clung to the remaining piece of stern. At dawn a few crew members swung the last lifeboat into the water. The lifeboat was tossed around like driftwood in the massive waves, but the battered men made it to the shore, only sixty feet away. Those left on the stern were gripped by shock and cold, and by the endless motion of corpses caught in the surf. The gale was still too fierce to bring them in.

The storm did not subside until Sunday morning. Using their remaining strength to build a raft, the last survivors hauled themselves along the lifeline to the shore. Altogether there were fourteen survivors. Forty-five passengers and crew were killed. Today the steel wreckage of the *Algoma's* stern is strewn in three different areas. The bow section has never been located.

Algoma *debris deposited by the storm*

ISLE ROYALE
Copper Mining—An Ancient Tradition

Copper was mined on Isle Royale dating back at least 3,000 years. Ancient ancestors of the Ojibwe, Sioux, and Iroquois extracted the pure metal from rock using simple stone hammers. They fractured the bedrock by lighting fires on the rock and then dousing it with water. They would then hammer away at the exposed copper. Thousands of stone hammers, from three to sixty pounds, have been found on the island. Some mines are open pits, thirty feet long.

Archeologists have discovered jewelry made from Lake Superior copper as far south as Alabama and Florida. It is believed that these ancient peoples were part of an extensive trading network in which they traded metal for perishable items, like corn and hemp.

Seventeenth century French missionaries and explorers were so impressed by the magnitude of the copper deposits that they wrote that Isle Royale and other islands were made of copper. They heard Ojibwe stories about the giant serpent, Mishepeshu. As manitou of the underworld, Mishepeshu controlled copper, or miskwabik. Ojibwe considered copper sacred. They carried talismans, carefully wrapped and handed down through generations. An early 19th-century Ojibwe elder named Keatanang called copper "our hope and our protection. Through it I have caught many beavers and killed many bears... through it too I have always remained healthy."

In a treaty of 1842, the Ojibwe ceded Isle Royale to the United States. Within five years, entrepreneurs had rushed there, creating small mining communities and a modest copper rush that lasted until the late 1870s. During these years, the miners discovered many of the ancient native copper diggings, with stone hammers left alongside.

The next decades proved to be more trial than treasure. In 1850, one Lake Superior newspaper described the grim

Prehistoric miner and tools

Above) Wendigo Mine had boarding houses for the single men, and modest company houses for married miners and their families.
Left) Miner with head candle

working conditions a typical copper mine, "Ankle-deep in black, glue-like mud, with claustrophobic black walls, illuminated by feeble yellowish flicking candles, and separated from instant death by a few rotten props, the men breathed bad, humid air, while tearing fiercely at dripping, ragged rocks."

Sarah Barr Christian, wife of a mine superintendent, offered a glimpse of the island population in her journals written between 1874-75,

> Our miners were almost entirely Cornish people from Cornwall England. Quite a number of them had families... For surface work the men were mostly Scandinavians—Norwegian and Swedish... For the forest work... the Finnish men were mostly used... with all these young Scandinavian men my maid was soon... a miner's bride. She had about fifty stalwart young men to choose from, and I fear chose the least desirable.

Miners graveyard on Cemetery Island

Jane Masters came to the island in 1851 to join her husband who was working in the Siskiwit Mine. In her journal, she recorded the hardships of the winter of 1852: "For six weeks all of us had to subsist on bread and syrup, and so weak did the men become that the mine was closed."

Desperate for meat, twenty men devised a scheme to cross the lake to Fort William. They skidded across the ice in an improvised boat and sleigh. When they hit water, the sleigh and passengers were loaded in the boat. The men rowed until the ice prevented progress, and then they returned to the ice. Once they reached Fort William, the men loaded meat into the boat and covered it with balsam boughs for protection. They got back to the island only to find that the balsam had tainted the meat, making it inedible.

From 1845 to 1893, Isle Royale's 18 mines produced about 2 million pounds of copper. Today, on long side trails, hikers will find collapsed shafts that have been cordoned off. The moss-covered miner's graveyard on Cemetery Island is another remnant of this historic era.

In 1875, Sarah Barr Christian visited the nearby Minong Mine where she happened on an amazing, ancient find,

> There stood in a pit of sand a mass of pure copper... It stood fully six feet high... The "mass" obelisk was later removed by some interested party, who brought a freighter into the cove, with hoisting machine and necessary equipment... I suppose it went into the common melting pot, a smelter, along with insignificant bars and ingots. But I do wish it might have gone to the Smithsonian Institute. It was so beautiful, and a silent monument to a lost tribe.

In fact, this over 5,000-lb. copper mass was brought to Philadelphia's Centennial Exposition in 1876.

Discovered in 1874 near the Minong Mine, this over 5,000-lb. copper mass was brought to Philadelphia's Centennial Exposition in 1876. Miners as early as 2500 BC had hammered off most of the rough edges. When it was found, it was buried under 16 feet of debris, including broken prehistoric stone tools.

ISLANDS OF SUPERIOR NORTH SHORE

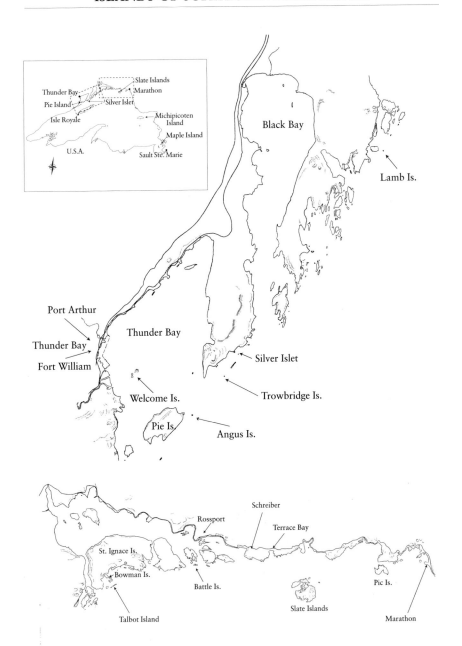

ANGUS ISLAND

The Doomed Monkshaven

1905 was a year renowned for storms on Lake Superior. After a three-day gale in November, fourteen ships were lost, their wreckage strewn along the shores.

The men on the steamer *Monkshaven* were lucky to survive. They had battled their way across the storming lake with a cargo of steel rails when suddenly Angus Island loomed out of the snow, dead ahead. One enormous wave lifted the vessel and brought it down upon a rocky outcropping, slicing the hull open like a can of stew. The *Monkshaven's* 21 men scrambled to nearby Angus Island where, for three days and nights in high winds and sub-freezing temperatures, they huddled beneath a crude shelter of boards and branches. Before them in the water, their doomed ship rolled and groaned with every wave. Several men went mad, unable to withstand the wind, noise, hunger and fear of dying from exposure.

On the fourth day, two men risked reboarding. They retrieved clothing, provisions and a lifeboat. Thirteen men rowed into the shipping lane and were rescued. The *Monkshaven* sat impaled at the edge of Angus Island for many years before it was finally sold for scrap.

The Monkshaven *aground on Angus Island*

PIE ISLAND

The Mermaid Sighting

Voyageurs at Dawn *by Frances Hopkins*

Thirty years had passed but Venant St. Germain recalled the evening clearly. It was 1782. St. Germain and three other voyageurs were returning to Fort Michilimackinac, when they stopped for the night at Isle Pâte (Pie Island). Their only passenger, an elderly Ojibwe woman from Grand Portage, crouched over the flames cooking. St. Germain had headed down to the water with a fishing net when he saw a human form bobbing—swimming like a fish—in the gentle waves.

St. Germain paused, and then cautiously approached, viewing the "animal" (as he called it) for approximately four minutes. The torso, visible above the water, looked like a child, maybe 7 or 8 years old. One arm was extended strangely in the air, the other hand resting on the hip. Its eyes were "extremely brilliant, head small but handsomely shaped, the mouth proportionate to the rest of the face, the complexion of a brownish hue." Alerted by St. Germain's stillness and fixed gaze, the others joined him. The creature stared back with what the group later described as "a mixture of unease and curiosity." Soon the little being vanished in the water.

The incident haunted St. Germain for years. Nearly thirty years later he stood before the Court of King's Bench in Montreal to sign an affidavit. *The Canadian Magazine* reprinted the deposition in 1824, claiming the testimony was proof of the existence of mermaids on Superior.

St. Germain's story was not the first to suggest the existence of mermaids on Superior. In the Ojibwe spirit world, mermaids and mermen—Nebaunaubaewuk and Nebaunaubaequaewuk—lured mortals to the watery depths, holding them captive until they eventually transformed into this half-human, half-fish being.

Pie Island

SILVER ISLET

The Battle of a Silver Mine

It was the summer of 1870 on Silver Islet. An ugly little island just 90 feet long (27 m), it would have been completely overlooked, if silver hadn't been discovered here. For the dozen immigrant workers, 18 hour days of bolting logs together was tedious, exhausting work. Under the supervision of Charles Palmer, civil engineer, they were assembling a crib and breakwater strong enough to protect the future mine shafts from Lake Superior. One of the new men surveyed the partially completed crib. It was going to be 13 feet thick! For weeks Superior had been a placid blue. The worker declared that the immense crib would be "overkill." The other men grinned. The newcomer had a lot to learn.

The savagery of the first October storm surprised everyone, especially engineer Palmer. He was sure his construction could withstand anything. Almost half of the breakwall had been ripped out. Rock and bent bolts were strewn everywhere as though Superior had spat them out in contempt. Even the 300-ton clay cofferdam, enclosing the silver vein, had been damaged. Palmer was stunned. How could he have so greatly underestimated the lake's power? He set about to rebuild, doubling the cribbing. He hoped that 26 feet would be wide enough. But he sensed the lake was not finished with him yet.

As an early Christmas present, Superior shredded huge portions of the breakwall. Then in March, the lake attacked again and again, ripping out

Bachelors lived on the island in three boarding houses. Other buildings included the shaft, engine, and rock houses, the pump house, blacksmith shop and library/saloon.

Silver Islet mine was exposed to Lake Superior's deadly autumn storms.

another massive section, and then destroying another 50,000 ft. (15,000 m) of timber cribbing. The mine managers kept building and expanding until the breakwall was 800 feet by 500 feet, and the tiny Silver Islet had grown to 10 times its original size!

To succeed in this location, the mine superintendent had to be tenacious. William Bell Frue was that and more. He was an inventor, speculator, manager, and engineer. The location was destined for fame and fortune he enthused, writing to an investor that "Silver Islet will be a paying mine long after you and I are moldering in our graves."

By the 1870s, from a distance, Silver Islet looked like a cluster of floating buildings. The mine had a work force of 480 men. Married men lived on shore, while single men lived in three bunkhouses on the islet. With little time to visit the mainland, bachelors rarely married. The island did not offer a homey atmosphere, with its shafthouse, engine house, rock house and pump house, hoists, and blacksmith shop. The saloon, which doubled as the library, was their only refuge. The mainland town of Silver Islet sprang to life with churches, houses for the workers and their families, an elegant three-story house for the president, a general store, and a jail.

After the force of nature, superintendent Frue's biggest challenge was how to keep his work force. He had originally hired miners from the copper region of the Keweenaw Peninsula in Michigan but they rarely stayed for the long

The 60-hour work week, and poor conditions were some of the miners' complaints about Silver Islet.

term. Then he paid passage for Norwegian and Cornish miners. He had high hopes for the miners from Cornwall. In the 1850s, England's exhausted tin and copper mines had put a quarter of a million men out of work. Cornishmen had known the hardship of the mines since childhood and for generations. But Silver Islet conditions were unpleasant, even by mining standards of the time. With blisters from calcium chloride from the mine walls, explosions from methane gas pockets and the constant fear of deadly floods, even the Cornishmen didn't stay long. But if threats to personal safety weren't enough, the indignity of rules offered the final straw. When it came to whiskey, the company tallied every man's consumption. And at they end of every shift, every man was searched for silver pieces he had tried to squirrel away. If he dared refuse, he was fined $10.

Superintendent Frue left Silver Islet in 1875. Although he was a capable replacement, Richard Trethewey could not maintain the level of production. It was only when they brought in a diamond-tipped drill—the first of its kind—that they struck a new vein and investors celebrated profits once again.

By 1883, one shaft was almost a quarter mile deep (1,250 ft.). The superstitious noticed they were nearing 1,300 feet in the 13th year of operation. There was only enough coal to last until March 1st. Without fuel, the pumps would cease to function, and the mine would flood. The steamer *H. B. Tuttle* was on its way with 1,000 tons of coal, more than enough to hold Superior at bay until spring. But the lake froze early and the boat was locked in ice somewhere off Houghton, Michigan. The *Tuttle* never arrived. Frantic, the miners fed wood into the pump boilers, even dismantling wooden buildings. But it was not enough. Within weeks the mine flooded and had to be abandoned.

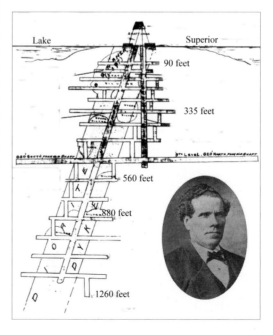

By 1883, Silver Islet mine was almost a quarter of a mile deep. (Inset) Mine superintendent William Bell Frue led his miners in a battle against Lake Superior.

Silver Islet from the air. Remnants of the break-wall are still visible beneath the water.

In its 13 years of operation, the Silver Island Mine had shipped more than $3,000,000 worth of ore, $1,300,000 in its first three years alone. The mine spawned a vibrant mainland community that continues today. The original general store now includes a tearoom. Many of the "camps" or cottages, along the waterfront date back to the mine era. Even the old jail has been converted to a cottage. In amongst trees at the far end of the Avenue, the tranquil cemetery is gradually returning to nature.

At the Islet, nothing remains of the mining operation but the odd fragment of twisted metal. Just off the island, the two shafts stare up through shallow water. Divers have been killed entering the shafts, so they have been sealed off. The remains of the massive cribs stretch out hundreds of feet around the perimeter. The island is privately owned and trespassing is prohibited. Silver Islet residents make it their business to notice transgressors! (Much of the information for this story was gathered from Elinor Barr's *Silver Islet: Striking it Rich on Lake Superior*.)

TALBOT ISLAND

The Lighthouse of Doom

Talbot Island's "lighthouse of doom" began auspiciouly enough. After 1867, the new Dominion of Canada quickly lit the waterways in order to assist the increased traffic on the upper Great Lakes. Talbot Island, miles out from the mainland, was chosen for Superior's first Canadian lighthouse. At that time, lightkeepers were expected to arrange their own way off the islands at the end of the shipping season. After the first year of Talbot's operation, lightkeeper Perry did not arrive at the Hudson's Bay Post where he was

Talbot Island

expected. The next spring, Perry's badly decayed body was discovered near his boat at what is now called Perry Bay on the Sibley Peninsula, nearly 14 miles (22 kms) off course.

The government's solution was to winterize the lighthouse, and double its size. Perry's successor was well acquainted with Superior. Thomas Lamphier, a former captain with twenty years on a Hudson's Bay schooner, came with his wife, a striking native woman from Hudson Bay with long raven hair. During the winter they received no visits, letters, or supplies. The Lamphiers settled into a routine, but not long after freeze-up, Thomas died suddenly.

Mrs. Lamphier added coal to the fire and sat back heavily into the rocking chair, worry and exhaustion shadowing her brown eyes. Hours had passed since she had looked in on her husband. His body had gone still, all expression lifted, his face had gone completely slack.

The following morning she looked for a place to bury her long-time companion. It was slow going, using the spade as a walking stick through the deep snow and the woods. It was not long before she realized that the ground was frozen so hard that a burial was out of the question. Not even a crow called in the forest. Nature, like her husband, had gone to sleep. She wrapped her husband in a canvas sail and dragged him to a cleft in the cliff face. Straining, she lifted the stiff figure and wedged him between the rocks.

That spring, the lighthouse tender anchored off the island. As they rowed toward the lighthouse, workers spied a white-haired stranger on the shore. But it was Mrs. Lamphier, her raven hair gone completely white. Relating her ordeal, she self-consciously touched her hair and half joked, "The winter took it."

A few years passed without incident for Talbot's third keeper, Andrew Hynes, until the early winter of 1872. Hynes prepared the boat for his return to the mainland. The lighthouse windows boarded up, the lamps

Lightkeeper Thomas Lamphier's grave on Bowman Island

Andrew Hynes was barely alive when he landed at the town of Silver Islet.

extinguished, he set off for Fort William, the sharp December sun glinting on the lapping waves. Then Superior changed moods.

Fishermen at the Silver Islet dock noticed a sailboat slowly coming towards them. One man gave a friendly wave but the figure, slumped over, gave no response. The barely conscious man was collapsed over the tiller, his oilskins encrusted in ice. Hynes had been stuck eighteen days on the storming lake, having travelled a mere 60 miles (96 kms).

After only six years of operation, the lamps were removed and a board was nailed across the door. Talbot Island lighthouse was the first to be abandoned in Great Lakes history because its risk to human life far outweighed its use to shipping.

BATTLE ISLAND

Battle Island lighthouse

Perched high on its cliff, the Battle Island lighthouse towers above the water. In 1977, the lightkeeper watched as the lake's waves broke near the shore at heights of fifty feet. They struck the cliff with such force that the spray alone smashed the glass out of the lantern-room about 120 feet above the water.

It is fabled that while the troops marched over twenty miles across glare ice, natives who were sympathetic to Riel opened fire.

The "battle" of Battle Island did not actually happen here. It occurred in 1885, at the time of the North-West Rebellion. It was early spring, and troops heading to the Northwest to quash Louis Riel's uprising had to contend with four gaps in the Lake Superior section of the incomplete railway. The men marched across the gaps in the line—86 miles (137 kms) in total— in temperatures that reached minus 35°F. They stumbled over stumps, fallen trees, and through snow drifts as deep as they were tall. Just when they thought the worst was over they faced a twenty-mile stretch across Superior's glare ice before they once again reached the rail line at Red Rock. And it is rumoured that during this march, local natives who were sympathetic to Louis Riel fired at the soldiers, trying to stop their advance west.

Soldiers were blinded by glare ice as they completed their march to Red Rock.

SLATE ISLANDS

A Meteorite Hit

Every year, our planet is bombarded by an estimated 10,000 lbs. (4,500 kgs) of space debris. But there is always the possibility of a "big hit." On two occasions, NASA scientists have scoured the Slate Islands to research just such an explosion—thousands of times more powerful than the atomic bomb that devastated Hiroshima. From the evidence, they concluded that a 19-mile-wide (30-km) asteroid struck the site of the

Slate Islands lighthouse towers from a cliff created by a massive meteorite strike.

Slates. When this hurtling space rock hit earth, the instantaneous transfer of energy into raging heat caused the rock to vapourize. Enough dust was tossed into the atmosphere to bring weeks of darkness. A mountain range thrust up, only to be slowly worn down over millions of years by weather and glaciation, finally to be flooded during the formation of Lake Superior. The gorgeous cluster of islands that are the Slates are what remain of the central cone from the original impact crater. Today, dramatic cliffs on the south side of Patterson Island form a bulwark against Superior's force. Within the sheltered areas of the Slates is an enchanting world—a fantastical sculpture garden of rock formations between Patterson and Mortimer, cobble beaches filled with surprisingly coloured stone, and peaceful waters, a refuge from the open lake.

The cooling effects of Superior have created a niche for arctic and alpine flora. The narrow leafed Dryas Drumondii thrives here and is not found again for another 1,000 miles (1,600 kms) to the northwest. Another unusual plant found here is Polygonum Viviparum, an Inuit delicacy prepared with seal oil. The Slates are home to the largest herd of woodland caribou in Ontario. These animals once roamed as far south as Manitoulin Island on the North Channel, but they were forced northward when humans altered their habitat. In 1985, the Slate Islands became a Natural Environment Provincial Park, a quiet haven and a sanctuary for wildlife. Boaters, kayakers, campers and sport fishermen enjoy its remoteness and beauty.

MICHIPICOTEN ISLAND

The Floating Island

Mine building on Michipicoten. Ojibwe were reluctant to show prospectors the source of their sacred copper.

In the 1600s, Indians told missionaries and explorers about Superior's islands of copper. Superior's most fabled "copper islands" were Michipicoten Island and Isle Royale. Long ago, an Ojibwe group was snowshoeing over the frozen lake when, without explanation, the ice began to break up. Terrified, the group ran towards Michipicoten. The closer they came, the further the island drifted away. And so was born the story of the mystical floating isle, and the Ojibwe's abiding fear of it.

Local Ojibwe traditionally believed that Michipicoten Island was also the domain of the powerful underworld manitou, Mishipeshu, the giant serpent who controlled copper. Anyone foolish enough to challenge him would suffer tragic results. A group of Ojibwe once visited the island to gather precious copper nuggets. They stayed the night before heading home, laden with treasure. Not far from the island, they

Depicted here are the Agate Island and Quebec Harbour lights. Both are now gone, but the Davieaux Island light (seen in distance) and the East End light are still in operation.

heard a thunderous voice: "Who are these robbers carrying off from me my children's cradles and play things?" The trespassers died in agony soon after returning to the mainland.

When the first surveyors arrived, they had to wade ashore because their Indian guides refused to land with them. Their fears had not diminished. In the late 1800s, lightkeepers and their families joined miners, fishermen, mill workers, a farmer, and a shopkeeper on this large mysterious island floating 28 miles (45 kms) offshore. Remnants of their lives are still visible.

MICHIPICOTEN ISLAND

Quebec Harbour Fish Camp

Quebec Harbour dock lined with net-drying reels

The Hudson's Bay Company started a commercial fishery in 1839 at Quebec Harbour. In 1860, American fishing tycoon, Alfred Booth set up an operation at Quebec Harbour that prospered for years. During the Great Depression of the 1930s, the Purvis family took over the site. The fishing station grew to a sizeable seventy people, with cabins, a store and cookhouse, a net house, and packing house. An icehouse made ice in a large brine tank. In an open room above the packing house, fiddlers played at dances running through the night.

When it came to knowing fish, no one could match the packing crew. Their ability to pinpoint a fish's origin was uncanny. One day, the Purvis tug rescued an American fishing boat. While packing the American's catch, the crew realized it was filled with fish only found in Canadian waters. They notified authorities, and the tug was towed to the Sault, where the Americans paid a hefty fine to get it back.

The general store. Men rolled dice to see who would pay for coffee.

Much of the once vibrant fishing station is still standing. Neat shelves line the walls inside the cookery and store. The old, square log, blacksmith shop—moved here from an early mine site—is still in good condition. A few drying reels are rusting in the overgrown grass. Above the door of the packing house is the name plate from the Captain Jim, one of several wrecks that can be seen in the harbour.

Fishermen at Quebec Harbour

Children at the fishing station

Without much to do on time off, many fishermen chose to "share-fish" in the evenings, setting nets in the harbour from small boats. For every pound of fish they caught, the company would split the profits.

The Quebec Harbour site

MICHIPICOTEN ISLAND: EAST END LIGHTHOUSE

A Deadly Policy

December 1916. Lightkeeper William Sherlock eased down the icy rocks. As he suspected, the dock had been swept away in the giant waves. "Good thing we moved the boat," he said as his son poured the morning coffee.

They were skirting around the real question: when should they make a break for the mainland? William had motorized the open sailboat, but it was still a 28-mile (45-km) trip. Still a terrifying gamble. Wait too long, and they would miss their opportunity to get off the island safely, starving at the lighthouse. Leave at the wrong time and they would be lost on the lake. William Sherlock was new to these decisions. Only the year before, the government had announced it would no longer retreive Lake Superior keepers at the end of season. Protests fell on deaf ears. And so, with the storm abated, the Sherlocks and their small dog pushed off in their sailboat, with twenty-five gallons of extra fuel, an emergency sail and some provisions.

There was no predicting Superior in December. William Sherlock just hoped for mercy. Halfway across open water, a dreaded nor'easter rose and the temperature plummeted. The lake turned grey and began to roll, fuelled by wind too strong for sail. Then, with a sputter, the engine died. William hauled out the oars. The dog went from spinning in panicked circles to shivering on James' lap. The freezing water lapped at their boots.

Before long it was like rowing a full bathtub. Bailing no longer worked so William resorted to lightening the load. He tossed the fuel, then the sails and provisions. But the water level kept creeping up. As the sides thickened with ice, so did the two men—they were scarcely able to bend their arms or knees. William refused to die entombed in a block of ice. He rowed harder. The snow was blinding. Then, reaching to retrieve an oar, James fell overboard. It was only William's quick response that prevented his son's certain death.

Finally James and William could hear the roar of the surf on a rocky beach. They managed to manoeuvre the boat to Leach Island where they found driftwood dry enough to build a fire. Warmer, the Sherlocks tried to chip away the ice from the boat and make repairs. Four days passed. They huddled by the fire and hunted for dried berries. The high winds and bitter cold would not let up, but they set off any way, afraid another day might render them too weak to journey on.

James leaned into the oars, pointing toward the North Shore. William did not stop bailing. Five hours later they reached land. But the nightmare

East End Lighthouse. In December 1918, Keeper William Sherlock died trying to cross to the mainland after the shipping season. His body was never found.

wasn't over yet. Severely weakened from exposure and hunger, it took them three more days, crawling much of the way, to reach the fishing station at Gargantua Harbour. It was here that they were transferred to hospital in Sault Ste. Marie. Although their hands and feet had been badly frozen, the Sherlocks made a full recovery. Their small dog was not as lucky. "We killed him when we reached the North Shore," William explained, "and this kept us alive until we struck Gargantua."

Clearly, Superior in December was no place for a sailboat. The Sherlocks wrote the Department of Marine. How in good conscience could the Department stop picking up lightkeepers at the end of season? But the Sherlocks' near miss did not move the Government. Two years later, in December 1918, William Sherlock did not arrive on the mainland. Sherlock and his boat were never recovered.

William's wife took over lightkeeping at East End light until 1925. In 1921 the Department of Marine finally resumed delivering and picking up lightkeepers. They sent the *Lambton*, a ship so poorly designed for Lake Superior that it was considered dangerous. The Department ignored advice on the matter, sending the *Lambton* any way. By chance, Mrs. Sherlock was not aboard when, in a spring storm of 1922, the *Lambton* vanished with twenty-two hands, including several other Lake Superior lightkeepers.

CARIBOU ISLAND LIGHTHOUSE

The Great Lakes' Most Isolated Lighthouse

Lonely Caribou Island is the most remote of all the Great Lakes islands. Over 65 miles (100 kms) from the nearest port and often obscured by Superior's dense fogs, it receives few visitors. Ojibwe avoided this "Island of the Yellow Sands" believing that it was guarded by a huge monster. In 1771, trader Alexander Henry of Sault Ste. Marie landed here, hoping that the yellow sands of legend were, in fact, gold. Henry was disappointed to find brilliant beaches of ordinary sand. It was nothing more than a flat, wooded island with small lakes, moss and honeysuckle, cranberry bogs and caribou.

Few others set foot on Caribou's sands until the 1860s. Shipping lanes to the north and south of the island became so busy, and passed so close to its shoals, that a lighthouse became necessary. The first tower was built on Caribou's tiny sister islet in 1886. It served until 1911 when it was replaced by a more prominent, concrete tower, ninety feet tall, hexagonal in design, and strengthened by six flying buttresses. The isolated location required Caribou's keepers and assistants to be hardy and resourceful. Among the most memorable of these men was George Johnston, the keeper of Caribou lighthouse between 1913 and 1921.

His first season as lightkeeper, George Johnston had packed a good supply of cartridges but had failed to bring his gun. He carved a makeshift weapon from a piece of sturdy driftwood, adapted a metal vapour tube as

Caribou lighthouse complex. Keeper George Johnston built a shed on the island just to hold the objects that drifted ashore from passing ships (mostly wood and wooden shingles).

a barrel, and fashioned a breech and firing pin. It had poor aim but was good for hunting rabbits to supplement the family's fish diet. While George was extending the breakwater, a ballast stone rolled and broke his leg. Gritting his teeth against the pain, he set the bone himself, attached a splint, carved a peg-leg and crutches, and was soon climbing the lighthouse stairs again.

In a demonstration of his grit and dedication, Johnston awoke one night to a ship calling in distress off the fog-bound island. Johnston followed the shoreline with his boat when suddenly the 536-ft. (160-m) freighter *Westmount* leaped out of fog, its bow nearly resting on the beach. She was not badly damaged but was firmly lodged ashore. Johnston took the Captain 30 miles (48 kms) to the Quebec Harbour fishing village on Michipicoten Island to call for assistance. Before long, a tug towing a barge removed enough cargo to refloat the *Westmount* and send her to dry dock.

Louise Johnston with her infant Pat in 1912. He was brought to the island when he was six weeks old. The hammock was made from a meat basket used to carry meat onto ships. Discarded baskets were often found on the island's shore.

The two eagles were family pets. The left eagle looks miserable because he just had a dunk in the lake. Johnston wanted to give the birds a chance to fly so he attached a rope to a rock and tied it to the eagle's leg. The eagle managed to fly away, but the weight caused it to plummet into Superior. The eagles spent their remaining days in the Toronto Zoo.

The Johnstons visiting neighbouring Caribou Island. It was a favourite place to picnic and to beachcomb.

L) The assistant lightkeeper, and San, Pat and Roger Johnston showing off a 52-lb. trout, 1915 R)George Johnston, keeper of Caribou light from 1912-21

In 1917, the government stopped transporting lightkeepers home in December. Johnston refitted the government issue sailboat with a cabin, coal-fired heater, and an engine. In December 1919, on the 60-mile trip home, Johnston and his assistant were trapped eight days on the Lake because of ice and storms. In 1922, the government sent the Lambton to deliver and pick up keepers.

After the government ignored Johnston's warnings about the Lambton's poor design, he refused to board the steamer for its first trip of the season on April 18, 1922. The following day, the ship foundered. George Johnston was in the search crew that discovered a Lambton lifeboat. The bodies of all twenty-two passengers, including George Penefold the new keeper of Caribou light, were never found.

Caribou light tower

MAPLE ISLAND

Treason, Conspiracy and Accessory to Murder

On August 18, 1816, three canoes set off from Fort William on Superior's north shore for Montreal to take the prisoners to trial. With deadly force, one canoe struck the shoal, sending its twenty-one passengers into the surging foam. The other canoes plunged toward nearby Maple Island where the bodies had been swept. William McGillivray jumped out at the water's edge, hauling corpses from the surf. Nine in all. All his friends and partners. All dead because of Lord Selkirk's vendetta.

In 1811, Lord Selkirk obtained a land grant on the Red River in what is now the province of Manitoba. On land twice the size of England, he promised to create the Red River colony, settling one thousand Irish and Scottish families within ten years.

The North West Company of fur traders (of which McGillivray was a director) opposed Selkirk's colony. The Company feared the settlers would cut off its corridor to the northwest fur supply, and its vital pemmican supply. The Métis sided with the Company. They were afraid Selkirk's settlers

would take their land. In June 1816, tensions at the Red River settlement exploded at Seven Oaks, resulting in twenty-one men being killed by armed Métis. Lord Selkirk burned with rage. He was told that these Métis had been directed by members of the North West Company at Fort William, and he vowed to punish those who had terrorized his colony. Selkirk and his

Twenty-one men were killed at the Seven Oaks Massacre in Red River Manitoba

Lord Selkirk arrested all the North West Company partners at Fort William.

Lord Selkirk sought justice for the Seven Oaks Massacre but instead destroyed his own reputation.

entourage made their way to the North West Company's Fort William to arrest William McGillivray and his partners for treason, conspiracy and accessory to murder. In the morning, they would leave the Fort as prisoners, on their way to Montreal.

Under Selkirk's seige, the partners set documents ablaze in the stealth of night. A disgruntled Métis blacksmith became Selkirk's informant, and led him to a stash of weapons and gunpowder. In Selkirk's mind, burning documents was tantamount to admitting guilt for the Seven Oaks Massacre. On August 18, Selkirk supervised the launch of three canoes, with the North West partners on their way to Montreal for trial.

En route, disaster hit with deadly speed. One of the canoes struck a shoal spilling its 21 passengers into the surging foam. Panicked, others in the brigade plunged their paddles toward the scene but the seas had already swept the struggling men away. By the time the canoes reached Maple Island, the crumpled bodies were near the shore, rolling in the surf.

The terrible task of identifying the dead began. Explorer Simon Fraser turned over one body to see the face of his acquaintance Kenneth Mackenzie, a North West Company partner. Another man identified an Ojibwe Chief, ironically renowned for his skill at the canoe. Little time passed before nine corpses had been identified.

Selkirk's life was shattered by the deaths of the North West Company men. His vigilante activities won him little support in Montreal and abroad, and led to a series of lawsuits in Canadian and British courts. Selkirk ended up in Britain bankrupt from legal fees, his reputation tarnished. Suffering from tuberculosis, he died in 1820, at aged forty-nine.

A year later, the famous enemy fur trading companies, The Hudson's Bay Company and the North West Company merged. The Red River settlement was restored, and slowly prospered. Most of the casualties of the Maple Island canoe disaster were buried on the Island.

Director of the North West Company, William McGillivray, survived the Maple Island tragedy.

ISLES PHILIPPEAUX AND PONTCHARTRAIN

The Imaginary Islands

In 1822, some time after the Revolutionary War, British and American commissioners sat down in Paris to re-draw the international border, declaring it to run through Lake Superior, "northward of the Isles Royal [sic] and Philippeaux, to the Long Lake." It was not discovered for many decades that Isle Philippeaux and Long Lake did not actually exist.

The first map of Lake Superior was drawn around 1671 by two Jesuit priests. Travelling by canoe using only a compass and an astrolabe, their work was astonishingly accurate, surpassing later maps. Seventy-five years later, Jacques Bellin, acclaimed for his accuracy and scrupulous sources, published his map of the Great Lakes. Remarkably, his 1744 map distorts Superior and includes five imaginary islands: Isles Hocquart, Ste. Anne, Beauharnois, Phillipeaux, and Pontchartain. Invented, some believe, by a man named Louis Denys, Sieur de La Ronde.

It was hard to pin La Ronde down. He had worked as a privateer, a spy, a naval captain, a fur trader and a prospector. One of the few Europeans on Lake Superior in the early 1730s, La Ronde, searched for copper along the south shore aboard his 40-ton barque. The German miners he imported located several veins, but the cost of extracting the copper slowed him down. La Ronde never found the pure copper islands fabled by the natives.

Published in 1671, this Jesuit map of Lake Superior was impressively accurate.

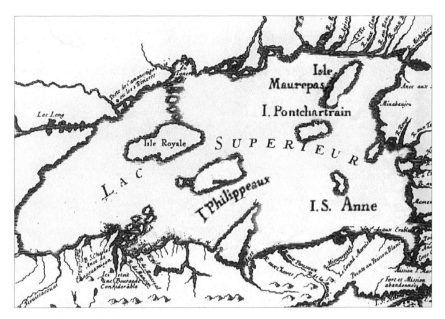

Jacques Bellin's 1744 map included La Ronde's imaginary islands.

His failure may have created pressure from officials who had given him the right to prospect. And what better way to placate superiors than to immortalize them, naming landmarks after them. Isle Hocquart was named after the Intendant of Justice at Quebec and Isle Beauharnois, after the governor of New France. These two islands may represent existing islands. But the islands of Phillipeaux and Pontchartain were completely fabricated. These were named for the French Minister of the Marine who had approved La Ronde's prospecting scheme, Jean-Frédéric Phélypeaux, Compte de Maurepas et de Pontchartrain.

La Ronde's information, imaginary islands included, found its way to the Département de la Marine in Paris and into the hands of eminent cartographer, Jacques Bellin. Bellin took La Ronde as an excellent source. After all, a French naval captain who had sailed the Lake extensively would surely have discovered more than priests travelling by canoe. Bellin incorporated Isles Philippeaux and Pontchartrain into his 1744 map, as did Dr. John Mitchell in his map of 1755. It is Mitchell's map that was used to redefine the international border in 1822.

Picture Credits

Archives de la Province du Canada Français, Saint-Jerome, Quebec:157
Archives Jesuit Fathers, Upper Canada:172(t)
Archives nationales du Québec à Québec:146
Archives of Ontario:12(l),28(l),41,84,134(t),135)b)149(t),152(t),192,248,249,250,255(c), 260,261(b),262
Apostle Islands National Lakeshore:220,221,222,225(b),226,227(br&l),228(b),229,231-237,239,242,246
Baldwin Room, Metro Toronto Reference Library:5,6,51(l),133(t),158,159
Bayfield Heritage Association:238
Beaver Island Historical Society:183(b),193-211
Bruce County Museum and Achives:105,106,136,138
Burton Historical Collection, Detroit Public Library:189,256
Caughey, Amy:19
City of Toronto Archives:3(map),10,12(r&b),13
Collingwood Museum:148
Detroit News:43,77
Follett House:71,72,73(r),74(b),91,92,93,94,95.96-97,99
Fort Malden National Historic Site:86
Gibson, Sally:9
Grand Hotel Archives:115(t&b),119-120
Great Lakes Historical Society:vi,98,100,101(t),252
Historical Society of Wisconsin:225(t)
Huronia Museum, Midland:140(t),141(b),162,163(b)
Isle Royale National Park:241,242,243,246,255(t)
Johnston, Pat:273,274,275
Kelleys Island Historical Society:ix,70(b),71,73(lb),74(t),88(t),89
Lake Erie Islands Historical Society:48,49,51(r),53(t),55(t&c),56,57,58,59,60,61,62,63, 64(c&b),65,66,69,70(t),90
Les Cheneaux Historical Association:124
Library of Congress:126(b),129,175,227
Lynx Images Inc.:vi,29(b),101(b),110(b),117(t),141(t),149(b),151(b),156(t),167,180(b), 213-215,228(t),255(b),259(b),263,264,267,268(t),270(b)
Mackinac Island State Park Commission:104,113(t&b),114,115, 116(t&b),117(b),118, 121,127
Marine Museum of the Great Lakes at Kingston:25(br),28,(br&l)
Marquette County Historical Society:216(t),217
Martyrs' Shrine:143(b),145
U.S. Naval Academy Museum (Beverley R. Robinson Collection):64(t)
Metropolitan Toronto Reference Library:1,2,3 (insets),7,8,11,12(r),14,16,17,31(b),32(b), 37(b),53(b),68,103,109,110(t),130,132,133(b),143(c),169(t),254,276(b),277(t)
National Archives of Canada:4,23(t),27,32(t),33(r),34,42,85,126(t), 134(b),135(t),137(t), 140(b),142,143,144,151(t),160,163(t),169(b),223,259(t),266,272,276(t),277(b),278,279
National Archives(US):244
Lange, O Hugh:78
Lilley, George (Queen's University Archives):23(b)
McKenzie, Peter (painted by):41
Osborne, Dr. Brian:15

Parry Sound Public Library:108
Pelee Island Heritage Centre:80,81,82, 88(b)
Perry's Victory and International Peace Memorial:52,55(b)
Phelphs, Edward: J.E. Evans Collection:139
Purvis, Mort:268(b),269,270
Thousand Islands Bridge Authority:40(t)
Thunder Bay Historical Society:137(b),253,258,261(t),265
Sapluski, Wayne:177,178,218,247
Sleeping Bear Dunes National Lakeshore:190
State Historical Society Wisconisin:186,187,189
Queen's University Archives:vii,24,25(t&c),26,28(r),29(trl&c),31(t),33(t),35-36,38-39,40b,45
Watertown Daily Times:37
Washington Island Archives:179,180(b):181,182,183,184,185
West Parry Sound District Museum, Dave Thomas Slide Collection:152(b),153,154
Windsor Star:44
YMCA, Sudbury:164,165

PUBLICATIONS:

Arbic, Bernard. *Sugar Island Sampler*:172(b),173
Bayliss, J. & E. Estelle. *Historic St. Joseph Island*:168
Cook, S.F. *Drummond Island: The Story of the British Occuptation 1815-1828*:170
Cosgrove, Winston M. *Wolfe Island Past and Present*. Queens University Archives:21,22
Grover, Frank. *A Brief History of Les Cheneaux Islands*:122
Hamilton, James. "Famous Algonquins: Algic Legends," Transactions of the Canadian Institute 6 (1889):156
LeRoy, Rudd Uldene. *Six on an Island*:123
McKenny Tour of the Lakes:Hambleton Colln.:224
McKenney, Thomas Loraine. *History of the Indian Tribes of North America*: 216(b)
Monkman, Irene. *Oliphant and its Islands, Lake Huron*:109
Schooner Days:14(b)
"The Charity Site: Guide to a 17th Century Huron Village on Christian Island."
Northeastern Archaeological Associates, Beausoleil First Nations:145(b)

SELECTED BIBLIOGRAPHY

BOOKS AND PAMPHLETS

Arbic, Bernard. *Sugar Island Sampler*. Sault Ste. Marie: privately printed, 1993.
Ashley, K. Beldon. *Islands of the Manitou*. Florida, Coral Gables: Crystal Bay Publishers, 1985.
Barr, Elinor. *Silver Islet: Striking It Rich in Lake Superior*. Toronto: Natural Heritage/Natural History Inc., 1988.
Barry, James P. *Ships of the Great Lakes*. Holt: Thunder Bay Press, 1996.
_____.*Old Forts of the Great Lakes: Sentinels in the Wilderness*. Lansing: Thunder Bay Press, 1994.
_____.*Georgian Bay: The Sixth Great Lake*. Toronto: Clarke, Irwin & Co. Ltd., 1968.
Bayliss, Joseph and Estell. *Historic St. Joseph Island*. Cedar Rapids: Torch Press, 1938.
Berton, Pierre. *Flames Across the Border*. Toronto: McClelland and Stewart, 1981.
Bigsby, John J. *The Shoe and the Canoe*. Vol. II. London: Chapman and Hall, 1850.
Bonvillian, Nancy. *The Huron*. New York: Chelsea House, 1989.
Boyd, Margaret A. Editor. *The Story of Garden Island*. Kingston: Honson and Edgar Ltd., 1973.
Bradford, Robert D., *Historic Forts of Ontario*. Belleville: Mika Publishing Co, 1988.
Castle, Beatrice Hanscom. *The Grand Island Story*. Marquette, Michigan: The John M. Longyear Research Library, 1974.
Cate, Adrian G. Ten. Editor. *Pictorial History of the Thousand Islands of the St. Lawrence River*. Brockville: Besancourt Publishers, 1977.
Chisholm, Barbara. *Superior: Under the Shadow of the Gods*. Toronto: Lynx Images Inc., 1998.
Cook, S.F. *Drummund Island: The Story of British Occupation, 1815-1828*. Lansing: R. Smith Printing Co., 1896.
Cooper, Barbara Allan. *Hotel Victory*. Published by author, 1985.
Cosgrove, Winston M. *Wolfe Island Past and Present*. Queens University Archives.
Eaton, Conan Bryant. *Rock Island: The Island Series*. Washington Island,WI: Door County Advocate, 1969.
_____.*Washington Island: The Island Series*. Sturgeon Bay, WI: Bayprint Inc. 1972.
Engelmann, Larry. *Intemperance: The Lost War Against Liquor*. New York: The Free Press, 1979.
Frohman, Charles E. *Put-in-Bay*. Columbus: Ohio Historical Society, 1971.
Gale, Thomas P. and Kendra L. *Isle Royale: A Photographic History*. Houghton: Isle Royale Natural History Association, 1995.
Gibson, Sally. *More Than an Island: A History of the Toronto Island*. Toronto: Irwin Publishing, 1984.
Grover, Frank R. *A Brief History of Les Cheneaux Islands*. Grand Rapids: Black Letter Press, 1912.
Gutsche, Andrea. *Alone in the Night: Lighthouses of Georgian Bay, Manitoulin Island and the North Channel*. Toronto: Lynx Images Inc., 1996.
_____.*Ghosts of the Bay: A Guide to the History of Georgian Bay*. Toronto: Lynx Images Inc., 1994.
_____.*The North Channel and St. Mary's River: A Guide to the History*. Toronto: Lynx Images Inc., 1996.
Henry, Alexander. *Travels and Adventures in Canada and the Indian Territories*. Toronto: George N. Morang & Co., 1901.

Hills, Norman E. A *History of Kelley's Island, Ohio*. The Kelleys Island Historical
  Association, 1993.
"Historic Structures, Grand Island National Recreation Area, Michigan." Escanaba, MI:
  Hiawatha National Forest, 1991.
Hunt, C. W. *Booze, Boats and Billions: Smuggling Liquid Gold*. Toronto: McClelland and
  Stewart, 1988.
Karmamanski, Theodore. *Narrative History of Isle Royale National Park*. Isle Royale
  National Park, Feb. 1988.
Keller, James M. *The "Unholy" Apostles: Shipwreck Tales of the Apostle Islands*. Chelsea:
  Bookcrafters, 1984.
Landon, Fred. *Lake Huron*. Indianapolis, The Bobbs Merill Co., 1944.
Lenihan, Daniel. *Shipwrecks of Isle Royale National Park: The Archeological Survey*.
"Historical Glimpses of Lennox and Addington County." The Lennox and Addington
  County Council, 1964. Queens University Archives.
LeRoy, Rudd Uldene. *Six on an Island*. Allegan Forest, MI: The Priscilla Press, 1995.
Lidfors, Kathleen, "Sandstone Quarries of the Apostle Islands: A Resource Management."
  Department of the Interior National Park Service, 1893.
Ligibel, Ted and Richard Wright. *Island Heritage: A Guided Tour to Lake Erie's Bass
  Islands*. Columbus: Ohio State University Press, 1987.
Lilius, Aleko. *The Romantic Thousand Islands: Their Towns and Times*. Toronto: Holiday
  Publications, 1948.
Mackinac State Historic Parks. *Mackinac: An Island Famous in These Regions*. Mackinac
  Island, Michigan, 1998.
Marchetti, Donna. *Around the Shores of Lake Erie*. Saginaw, MI.: Glovebox Guidebooks of
  America, 1998.
Marshall, James A. Editor. *Shipwrecks of Lake Superior*. Duluth: Lake Superior Port Cities
  Inc., 1987.
McCabe, John. *Grand Hotel: Mackinac Island*. Mackinac Island, Michigan: The Unicorn
  Press, 1987.
McConnell, Barbara. *Ste. Marie Among the Hurons*. Toronto: University of Toronto Press,
  1980.
McKenna, M.J. Katherine. *The Impact of the Upper Canadian Rebellion on Life in Essex
  County Ontario 1837-42*, Parks Canada.
Mifflin, R. *The Light on Chantry Island*. Erin: Boston Mills Press, 1989.
Monkman, Irene. *Oliphant and its Islands*, Lake Huron. 1912.
Newell, Amy. *The Caves of Put-in-Bay*. Put-in-Bay, Ohio: Lake Erie Originals, 1995.
Organ, John Gray. *Lord Selkirk of Red River*. Toronto: The Macmillan Co., 1963.
Pearen, Shelly. *Exploring Manitoulin*. Toronto: University of Toronto Press, 1993.
Porter, Phil. *Mackinac: An Island Famous in these Regions*. Mackinac Island, MI.
Quaife, Milo. *Lake Erie*. Indianapolis, New York: The Bobbs-Merill Co., 1945.
_____.*Lake Michigan*. Indianapolis: Bobbs-Merill Co., 1944.
Richardson, Jean K. *Wolfe Island Sketches*. Queens University Archives.
Rollason, Bryan. Editor. *County of a Thousand Lakes: The History of the County of
  Frontenac 1673-1973*. Kingston: Frontenac County Council, 1982. Queens
  University Archives.
Ruchhoft, Robert H. *Exploring North Manitou, South Manitou, High and Garden Islands
  of the Lake Michigan Archipelago*. Cincinnati: The Pucelle Press, 1991.
Ryall, Lydia J. *Sketches and Stories of the Lake Erie Islands*. Norwalk, Ohio: The American
  Publishers Co., 1913.
Scott, Ina. *Yesterday's News, Today's History*. Gananoque: 1000 Islands Publishers, 1982.
Smith, Susan Weston. *The First Summer People: The Thousand Islands 1650-1910*.

Toronto: Stoddart Publishing Co. Ltd., 1993.

Stonehouse, Frederick. *Haunted Lakes*. Duluth, MN: Lake Superior Port Cities Inc., 1997.

Sundland, Judi. "A Visit to Rossport, Ontario Canada." Rossport Historical Society.

Swainson, Donald. *Garden Island: A Shipping Empire*. Kingston: Marine Museum of the Great Lakes at Kingston with the assistance of the National Museum of Canada,1984.

Tanner, H. H. *Atlas of the Great Lakes Indian History*. Norman, Oklahoma: University of Oklahoma Press, 1995.

The Journal of Beaver Island History. Vol. 1. Beaver Island, MI: Beaver Island Historical Society, 1996.

Thompson, Shawn. *A River Rat's Guide to the Thousand Islands*. Erin: The Boston Mills Press, 1996.

_____.*River's Edge: Reprobates, Rum-runners and Other Folk of the Thousand Islands*. Burnstown: General Store Publishing House, 1991.

Thorndale, Theresa. *Sketches and Stories of the Lake Erie Islands*. 1989.

Tiessen, Ron. *The Vinedressers: A History of Grape Farming & Wineries on Pelee Island*. Pelee Island, ON: Pelee Island Heritage Centre, 1996.

Weeks, Robert. *King Strang: A Biography of James Jesse Strang*. Ann Arbor, MI: The Five Wives Press, 1971.

Wilson, Catherine Anne. *A New Lease on Life: Landlords, Tenants, and Immigrants in Ireland and Canada*. Montreal: McGill-Queen's University Press, 1994.

Wilson, Mark L. and Stanley J. Dyl II. *The Michigan Copper Country*. Tucson: The Mineralogical Record. March-April 1992, vol. 23, number 2, 1992.

ARTICLES, REPORTS, INTERVIEWS AND WEB SITES

"Angelique: Story of Suffering and Heroism Retold in Prose—The Narrative in Her Own Words." Detroit Tribune, 1925.

"Apostle Islands General Management Plan." Apostle Islands National Lakeshore, 1989.

"Ashland and the Brownstone Excelsior Quarry." *Ashland Daily Press*. Jan. 1892.

Carruthers, Peter. "Preliminary Excavations at the Supposed Site of Ste. Marie II—Christian Island Ontario." 1965. Archeological Sites Data Base, Public Archives of Ontario, Series RG 47-47.

"Childhood Passage." *Outlook*, Kalamazoo MI, 1987

"Dr. Thordur Gudmundsen: The Icelandic Doctor of Washington Island." *The Wisconsin Medical Journal*, May. 1939.

"Drama of the Lonely Men: Rock Of Ages." *Keeper's Log*. Fall, 1995.

"Four Days of Terror: Winter on Michigan Island." *The Lightkeeper's Log*, Spring, 1996.

Francis, David W. "Johnson's Island: A History of the Resort Era." *Inland Seas*. No. 2, Vol. 36, 1980.

Gilbert, Bil. "Americas Only King Made Beaver Island His Promised Land." *Smithsonian*, August, 1995.

Holden, Thom. "Sinking of the *George M. Cox*." *The Nor'Easter: Journal of the Lake Superior Marine Museum Association*. Vol. 8, No. 3, May-June 1983.

"Island Memories: Lighthouse Makes Anna Hodge Beam." *Kalamazoo Gazette*, May 5, 1995.

"Journal of Jane Masters." *The Calumet News*. March 17, 1913.

Jury McLeod, Elise. "Ste. Marie-on-the-Wye." *Inland Seas*. Vol. 4. No. 3, 1948.

Karrow, Robert. "Lake Superior's Mythic Isles: A Cautionary Tale For Users of Old Maps." *Michigan History*. Jan./Feb., 19—.

Landon, Fred. "Disaster on Isle Royale." *Inland Seas*, Vol. 21, No. 4, 1965.

_____."Shipwreck on Isle Royale." *Inland Seas*, Vol. 6, No. 1, 1960.

Long, Roger. "Johnson's Island Prison." *Blue & Gray Magazine*. Vol. IV, Issue 4, February-

March 87.

⸺."The Castle in the Lake." *Seasons of the Sandusky*, Spring 1994. Mackinac State Historic Parks.

Macrath, Robert. "On the Trail of the Hermit." Collected articles pertaining to Hermit Wilson. Apostle Islands National Lakeshore.

Martin, Patrick E. "Mining on Minong: Copper Mining on Isle Royale," *Michigan History*, May, 1990.

McDermott, P.W. "Snake Stories of the Lake Erie Island." *Inland Seas*, Vol. 3, No. 2, April 1947.

Neuman, Martha. "What Are Those Cabins Doing There?" Student Paper. University of Wisconsin, 1993.

Rainey, Lee. "Lake Erie Limestone Carriers: The Shays of Kelley Island." *Railroad Model Craftsman*, Dec. 1986.

Rathbun, Peter. "Special History Study: Light Station of the Apostle Islands National Lake Shore," National Park Service, Feb. 1988.

Snyder, David. "Isle Royale Lighthouse and the Malones," *The Daily Mining Gazette*, 1988.

⸺. "Raspberry Island Lighthouse Historic Structure Report." Apostle Islands National Lakeshore.

"Steamer Sevona Wrecked on Sand Island Reef."Apostle Islands National Lakeshore Historic Resources—Working Data Base. www.nps.gov/apis.

Stonehouse, Frederick. Interview with Joel Blahnick, June 1, 1994.

"The Journal of Sarah Barr Christian." *Quarterly Newsletter of Keweenaw Historical Society*, Feb. 1992.

Zornow, William Frank. "John Wilson Murray and the Johnson's Island Plot." *Inland Seas*, Vol. VI, 1950.

INDEX

ACKNOWLEDGEMENTS

This book could not have been compiled without the generous assistance of the following individuals. While many have contributed to the project, any errors or omissions found in the text are ours alone.

We would like to extend a special thanks to those who helped in researching areas that encompassed many sites, and those who graciously allowed us to draw on their published material. Our gratitude also goes to all others who helped in our research, fact-checking and picture gathering:

Kim Alexander, Rock Harbor Lodge; Gerard Altoff, Perry's Victory and International Peace Memorial; Goodwin Berquist and Barbara Ellefson, Washington Island Historical Society; Christine Bourolias, Archives of Ontario; W. G. Breck; Steven Brisson and Phil Porter, Mackinac Island State Park Commission; Kathleen Burtch, St. Lawrence Islands National Park; Margaret Calvin d'Esterre; Peter Carruthers; Bill Cashman and Joyce Bartels; Beaver Island Historical Society; Steven Catlin and Terry Gainer, Martyrs' Shrine; Amy Caughey; Carmel Cosgrove; Kip Courier and Susan M. Schwerer, Follett House; Mark Eggleson, Rock Island State Park; John G. Franzen, Grand Island: Hiawatha National Forest; Bob Garcia, Fort Malden National Historic Site; Annegret Goehring, Les Cheneaux Historical Association; Bill Heard, Sleeping Bear Dunes National Lakeshore; George Henderson, Queen's University Archives; Kaye Hiebel, Marquette County Historical Society; Jamie Hunter, Huronia Museum-Midland; Ed Isaly and Ruth Griebel, Lake Erie Islands Historical Society; Lawrence Jackson; Pat Johnston; Brenda Klinkow, McCord Museum of Canadian History, Montreal; Andy Kraushaar, State Historical Society of Wisconsin; O. Hugh Lange, Kelleys Island Historical Association; Uldene Rudd-Leroy; Bob Mackreth, Apostle Islands National Lakeshore; Kay Masters, Michigan Technological University; John McCabe; Kally McCarney, Kally's Gift Shop; Craig Morton, Kelleys Island State Park; William A. O'Brien and Carla Levigne, The Great Lakes Historical Society; Dr. Brian Osborne, Queen's University; Joe Parker; Stewart Renfrew, Queen's University Archives; Bob Tagatz, Grand Hotel, Mackinac Island; Dave Thomas; Shawn Thompson; Ron Tiessen, Peele Island Heritage Centre; Shane Sanford, Thousand Islands Bridge Authority; Liz Valencia, Isle Royale National Wilderness Park.

Our deepest thanks go to those on the front lines: Janice Carter and Katharine Knowles for the maps, Jennifer Hart and Janet Looker for proofreading, and Margaret Graham for additional research. Special thanks to Steve Gamester for his enormous and enthusiastic contribution, and to Deborah Wise Harris, editor extraordinaire, whose love of language and precision of thought shaped this book.

SUPERIOR

UNDER THE SHADOW
OF THE GODS

SUPERIOR

Under the Shadow of the Gods

The history of Lake Superior's magnificent Canadian shore is explored in all its drama in this remarkable book and film. The book follows the Canadian shore from Sault Ste. Marie north past Thunder Bay to the American border. Past and present are linked through historical stories, ghost towns, shipwrecks and other fascinating abandoned sites. Included are over 200 sites, maps and archival photographs.

The breathtaking film reveals Lake Superior as a world belonging to the gods—with its mystical islands, rugged shorelines, and dramatic tales. Rare archival footage and photographs, voices from the past, stunning cinematography, and a haunting score enrich these compelling sagas.

Silver Screen Award Winner for History, U.S. Film & Video Festival

ISBN 0-9698427-9-1 Bk/Video $49.95 CN/$39.95 US
ISBN 0-9698427-8-3 Video $29.95 CN/$24.95 US
ISBN 0-9698427-7-5 Book$24.95 CN/$19.95 US

TO ORDER THESE BOOKS AND VIDEOS OR TO RECEIVE A CATALOGUE WRITE TO:
LYNX IMAGES
P.O. BOX 5961, STATION A
TORONTO, ONTARIO
CANADA, M5W 1P4
WEB SITE:WWW.LYNXIMAGES.COM

TO ORDER SEND CHEQUE OR CREDIT CARD INFORMATION WITH THIS ORDER FORM

	Item #	Description	Qty	Unit Price	Total
Name					
Address					
Province/State Postal/Zip code					

	Total Merchandise	
Telephone	Shipping	
	Sub-total	
Credit Card # Visa/Master Card only (circle) Exp. Date	PST 8% (Books are exempt)	
	GST 7% (Canadian customers only)	
Signature	Total enclosed	

LYNX
IMAGES

	CAN	U.S.
Shipping under $ 70	$4.00	$6.00
Shipping over $ 70	$6.00	$10.00

Send to Lynx Images, PO Box 5961, Station A, Toronto, Ontario M5W 1P4

THE NORTH CHANNEL AND ST. MARY'S RIVER

A Guide to the History

For centuries, Lake Huron's North Channel and the St. Mary's River (leading to Lake Superior) have provided an essential passageway, first for native peoples and then for successive waves of Europeans. The footprints of natives, explorers, missionaries and fur traders, soldiers and settlers, entrepreneurs and scoundrels are ever visible. Brimming with stories, folklore and eccentric frontier characters, the book pulls you through a fascinating history of this region. Over 125 sites, maps and archival photographs highlight shipwrecks, abandoned forts, frontier towns and hidden places.

ISBN 1-894073-00-2 $24.95 CN/$19.95 US

GHOSTS OF THE BAY

The Forgotten History of Georgian Bay
Guide Book and Video

The 90-minute film leads viewers on an expedition to the haunting vestiges of Georgian Bay's past (now an eerie world of shipwrecks, ghost towns, fishing camps, lumber villages, and native sites). Bring the book along on your own journey, and transform your experience of Georgian Bay. The 300-page book includes 140 sites, 50 maps, and fascinating archival photographs.

ISBN 0-9698427-1-6 Book/Video $49.95 CN/$39.95 US
ISBN 0-9698427-0-8 Video $29.95 CN/$24.95 US
ISBN 0-9698427-3-2 Book $24.95 CN/$19.95 US

ALONE IN THE NIGHT

Lighthouses of Georgian Bay, Manitoulin Island
Book and Video

Lighthouses capture the imagination with their fascinating stories and forgotten memories. Together the book and 72-minute video take you on a compelling journey to the lighthouses of Georgian Bay, Manitoulin Island, and the North Channel, and return you to a time when the Great Lakes were the lifeblood of the country. *Alone in the Night* traces the evolution of lightkeeping, revealing the heroic and the scandalous, the gritty and the routine aspects of this remarkable chapter of Canada's marine heritage.

Discover the over 50 lighthouse sites through stories, photographs, and maps.

ISBN 0-9698427-4-0 Book/Video $49.95 CN/$39.95 US
ISBN 0-9698427-6-7 Video $29.95 CN/$24.95 US
ISBN 0-9698427-5-9 Book $34.95CN/24.95 US

About Lynx Images

Lynx Images is an award-winning book publishing and film production company that specializes in exploring and documenting vanishing pieces of Great Lakes history. Partners Barbara Chisholm, Russell Floren and Andrea Gutsche have travelled across the Great Lakes exploring the fascinating stories and characters, cultures and locations that make up our collective past. The result has been several best-selling titles:

Superior: Under the Shadow of the Gods
Ghosts of the Bay: the Forgotten History of Georgian Bay
Alone in the Night: Lighthouses of Georgian Bay and Manitoulin Island
The North Channel and St. Mary's River: A Guide to the History

The past is brought alive through juxtaposing historical photographs and rare archival footage with sites as they appear today—ghost towns, shipwrecks—sites abandoned by time. Next to be released is the book and film package, *Castles in the North: The Grand Hotels of Canada.*

LYNX IMAGES
P.O. BOX 5961, STATION A
TORONTO, ONTARIO
CANADA, M5W 1P4
WEB SITE: HTTP//WWW.LYNXIMAGES.COM

Author/Director Andrea Gutsche with Producer/Cinematographer Russell Floren at the Kelleys Island glacial grooves, Lake Erie

A Brief History of Pelee Island Winery

History is predominant when one speaks of Pelee Island Winery and the vineyards on the island. The tradition of winning awards for its wines, on both a national and international level, continues since receiving a medal in 1878 in Paris. The first estate winery in Canada, Vin Villa was founded in the 1860's and can still be seen on the island today. Since the early 1980's, Pelee Island Winery has planted the European *Vitis vinifera* varieties such as Chardonnay, Riesling, Pinot Noir and Cabernet Franc on approximately 500 acres of land. These new plantings have ushered in a new era of success for the winery.

Pelee Island is the largest of the Lake Erie Islands and is nestled in the centre of the lake. The extended growing season of Canada's most southern island allows our grapes to reach their full potential and maturity. All these factors of sun, soil, climate and southern latitude sum up to help create an internationally recognised microclimate.

Since 1982, the production facilities have been located on the mainland in Kingsville. Visitors are welcome to visit our extensive retail store and take a comprehensive tour of the winemaking establishment.

On the island we offer an equally exciting experience, where one can join a vineyard tour, wine appreciation seminar and taste our fine wines. A barbecued lunch can be savoured in the wine garden at the Pavilion overlooking Lake Erie with a children's play area, beach volleyball and soccer facilities.

Pelee Island also offers activities: hiking the Red Cedar Savannah Trail, biking, fishing, canoeing and kayaking. A wonderful weekend getaway destination!

Pelee Island Winery is Canada's southermost and largest estate winery, and we invite you to take the opportunity to visit our winery and vineyards.

Call or email us now for more information!

Phone	(800) 59-PELEE
	(519) 733-6551
Fax	(519) 733-6553

www. peleeisland.com
Email: pelee@mnsi.net

M.V. Jiimaan ferry schedule:
(800) 661-2220